COINage Guide

Robert Irwin Wolenik

COINage GUIDE

To Collecting and Investing in Coins

FRANKLIN WATTS
NEW YORK | TORONTO
1987

Illustration for page 76 from *The Official
American Numismatic Association Grading
Standards for United States Coins*. Illustrations
© 1984, 1981, 1977 Western Publishing Company,
Inc. Used by permission.

Library of Congress Cataloging-in-Publication Data

Irwin, Robert, 1941–
Coinage guide.

Includes index.
1. Coins—Collectors and collecting—Handbooks,
manuals, etc. 2. Coins as an investment. I. Title.
CJ81.I78   1987   332.63   86-29009
ISBN 0-531-15511-0

Contents

COINage Guide

Preface

When we began publishing COINage magazine in 1964 the world of numismatics or coin collecting was in turmoil. The country was faced with a coin shortage and the government was convinced that coin collectors were to blame. The annoying hobby was going to be stopped by freezing the dates and eliminating the mint marks on coins.

But coin collecting continued to thrive and the shortage managed to solve itself. Since that time exciting events have kept coins in the public's attention and an army of new collectors have joined this hobby that combines the fascination of history with the lure of rising profits.

In the '60s U.S. coinage was altered drastically with the removal of silver from its content and the substitution of cupro-nickel. It was a sad time for many collectors as literally millions of coins were melted down for their metallic value, but that great melt had the effect of making the surviving coins skyrocket in value.

The '70s were years of major developments. We had brand new coins in the Eisenhower and Susan B. Anthony dollars. The government released to the public some 2.8 million Carson City silver dollars that had been lost for decades in the Treasury's vaults. Gold was legalized in the U.S. and began its upward climb with a value of approximately $150 an ounce.

The '80s have already been as exciting. The decade started with a gold and silver market driven to record highs by world inflation. The U.S. Mint began a new era of commemorative coinage with a Washington half dollar and coin series for the Los Angeles Olympic games and the Statue of Liberty. The latest addition has been the American Eagle gold and silver bullion series.

With all of this activity the coin investment market has grown more and more sophisticated. Analysts have discovered that rare coins have an outstanding history of appreciation and large funds have been targeted for numismatic investment. Nationwide electronic networks control thousands of transactions daily while fortunes are made or lost on the interpretation of a coin's condition.

It's exciting. It's fun. But it's also dangerous. Just as in any other field of investment, the newcomer can be easily led into disastrous gambles if he isn't guided with knowledge and integrity. Success and safety are best guaranteed by your own knowledge of the field. Learn about coins before you invest.

And there is a bonus that comes with this acquisition of coin knowledge. Lured to coins because of the profit potential, many investors have become true numismatists. The fascination of this centuries-old hobby has captured them and they have discovered a wonderful avocation with enough challenges to last a lifetime.

James C. Miller
Publisher
COINage

Introduction

Awell-dressed young man walked into a coin dealer's shop and asked to see a few coins; nothing specific, just rare coins. The proprietor, a stocky man in his fifties dressed in a sport shirt and slacks, moved his unlit pipe to the other side of his mouth and carefully looked the younger man over. Just what did the fellow want? There was no one else in the shop, so the proprietor had time to talk and listen. He took out two coins.

The first was an 1883-S Morgan dollar (G. T. Morgan was the name of the coin's designer; the S stands for the old San Francisco mint). It was a shiny piece.

The other coin was a 1918 Lincoln centennial half-dollar. It had a portrait of the president on the obverse (front)—also designed by Morgan—based on the Lincoln statue by Andrew O'Connor in Springfield, Illinois. It also was shiny, but it was discolored, with a gold-to-blue patina drifting across its surface.

Both coins were in plastic holders, and the young man lifted them, trying to get a better view of the coins. The dealer said nothing, waiting.

Finally the younger man asked, "What are these coins worth?"

"To buy or sell?" asked the dealer with a smile. When the man looked puzzled, he continued. "I have a buy price, which I use to purchase coins, and a higher sell price. In between's my profit. I'll sell you either coin for one hundred dollars."

The young man looked at the coins again and then asked, "Are they worth it? If I come back in six months, can I sell them back to you for more than I paid?"

LEFT: 1883-S MORGAN SILVER DOLLAR
RIGHT: 1918 ABRAHAM LINCOLN
CENTENNIAL HALF-DOLLAR

Again the dealer smiled. "That depends," he said. "If the market's up, perhaps you can sell them for more."

"But are they good investments?" the young man persisted.

The dealer looked around. There were still no other customers. "I tell you what. You seem like a bright young fellow. I'm going to take the time to explain how you can make your fortune in rare coins, if you're willing to listen."

The young man nodded, so the dealer proceeded. "There's only one rule. *To make money in rare coins, become a collector.*"

The young man waited, but when the dealer didn't say anything more, he tried to encourage him to continue. " 'Become a collector.' Yes, I understand. But I really don't have a lot of time. I just want to invest a few hundred dollars wisely."

"It doesn't take long to become a collector," the dealer said.

"I only want to invest," the younger man repeated. The dealer began to look annoyed. He said, "Ninety percent of the investors I know lose money in rare coins. Ninety percent of the collectors I know make money. Become a collector."

"But you don't understand," the young fellow persisted. I don't want to collect rare coins, I want to buy them just for profit."

"No, *you* don't understand, sonny." The dealer had a rough scratch to his voice now. "You walk in here and you don't know what coins you want, you don't know what a coin grade is, you don't even know how to hold a coin to examine it. I could tell that about you in thirty seconds. You don't know if this Lincoln is an MS-65 or an AU-55 [different coin grades]. You didn't even notice that it was discolored or if that discoloration made it more or less valuable. You put yourself in my trust and said, 'Sell me something, anything, I can make money on.' Why, you wouldn't care if I sold you a load of bananas as long as you could come back in six months and sell it for more than you paid."

"I didn't mean to upset you," the younger man said.

"I'm not upset. I'm saving you money," the dealer continued. "Rare coins are *not* like other investments. They're *not* like stocks and bonds. Rare coins are unique. No one coin is exactly like any other and that's the truth no matter what anyone says!

"To make money, you have to learn enough about rare coins to perceive value yourself. Else you'll always be at the mercy of some seller or buyer who immediately recognizes that you don't know what you're dealing in."

"Look," said the young man. "Forget I came in. I'm sorry I bothered you. I'll buy elsewhere."

"That just proves what a fool you are," said the dealer.

The young man had started to leave, but now he was getting a bit hot under the collar himself. He turned back and said, "What do you mean?"

"You see this coin here?" the dealer asked, pointing to the discolored Lincoln half. "I offered it to you for one hundred dollars. It's an MS-Sixty-five coin worth at least five hundred fifty dollars."

"It's worth five hundred fifty dollars?" the young man stammered. "What about the other coin?"

"It's a common-date dollar in worn condition. Maybe it's worth twenty dollars."

"You gave me a choice," the young man said.

"It was my test," said the dealer. "Just to prove to myself that you were a greenhorn and didn't know anything. I figured you'd want the dollar because it was bigger and shinier." He smiled.

"That's the one I would have taken," admitted the man. "But you didn't sell me either."

"I'm not here to cheat you." The dealer looked offended. "I'm here to make a market in rare coins. You tell me what you want, I'll get it for you at the best price. You tell me what you want to sell, and I'll give you the most I can for it. But you'd better be able to recognize what you're dealing in. Else someone not quite as nice and honest as I am will sell you a pig in a poke."

The younger man nodded. "But is it hard to learn about rare coins? Does it take a long time?"

"No, it's not hard, and it doesn't take long. But it does require that you get started."

GETTING STARTED
IN RARE COINS

I thought it important to place the above story at the front of this book. The reason is that rare coins today are approaching a billion-dollar-a-year market in the United States alone. Thousands and tens and hundreds of thousands of dollars are traded each hour in rare coins. Fortunes are made in just a short while, and even those who don't make fortunes frequently make enormous returns on their investment.

To put it another way, word has gotten out that rare coins are a magnificent investment. An annual investment survey conducted by Salomon Brothers, the highly regarded New York brokerage house, regularly lists rare coins as one of the best investments. The June 1985 survey ranked rare coins fourth for the previous period behind stocks, bonds, and old master paintings. Going back over fifteen years, rare coins rated second amongst *all* investments, falling behind only to oil. (With the drop in oil prices through 1987, this could change.) Today, many prudent investment counselors advise their clients to invest a *minimum* of 5 percent of their portfolio in rare coins. Rare coins are definitely the investment field of the future.

Yet very few people who invest in rare coins really understand the field. Most think it is like any other investment, from pork bellies to gold bullion. It's not. To show the difference, here's a comparison between investing in a stock and a rare coin.

CHARACTERISTICS	STOCK	RARE COIN
Government-supervised transactions	Yes	No
Homogeneous (one unit exactly like another)	Yes	No
Liquid (national market available for buying and selling)	Yes	Local market-makers
Profitable	?	Sometimes very

Investing in a rare coin is more like buying a Rembrandt than like buying a share of AT&T. It's more like picking a fine Burgundy than it is like ordering a Coke. It's more like owning a stable of fine Arabian horses than like having a Chevy and a Honda in the garage.

To succeed, regardless of what others may suggest, means that you *must* get involved. As one dealer recently told me, "Investors typically buy at the market's peak and then panic-sell when it drops. Also, most don't really know what they are buying, and that enormously increases their chance of getting a misgraded coin."

HOW TO GET INVOLVED

That's why this book was written. It will explain what's happening in rare coins today and show you how to get started for yourself. It will help you to understand coin grading and coin valuation (they are two different things). It will tell you what to look for and what to avoid.

This book is designed to help you survive and prosper in the fantastically profitable world of rare coins.

Chapter

1

WHAT THE EXCITEMENT'S ALL ABOUT

Rare coins have made their impact on investment markets. In an annual survey by Salomon Brothers, the Wall Street financial institution, rare coins have consistently done well. A recent survey suggested a 17.7 percent average annual return over the previous fifteen years and a 20.4 percent annual return over the previous ten years in rare coins. That's almost unbeatable in terms of investment opportunities.

Yet for many the idea of investing in rare coins seems strange, almost contradictory, and at best confusing. After all, coins are everywhere in our lives. Chances are all we have to do is put a hand into a pocket and we'll pull out a dozen different coins. Are any of these worth more to collectors than the value stamped on them?

At one time the answer to that question would have been yes. Years ago the chances of finding a rare coin in pocket change were fairly good. But, for the most part, those times are past. (Collectors have already taken most potential rarities out of circulation.) Today rare coins are to be found in dealers' showrooms, in collections, and in safety deposit boxes. Only in unusual circumstances (such as the mint producing an error coin) is there much chance that a rarity could be found in circulation.

WHAT MAKES A
RARE COIN VALUABLE?

Three elements make a rare coin valuable, and we'll be discussing them throughout this book. They are grade (the quality of the coin), scarcity (how many specimens exist), and popularity (whether anyone collects them).

COINAGE PHOTO BY LARRY STEVENS

RARE COINS (IN HOLDERS)
ALONG WITH COMMON COINS

But before we get into a discussion of value, let's be sure we understand what a rare coin really is. Nearly every coin has a value stamped on its face. (Gold bullion coins sometimes are an exception.) A nickel says five cents, a dime says "dime" right on it, and so forth. The amount stamped on a coin is called its face value, and with U.S. coinage you know that the piece will always be worth at least that much.

However, certain coins—because they are very old and scarce and because they are in excellent condition—may be worth more, far more, than their face values. These are the rare coins. For example, a 1914 nickel with a buffalo design is always worth five cents as U.S. coinage. But to a collector that coin in top condition is worth about $400.

In this field we deal with the rare coins, those worth more than face value. Some coins are worth a great deal of money—tens of thousands of dollars. Others can be purchased for under fifty dollars. But all of them have in common the fact that for several reasons they are prized far more than their face value states. (Also, you can be quite sure no one is going to waste one of them in a vending machine!)

WHAT MAKES
A COIN VALUABLE

Notice that in the above example we said a 1914 buffalo nickel was rare. On the other hand, if we had chosen a 1987 nickel, we probably wouldn't be able to make that statement. Being old usually (but not always) makes a coin rare and valuable. The reason is obvious: They aren't making any more of the older ones. And the vast majority of those that they did make have long since fallen by the wayside, either worn out or melted down for their metal to make other things. Thus, those that remain are highly prized.

SCARCITY

In general, the fewer examples there are of a coin, the more valuable that coin will be. The very word *rarity* means "scarce" or "few in existence." If there were millions of Picassos available, their price wouldn't be very high regardless of their quality. They simply would be too plentiful, like granite. Granite, for example, is quite a pretty kind of rock. But it's hardly scarce or highly valued. A diamond, another type of rock, is highly prized primarily because of its scarcity. Rare coins are like Picassos or diamonds. The fact that there are only a very few of them out there contributes to their value.

BEAUTY

Just being rare or scarce, however, isn't always enough. Ammonia is a relatively scarce item on this planet, but that hardly puts it in high demand. There must be a desire for

SAINT-GAUDENS HIGH-RELIEF
TWENTY-DOLLAR GOLD PIECE
IS COLLECTED BOTH FOR ITS
RARITY AND ITS GREAT BEAUTY

the commodity that is scarce. With coins, the demand originally came from collectors who admired the beauty of coins. They collected coins—such as the twenty-dollar gold piece designed by Saint-Gaudens, for example—because they felt that more than coins, they were striking works of art whose beauty they admired and longed to possess.

More recently investors have replaced collectors as the dominant force in the rare coin field. Their demand is based less on an admiration for a coin's beauty than a desire to take advantage of its price appreciation. While collectors are very discriminating in what they purchase, going after their favored pieces, investors tend to be indiscriminate. Naturally enough, investors don't really care what the coin looks like as long as it makes money. Thus, the investors have relied on the collectors' judgment as to beauty. Hence, coin appreciation has generally gone back to the collector and his eye for beauty.

QUALITY

Finally, and most important, there is the quality of the coin. Collectors will pay a higher price for coins that are in good condition than they will pay for similar coins in poor condition. In fact, of all the factors that determine value, condition is the single most important.

Look at it this way: Any piece of sculpture by Michelangelo is going to be valuable. However, one of his major pieces that is intact is going to be worth vastly more than a broken piece of one foot of a minor work. The quality of the coin, more than anything else, determines the value.

TOP QUALITY

It's important not to be misled about quality. One might think from our Michelangelo example that quality is simply a matter of preservation. Quality, by this reasoning, might mean how close to the original condition the work of art is. Thus, coins might be graded just on how little wear they've accumulated over the years.

However, that would be to assume that every Michelangelo painting or sculpture was equally good. As we all know, however, some were better than others—in the original. And so it is with coins. Some coins—because of the way they were struck at the mint, because of their brilliance, or because of their toning—are simply better pieces than others.

Thus, while how well preserved a coin or a work of art might be is a first consideration, once we've determined that the preservation is perfect, we move on to other considerations. In coins these other considerations are strike, brilliance, toning, and lack of marks or scratches. These features can make a tenfold difference in a coin's value. (A coin with no wear but poor strike, brilliance, or toning might be worth only a tenth of a coin that also has no wear but in which these other features are present.)

If this seems confusing, welcome to the chaotic world of coin grading. We'll delve deeper and deeper into this subject in the next chapter and even show you how to grade your own coins. But for now, let's stick with some basics, namely wear and tear—preservation.

Preservation, or the lack of it, is the single most important reason that pocket change seldom produces rare coins. Even the slightest scratch or abrasion on a coin's surface will severely impinge on its value. Just the handling by our fingers as we hand a coin to another person will produce rub marks on its surface that dramatically lower its value.

This last fact is one that is most frequently misunderstood by noncollectors. My mother was a good example. She was not a coin collector; however, she had heard that people often put away coins for years and later on they turned out to be great and valuable rarities. Consequently, in the 1930s she put away several dozen silver dollars. She felt that someday they would be valuable. Eventually I inherited this small collection.

The coins she had saved were from the late 1800s, mostly from the old Carson City mint. (Mint marks are important in determining coin scarcity; the Carson City coins have a tiny CC placed on them.) As it turned out, if my mother had originally obtained coins with no wear and then had carefully preserved them, they would indeed have been valuable, worth an average of several hundred dollars apiece on today's market. However, my mother was not aware of the importance of condition. She simply took some shiny coins she found in circulation and tumbled them all together in a wooden box. Over the years they rubbed against each other, producing nicks, scratches, and other marks.

Eventually, when I received the collection and took it to a coin dealer for evaluation, I learned that although the coins were rare (based on age and scarcity) and in demand (based on popularity), they were worthless as collectors' items because of their poor condition. (Of course, they were still worth substantially more than face value for their silver content.)

COINAGE

CARSON CITY CC MINT MARKS
(SHOWN IN CIRCLE) ARE STILL
POPULAR WITH MANY COLLECTORS

TOP COINS

The top rare coins are those that combine all the above elements: They are popular, scarce, and in top quality.

HOW TO EXAMINE
A RARE COIN

Before proceeding further, it's important to understand that rare coins cannot be treated like pocket change. Since any marks, scratches, or rubs will dramatically reduce their value, we must have a special way of holding them up for examination. This doesn't mean we need to be intimidated by them. It's just that we must be careful not to damage them.

When looking at a rare coin it is important that it be seen without anything between the eye and the coin. This isn't always possible, since the coins may sometimes be encased in glass or plastic that the owner will not want us to remove. However, whenever making a purchase, the naked coin should be viewed *if at all possible*.

The reason has to do with lighting and refraction. Any coin is relatively small, yet it has many details. Plastic or glass can refract light in such a way as to cover up some of the details, perhaps making the coin seem better or worse than it really is. This is particularly true when we want to examine a coin to see if there has been any wear to the rim.

Therefore, if you're going to buy a coin, first *ask* the owner if you may take it out of the holder. If the owner recognizes that you understand rare coins and are a serious purchaser, he or she will often allow this.

THE PROPER WAY
TO HOLD A COIN

Before taking the coin out of its holder, be sure that you have a piece of cloth beneath where you will hold it, in case the coin should fall. A piece of jeweler's felt works best.

Next, be sure that the coin isn't damaged as you're taking it out. *Avoid touching any surface but the rim.* Be careful of staples or other sharp objects that could scratch the coin. Be sure the holder's opening is clear. Then ease the coin out of the holder without touching the front or back (obverse and reverse) surfaces. *Remember, never touch a rare coin's surface!* Acids and other chemicals in our skin can damage the surface of the coin.

It is normally permissible to hold a coin *gently* by the rim. The best way is between the thumb and index finger, applying as little pressure as possible. But don't drop it! Too little pressure, particularly if we're nervous about its value, can cause it to pop out of our hand. A coin that bounces on the floor and rolls around in the dust can lose 90 percent of its value in just a few moments. (Some owners require purchasers to wear special neutral plastic gloves when handling a coin, just in case.)

Hold the coin up to your eye to see it better, and use a magnifying glass of about 5-power. Don't hold the coin in front of your nose or mouth—exhaled moisture droplets can damage it.

THE CORRECT LIGHT SOURCE

Once you know how to hold a coin to examine it, be sure your examination takes place under the correct light source.

Here a lesson can be learned from photography. Contrary to popular belief, photographers know that the best way to shoot a coin photo is to saturate the coin with diffused light. This cuts down on the mirror effect that a coin's natural surface often has. It also makes the details of the coin stand out. (Putting a "hot," or direct, light on the coin highlights parts of the coin for the camera as well as the eye and can make some items, such as scratches, stand out unnecessarily.)

Unfortunately, using just diffused light tends to soften and lose some of the coin's brilliance. Consequently, photographers will often use two light sources—a diffused light for overall effect and then a tiny spotlight to "raise" the image off the coin, to make it more appealing.

Since the eye works much like a camera, the same holds true for us. If we view a coin in diffused light (outdoors in the shade), we will see many of the details, but we won't see all of its brilliance. If we move it into the sun, we'll see nothing but brilliance and perhaps some scratches.

The correct compromise is to view the coin under a light that will imitate the kind that photographers use. The easiest way to do this is to view the coin under fluorescent light, which tends to be very diffused. In addition, a tiny spotlight such as a Tensor lamp should be added to show the coin's highlights.

If you attend a coin auction, don't be surprised to see the coins displayed under fluorescent lighting on a long table filled with small spotlights and buyers sitting under the lights carefully examining the coins. This is considered good lighting.

Hints • Remember, the lighting affects how we see the coin. Lighting can make a coin seem in either better or worse condition than it actually is. Watch out for the following light sources, which will tend to throw off a coin's appearance:

> sunlight
> shadow
> bare light bulbs
> floodlights alone
> fluorescent alone

WHAT TO LOOK FOR

Now that we know how to hold a coin and how to view it, what are we looking for? How can we tell a rare coin from its more common cousins?

As noted earlier, when we hold the coin up to our eyes we will be looking for five separate features:

> preservation (lack of wear)
> marks or scratches
> strike (how detailed the image)
> luster (brilliance of the
> background and raised areas)
> toning (discoloration)

It takes a lot of experience to weigh all these factors adequately and to make a decision as to a coin's true condition, so don't feel disappointed if you can't do it the first time out. You can, however, learn the basics of grading in a very short period of time—see Chapter 3 to learn how.

At first, however, you can make one decision about the

coin's appearance without being any kind of expert at all. You can decide whether or not you like it. This is often the first and most important step toward becoming more than just an investor—toward becoming a collector.

BUYING AND
SELLING COINS

When we want to buy or sell a stock, we go to a broker, and frequently the trade is handled by the New York Stock Exchange or some similar exchange.

If stocks have Wall Street, what do coins have?

The question is really one of liquidity. Where is the market where coins are bought and sold? Where is the rare coin equivalent of the New York Stock Exchange? The answer is that no equivalent exists. There is no official market for rare coins.

Instead, coins are traded between individuals, bought and sold at auctions, and traded by dealers who make markets in them. By far the largest exchange of coins takes place amongst dealers. There are now coin dealers in virtually every city and community in the country; big cities sometimes have hundreds of dealers.

Dealers usually specialize. For example, ABC dealer on Temple Street may deal in silver dollars. She has a bid price (what she'll buy our coins for) and an ask price (what she'll sell them to us for). The spread is her cost of operation and profit. When we want to buy or sell silver dollars, she'll handle our business.

On the other hand, XYZ dealer on Huron Street makes a market in Mercury dimes and commemorative silver half-dollars. When we want to buy or sell these coins, we see him for his bid and ask prices.

These two dealers make a market, or specialize in certain types of coins. Of course, virtually all dealers will handle all coins. It's just that they won't make a market in them.

Let's go back to XYZ dealer, who makes a market in Mercury dimes and commemorative halves and try to sell him a Standing Liberty quarter. He doesn't make a market in these coins, but he will try to service us. He'll buy and sell any coin we offer, but he will then usually wholesale them out to a dealer who does specialize or make a market in them. Consequently, XYZ may not always be able to offer us top dollar for this coin, not be able to offer us quite as good a deal as on a coin in which he specializes.

DEALER NETWORKS

All of the major dealers are connected by one of at least two different teletype networks. (One network, FACTS, actually uses satellite broadcasting to send information to dealers via individual satellite receivers!) The dealers broadcast their "want" lists as well as their "offer to sell" coins. Thus, they maintain a sort of wholesale coin network between them.

Because of these networks, whether buying or selling, we can work with virtually any major coin dealer. If we go to a dealer who makes a market in the coin we want, we will certainly be shown a wide selection and give bid-ask prices.

On the other hand, if the dealer doesn't happen to make a market in that coin and doesn't have it in stock, yet feels that we are serious buyers, he or she can make a "want" call on the teletype. Another dealer who has the desired coin will then send it. Dealers sometimes swap coins in this fashion or sell wholesale.

How do you know who's a market-maker and who isn't? Ask. Dealers will usually tell you what they specialize in. If they don't specialize in the coin you have or want to get, they may be able to recommend someone else who does.

THE AUCTION MARKET

Rare coins are also sold at auction. Auctions are usually held as part of a coin show. In addition, there are hundreds of companies—such as Superior Coins in Los Angeles,

COINAGE PHOTO BY ED REITER

A TYPICAL REGIONAL COIN SHOW,
WHERE TENS OF THOUSANDS OF
VISITORS ARRIVE TO TRADE COINS

Bower and Merena in New Hampshire, Stack's in New York, and others—that handle mail-order auctions. We'll devote a chapter to how to buy a coin at an auction.

THE COIN SHOW

Finally, there is the matter of a coin show. A few years ago coin shows were few and far between. The national ANA (American Numismatic Association) show always attracted a big crowd, and there were a few large regionals, but that was it.

Today, however, there's a major coin show somewhere in the country virtually every week, and on some days two or three major shows are in full swing. (The ANA even has a midwinter or half-yearly coin show.)

Coin shows are an excellent opportunity to buy and sell and to learn about coins. Like other trade and consumer shows, dealers rent booths and table space. Then they spread out coins that they have to sell and await customers who may want to buy or who have their own coins to sell.

A typical show will have 100 or more dealers. Shows with 500 or more dealers are not uncommon. You simply walk up and down the aisles until you find something of interest.

Hint • Today rare coins are big business. That means that many dealers at coin shows are not really retailers but instead are wholesalers. They are there not so much to deal with you, the public, as to buy and sell coins from other dealers. In some shows as much as 90 percent of the business (dollarwise) consists of interdealer transactions! Therefore, don't be surprised if many dealers are just too busy to talk. They may already have a backlog of clients and are just looking for coins from other dealers to fill their want lists.

If you're new, find a quiet dealer who has some time to talk. He or she may not be in the big time, but you'll probably be able to learn a great deal about coins in just a few moments' conversation.

INVESTMENT
COUNSELOR MARKET

Coins have become such a good investment in recent years that many investment counselors have taken to handling them. Many times such persons will offer to buy or sell coins for you in much the same fashion as they buy or sell stocks, bonds, or any other investment. Almost always the investment counselor is not a dealer but instead works *with* a dealer, usually making a small commission.

There is nothing wrong with this—it may be a preferred

method of investing in coins for some people. But remember that coins bought in this fashion are only as good as the investment counselor (and dealer). If the counselor is fooled, tricked, or cheated, the same happens to you.

WHAT CAN YOU EXPECT
TO PAY FOR RARE COINS?

The sky's the limit. Individual rare coins have been sold for over a million dollars. On the other hand, it's possible to buy many rare coins in top condition for under fifty dollars apiece.

A lot depends on what you're looking for. If you want topgrade coins in the most popular series, expect to pay top-dollar prices, up to several thousand dollars a coin. If you're willing to accept a lower grade, however, or are willing to buy coins in currently unpopular series, you can purchase coins for much less.

Remember, though, you're not going to get rare coins for their face value. Except for some error coins accidentally placed in circulation, that hasn't happened in decades.

Rare coins have become big business, and you're out there competing with investors who have tens and hundreds of thousands of dollars to throw around. (That doesn't mean you can't do better than they do if you learn the market.)

WHAT TO WATCH OUT FOR

We'll have a great deal more to say about this in later chapters, but to begin with there are five general areas that might be termed pitfalls. This is not to say that you're necessarily going to fall into them. Thousands of people invest in rare coins daily with hardly a misstep. Nevertheless, it doesn't hurt to be on the alert. Here's what to look out for:

1. *Overgrading*—As we'll see, grade can be vital when determining price. If you buy a coin as one grade, say an

MS-65, and then, when you sell, discover that it's really a lower grade, say an MS-63, you could lose 90 percent of your investment. (On many coins the current price differential between these two grades is a factor of 10.)

Buying the right grade is the single most important key to success in rare coins. (We'll see how and why in the following chapters.)

2. *Overrated certificates*—As we'll see, the trend today is to give a certificate of grade with a coin. Many investors, however, make the mistake of paying more attention to the certificate than to the coin itself. Certificates can be incorrect. Good judgment (either your own or someone's you trust) is better.

3. *Buying wrong*—The rare coin market has cycles. Buying at the peak and panic selling on the way down has caused many a poor investor to loose a bundle.

4. *No income*—Stocks pay dividends, CDs pay interest, and houses pay rent, but coins pay nothing until they are sold. Don't tie up in rare coins money that you can't afford to let sit. If you need the money to bring you a monthly return, consider placing it elsewhere.

Profit from rare coins can only be made by selling for more than you paid. In the meantime you've got insurance, safety deposit box fees, and lost interest on your money to contend with.

5. *Shysters*—Like any other investment field, rare coins has its share of shysters. At one time counterfeits were a serious problem. However, today with authentication services available, it is no longer really serious. We'll have more to say on this in the chapter on grading.

More of a problem today are the telemarketers. These are individuals who call naive investors and try to get them to buy coins over the phone. Some telemarketers are honest businesspeople. But too many are just plain shysters selling incredibly overgraded coins to unsuspecting investors. If a person hasn't read a book such as this, it would be easy to see how a crooked telemarketer could take advantage of them. (We'll also discuss telemarketing in detail in Chapter nine.)

RARE COIN JARGON

Every field has its own special words—words that have precise and often unusual meanings to those involved. If you're new to the field, not knowing these words can immediately mark you as a novice and put you at a disadvantage. You need to learn the language to be successful in rare coins.

Then again, no one wants to spend hours memorizing a long list of words and meanings. Therefore, I've selected the following words as the most important ones you'll need to know. Look over this short list, learn, and you can talk "rare coineze" with the best of them!

American Numismatic Association (ANA)—most widely recognized coin organization in this country.

Ask price—retail or sales price a dealer is asking for a coin.

Bag mark—abrasion or scratch that a coin gets from being banged around in a mint-sewn bag with other coins.

Bid price—wholesale or bidding price a dealer is asking for a coin.

Bourse floor—room where a coin show is held and coins are bought and sold is called a bourse; floor where the dealers trade is the "bourse floor."

Bullion—physical gold, silver, or other rare metal, usually found in ingots or bars.

Business strike—regular strike on the mint's coin press intended to create a regular coin intended for circulation (see *Proof strike*).

Consignor—person who signs over his or her collection to an auction company for sale.

Device—anything on a coin's surface above the background; this includes the image and lettering.

Die—metal into which the reverse of a coin's design is cut and which is then used in a press to stamp out coins.

Double-die—error in which the press inadvertently struck the coin twice, producing a doubled image, usually visible in dates or mint marks; these can be very valuable.

Eye appeal—overall beauty of a coin.

Field—background of a coin.

Luster—brilliance of a coin, usually associated with its field.

Mint error—error in a coin introduced at the mint.

Mint state—showing no wear, perfectly preserved, as it was when it left the mint; uncirculated.

Numismatist—coin collector.

Obverse—front of the coin, which normally holds the face, or design, pattern.

Patina—discoloration on a coin often caused by contact with another metal or substance. When it refers to copper coins, it is usually brown in color and may detract from value; when it refers to silver coins, it is sometimes called "toning," is often green or blue, and may add value to a coin for collectors.

Proof—*not a grade* but rather a special kind of coin minted exclusively for collectors. (The presses are slowed down and the coin is struck two or more times.) These can easily be distinguished from business strikes by their highly polished and reflective surfaces.

Prooflike—regular circulation coin that looks as though it were a proof.

Restrike—coin struck from old dies at the mint; for example, if the mint today were to strike a 1916 Mercury dime using the original dies, it would be a restrike.

Series—all the coins (by date and mint mark) of a particular type of coin.

Strike—detail imparted to a coin by the die and press.

Toning—natural discoloration of a coin caused by exposure to air and moisture; also sometimes called patina.

Type—category of coin, such as quarters or halves; often further broken down into major design categories such as Morgan dollars.

Uncirculated—coin in mint state, never circulated.

Vest-pocket dealer—dealer without a booth at a coin show who tries to buy or sell coins in the aisles.

Whizzing—polishing a coin with a wire brush or other abrasive. This produces a luster, and the coin is often passed off as a higher grade. Whizzed coins are easily spotted (see Chapter 6.)

Chapter

2

DETERMINING A COIN'S VALUE

We all hope to get what we pay for. In some areas this is easy. We go into a supermarket and buy a bottle of ketchup. The price and value are plainly marked. We purchase a new car. While there may be some dickering with the dealer, by law the manufacturer's suggested retail price—the car's base value—is affixed on a sticker pasted to a window.

Unfortunately, determining value is *not* so easy with rare coins. In fact, as more and more investors have poured into the rare coin field, it has actually become increasingly difficult to determine rare coin values.

Yet value is everything when investing in a coin. Buy a rare coin valued at $1,000 and discover later that its real value is only $500, and you've sustained a substantial loss. The trouble is that most newcomers, as well as some who have been in the field for a while, don't really see the complexity of the problem. Some aren't even aware that there *is* a problem, and some react angrily when the subject of problems with coin valuation is brought up.

For many the word *value* is the same as the word *grade*. They hasten to point out that a coin has a certain grade. Simply determine the grade, see what that grade is currently selling for in one of several pricing guides available, and you have the value.

What could be simpler?

Oh, if things were only so easy!

Let's take an example that will shed some light on what has come to be known as the great grading controversy of the 1980s.

AN ILLUSTRATIVE EXAMPLE

You are an investor who decides to buy an 1880-O silver dollar. (The O refers to the mint mark, in this case the old New Orleans mint that struck coins between 1838 and 1909.) You have been told that for investment purposes, you should buy the best grade possible and that this is an MS-65 grade. (As collectors know, MS stands for "mint state." MS-70 means a state of perfect preservation. MS-65 is nearly perfect. We'll have more to say about this later.) You find a dealer who offers the coin to you with an ANACS (American Numismatic Association Certification Service) certificate stating that the grade is MS-65/65. (The double "65" means that both sides of the coin grade the same.)

The dealer brings out the *Gray Sheet (The Coin Dealer Newsletter,* a weekly publication that lists coin prices and is widely accepted as a determiner of price) and you read that the 1880-O dollar that week in MS-65/65 (both sides having a grade of 65) is worth $3,150.

As an investor, you feel you have concrete value in your hands—a certificate from ANACS, the leading certification service, showing the grade of the coin, and a statement from a leading publication as to the value of a coin of that grade. You buy for $3,150.

AN 1880-0 (NEW ORLEANS MINT) SILVER DOLLAR IN MS-65 CONDITION

AMERICAN NUMISMATIC ASSOCIATION

Later that same day you take that same coin to another dealer. You present the ANACS certificate, and you open a copy of the *Gray Sheet.*

The second dealer nods, then comments, "I wouldn't have paid more than twenty-five hundred dollars for this coin at retail. Were I to buy it from you right now, I couldn't offer you more than two thousand."

You go through a series of emotions—disbelief, alarm, anger. Finally you lash out, "You're a crook! You're offering me a third off of the value of this coin!"

The dealer nods sadly, indicating she understands your frustration. "I'm not a crook," she explains. "I'm just giving you a statement of value. To my eyes, the coin is weakly struck, it has little eye appeal, and, quite frankly, it's a fairly rare piece and I don't have a buyer for it. Therefore, to me, it's only worth a thousand—take it or leave it."

If you had indeed paid over $3,000 for that coin, you would be angry, frustrated, and probably more than just a little inclined to blame someone. But who to blame?

What about ANACS? ANACS in the past has graded primarily on the basis of preservation. Indeed, the entire MS grading system that ANACS uses, even to its very name "mint state," presumes that grade refers to how well preserved a coin is. The grade MS-65, hence, is primarily a statement of how the coin has survived since minting.

However, some coins leave the mint with a better appearance than others. For example, there's the matter of strike. The coins are created on heavy mint presses that stamp them out. While the U.S. mint aims for quality control, some presses work better than others, and some dies that are used to stamp the coins are more highly defined than others.

As a result, the coins, even the same issue from the same mint, will vary somewhat. Some will be struck better than others. Some coins will have a higher luster and will have greater eye appeal.

These characteristics (eye appeal and strike) may not have weighed heavily in the ANACS determination of grade.

(On the back of recent—1986 or later—ANACS certificates is an estimate of these features. See Chapter 3.)

As a result, a coin could *technically* be an MS-65/65 yet commercially be a somewhat lower grade.

But you as the investor have potentially lost a lot of money. You still want someone to blame. Could it be the *Gray Sheet?*

According to a recent comment (November 1985) in the *Gray Sheet,* "In some series of coins the market may be very thin and one buyer's higher bids may be the ultimate indicator. However, gem dollars are not a thin market. MS-65 dollars may be too low, or too high; *we don't know,* but what we do know is that there are plenty of buyers." (The italics are mine.)

Thus, if the *Gray Sheet* reports that the 1880-O silver dollar in MS-65 sold for $3,150, that probably means that one or more coins in that grade, perhaps with good eye appeal and a solid strike, have indeed brought that price.

But how many sales have occurred *at that price?* Were the coins that were sold particularly beautiful? Was it a "personality" purchase (someone with lots of money who was willing to pay any price for that coin)? Is that what *every* 1880-O in that grade is worth? The *Gray Sheet* can't really say, and we don't really know. Price guides are just that, *guides.* They are not offers to buy.

In other words, although the *Gray Sheet* may be doing its level best to present accurate prices, we have to understand that there is no fixed price for a coin. The price is whatever a buyer and seller agree on in an individual sale.

Unlike stocks, bonds, or other investments that are publicly traded minute by minute so that value can easily be determined, rare coins are "occasionally" traded and then often in private sales usually between dealers and customers. Drawing conclusions from these private sales or even from public coin auctions is, at best, difficult.

Well, if you can't blame ANACS or the *Gray Sheet,* why not blame the dealer? After all, isn't he or she offering to buy that coin for $2,000 and can't he or she then turn around to some other uninitiated investor and sell it for over $3,000? That certainly would be underhanded.

Again, the reality is far more complex than what seems obvious. Any dealer who's successfully in business knows what the commercial value of a coin may be. That is, he or she knows what he or she can sell it for. The second dealer you took the coin to was probably being straightforward. She didn't like the appearance of the coin, didn't have a market for it, and couldn't afford to spend more than $2,000 for it. That's what it was worth to her.

Well, then, what about the first dealer, the one who sold it for $3,150? Was he being honest?

He certainly did have a market for the coin—you!

Of course, that skirts the issue of value. Did he sell an overpriced coin?

Maybe. But now we get down to the nuts and bolts of grading. Here we have a coin that holds an ANACS certificate stating it is MS-65/65. Yet two different dealers calculate its value at two vastly different prices. Who's right?

The honest answer? They both could be!

The first dealer may put a lot of faith in technical grading. He may grade highest for preservation. He may have a strong and ready market for the coin. Hence to him it's worth a lot. The second dealer may not care a whit for technical grading. Assuming the coin is uncirculated, she may just look for luster and strike. She may not be able to make a market in the coin, hence won't pay much for it.

What it all comes down to is that if we need someone to blame, the only person who can reasonably be blamed is the investor! That's right. If we buy a rare coin unaware of the valuation problems we've only begun to unveil here and we get stung, we have only ourselves to yell at. Nobody did us in; our lack of knowledge was the culprit!

This is not to suggest, however, that it is impossible to buy rare coins successfully because of grading problems. Far from it—it is not only possible, but in some cases for those who understand the situation, it can be highly profitable. This example was given to point out that today the rare coin field is complex, not simple. The grading issues are tricky. And if you want to play this game to win, you're going to have to spend a little time figuring out all the rules.

Chapter

3

HOW COINS ARE GRADED

It's important to emphasize a subtle distinction made in this book. The last chapter was entitled "Determining a Coin's Value." This chapter is called "How Grading Is Done." The point is that grade and value, despite arguments to the contrary, are *not* the same thing.

Grading may be the single most important factor in determining value, but it is not the only factor. As we've seen and will elaborate on, there are others including liquidity, popularity, and scarcity.

WHAT GRADING REALLY IS

To be honest, grading can only be seen as an attempt to quantify, or rate, the appearance of a rare coin. This is not nearly as difficult to understand as it may at first seem. There are many comparable attempts in other fields. Take the game of bridge, for example. Prior to the 1930s, few people could play the game successfully. This was mainly because it was so difficult to evaluate a dealt hand of thirteen cards. However, Charles Goren came along about then and gave a point value for each card in the deck. All a player had to do in the Goren system was count up the points in his or her hand. If they added up to thirteen or more, that player could open the bidding. There were also point counts for all of the other important bids in the game. Goren's quantifying of bridge was so successful that he toured the world, meeting and beating virtually all the previous champions. It also allowed millions to play successfully.

Quantifying has been attempted in many other fields. Even beauty contests are frequently quantified. So many points are given for appearance in a swimsuit, in an evening gown, for talent, for composure, for personality, and so forth.

Quantifying allows a sense of objectivity. It tends to bring order out of confusion. For rare coins, quantifying is absolutely necessary if there is ever to be any investor confidence in the field.

Thus, it's no wonder that experts have long attempted to give quantity values to the surfaces of rare coins. The first such attempts involved descriptive terms.

THE DESCRIPTIVE SYSTEM

Under the descriptive system, certain words were used to describe the surface appearance of rare coins. Presumably any well-versed collector who read these terms (as used by another well-versed collector) would know exactly what was meant. Among the terms that were widely used (and are still used by some today) are:

Proof—not a grade, but a special, easily identifiable coin struck at the mint just for collectors. The following grades *do not* apply to them.

Uncirculated—"business strike," or coin intended for circulation; however, never touched by human hands, pristine, perfect, and new.

Extremely fine—very little wear and that entirely on the high points of the design. Some of the original mint luster (shine) should still be visible.

Fine—fair amount of wear. This coin has been in circulation for a while, but the design is still bold.

Good—this coin is almost worn out; however, the design is still visible.

Of course, there were many intermediate grades, such as "very fine" or "about good." Nevertheless, the idea should be clear that the coin grade was determined by descriptive adjectives.

INVESTOR PUSH

In the late 1960s and early 1970s, when the first waves of modern inflation hit America, there was a big surge of investment interest in rare coin collecting as an inflation hedge. The question most frequently asked by investors was, "What grade coin should I buy?"

Long-time adherents of the field, myself included, said and wrote, "Buy the *best* grade you can afford. It will appreciate fastest in value and will be the easiest to resell later on."

The wisdom of these words quickly became evident as coin prices rose and UNCs (the top-graded coins) rose faster and farther by a long shot than any other grade.

However, with so much demand for UNC coins, there was a natural tendency on the part of some to slip in some slightly lower-grade coins and call then UNCs. For example, a coin that was a bit better than the next grade down but still not an UNC tended to be upgraded during a hot market and called an UNC.

At the same time there were some supercoins that were clearly better than the run-of-the-mill UNCs. Dealers fretted that they were "giving away" these finer coins by having to sell them as UNCs. Thus, the one grade, UNC, was actually too broad to encompass all the coins it was supposed to cover. As a result, grade "slippage" occurred, and two new descriptive terms came into widespread use:

Choice (or Brilliant) Uncirculated:
a step above UNC.

About Uncirculated:
A step below UNC.

These new words sometimes did more harm than good. Some investors who had paid good money for UNCs were now told their coins were only "about UNC" and worth substantially less. Dealers who had previously been selling all UNCs for about the same price now began selling "choice UNCS" for more and "about UNCs" for less. Investors were confused.

THE MINT-STATE
GRADING SYSTEM

In an attempt to bring order to the confusing and rapidly fragmenting grading of rare coins, the American Numismatic Association (ANA)—under the guidance of a wise and experienced dealer, Abe Kosoff—adopted a grading standard called the MS (mint-state) system.

This system was originally introduced by William Sheldon, M.D., in his book *Early American Cents 1793–1814* (published n 1949 by Harper & Row) which was reissued as *Penny Whimsy* in 1958. (We'll have a great deal more to say about Dr. Sheldon and his book in a few pages.)

They took the Sheldon system and applied it to all U.S. coins. The system is based on a scale of 1 to 70. A grade of 70 was the top grade a coin could get. It meant the coin was in the same condition as when it came from the mint.

Grades below 70 indicated a less-than-perfect coin. Not all the numbers were filled in. In fact, Dr. Sheldon's original eighteen numerical grades were reduced to thirteen. Here are those thirteen, with their correlation to the older descriptive system.

MINT-STATE SYSTEM	DESCRIPTIVE SYSTEM
MS-70	Perfect
MS-65	Choice uncirculated
MS-60	Uncirculated
AU-55	Choice about uncirculated
AU-50	About uncirculated
EF-45	Choice extremely fine
EF-40	Extremely fine
VF-30	Choice very fine

VF-20	Very fine
F-12	Fine
VG-8	Very good
G-4	Good
AG-3	About good

THE POWER OF THE
NEW GRADING SYSTEM

On the face of it, it would seem that what had been done was to substitute one system for an equivalent one. Except for the grade of MS-70, there was a corresponding descriptive term for virtually every grade.

However, the difference was in the addition of numbers. Grading by numbers implies (whether or not it actually accomplishes) objectivity and quantification. It suggests that there is a standard that all can agree on.

At first this system proved satisfactory. In fact, some claim with good justification that this grading system is what propelled the rare coin upward into the realm of a credible investment.

However, in recent years it has become controversial. In fact, as this is written, rather than saying that grading has become confused, it might be more appropriate to say that it has become chaotic.

Dozens of grading services that will grade your coin for a fee have come into existence. Each of these potentially could grade the same coin somewhat differently.

In addition, in mid-1986 the ANA adopted new grading guidelines for uncirculated coins. The grades between MS-60 and MS-70 were all filled in. Thus there are now official grades of MS-61, MS-62, MS-63, MS-64, MS-65 and so forth all the way to MS-70.

However, at the same time the ANA *dropped* the adjectival references for these (MS-60 to MS-70) grades. Thus, officially, there are only numerical grades for uncirculated coins, no corresponding adjectival description.

Thus, when a collector or investor asks, "What exactly is an MS-64 coin?", the "official" answer is that it is a coin given that grade by ANACS.

Dealers in response have come up with a whole series of adjectival references for each grade including: brilliant; select; choice; gem; prime; perfect.

Of course these adjectival descriptions do not officially apply to any designated grade between MS-60 and MS-70.

How did this chaotic situation occur?

INVESTOR DEMAND

The problem is that recently the already great numbers of investors in the rare coin field have increased enormously. They've all heard that fortunes are to be made and all have been given the same advice, buy the highest quality coin you can afford. For most investors this has meant MS-65 coins.

Thus, today we have a huge investor demand for MS-65 material and the relatively scarce numbers of these coins has driven their price up. As a result, the price of MS-65 grade coins is many times more than the next lower grades. For example, the price differential between MS-65 and MS-63 is often a factor of ten! (MS-65 and MS-63 are two widely recognized grades.)

There is so much demand around the MS-65 category that many dealers have discovered (or invented) whole new subtleties of grading. For example, although the ANA has officially endorsed the MS-64 grade, there has been very little dealer acceptance of it as a distinct grade. Instead dealers have discovered (or invented) subtle sub-grades. For example, some dealers use the designation "MS-64A or MS-64B." Others use "MS-64+ or MS-64−." Some have even gone so far as to have "MS-64.1, MS-64.2, MS-64.3, MS-64.5" and so forth. The whole idea seems to be to try to grade a coin as close to MS-65 (the grade all the investors want) as possible, even though it isn't an MS-65 coin.

To put it another way, the more inventive a seller can be in creating the impression that the coin is "near MS-65," the more the coin will be worth.

On the other hand, there has been pressure to advance true MS-65 graded material into the new grades of MS-66, MS-67, MS-68, and MS-69.

As a result, dealers have been blamed in some quarters for the turmoil in the grading of rare coins. "If only they would stick to accepted standards, then everything would still be fine," I've heard one investor lament. (The trouble, of course, is that the "accepted standards" aren't really accepted or standard.)

Finally, it's just as easy to blame the investors. If they weren't swarming into the field pushing up the price of top grade material, then our present problems might not exist. (Investors generally don't want material graded lower than MS-60 and, consequently, there is no grading crisis in that area.)

AN INADEQUATE SYSTEM

Putting the blame on dealers or investors, however, really misses the point. The problem is not here because dealers or investors want it. (Both would be delighted to see it go away, if only it would.) The problem is here because the current coin grading system is no longer adequate to handle the needs of today's market.

Until a grading system comes along that so clearly defines *all* the grades that there is little to no disagreement, the chaos will continue. This certainly hasn't deterred investors nor kept profits down and that, undoubtedly, won't change in the future, either.

Chapter

4

CERTIFICATION

I've never known a collector who felt it was necessary to obtain a certification for a coin. On the other hand, I've never met an investor who didn't jump at the chance to get a coin certificate. Therein lies a critical difference.

A coin certificate, or certification, is a piece of paper that usually states that a particular coin is authentic and/or that it is of a specific grade. It is a document that goes along with the coin. (It normally contains a photo of the coin, thus linking the two.)

Certification is a means whereby standards can be applied so that anyone, knowledgeable or not, can immediately know the quality of a rare coin. It is neither an unusual nor a unique idea. Lots of things are certified, from milk to diamonds to dogs (pedigree).

INVESTORS AND CERTIFICATION

For coin investors, certification offers the promise of a panacea. It takes away the necessity of having to become familiar with coins. With certification an investor need only look at the certificate to determine the coin's grade and its authenticity. In no small part certification has been responsible for the latest wave of investors to enter the field of coin collecting.

Unfortunately, certification is not without its problems.

In this chapter we're going to look at both the benefits and the pitfalls of coin certification.

USA 1921 $1

In our opinion this is a genuine original item as described.

ANACS No.   ᴱ-0ː⸱⸱   GRADE: Proof 65/65

Registered To: _____   2-28-79

ANACS CERTIFICATE INDICATING
THAT THE COIN IS GENUINE AND
ALSO GIVING THE COIN GRADE—
IN THIS CASE PROOF 65/65 (BOTH
OBVERSE AND REVERSE GRADE 65)

FIRST ATTEMPTS
AT CERTIFICATION

It was in the 1970s that the first widespread use of certification took place. At the time there was concern about fake coins entering the market.

To combat this problem, the ANA determined to begin certifying the authenticity of coins. It would look at rare coins and then render an opinion as to whether or not they were counterfeit.

ANACS (the American Numismatic Association Certification Service) was founded to authenticate coins. For many years it served its function well. It performed so admirably, in fact, that investors began asking to see an ANACS certificate of authenticity before they bought a coin.

The old ANACS certificate became a standard by which coins were judged.

Then, in the late 1970s, amidst the confusion over grading standards brought on by the influx of investors, the ANA decided to expand its ANACS services. Building on the excellent reputation of ANACS, it determined that the service would not only determine authenticity but also give coin grades. Anyone could submit a coin to ANACS, which would then issue a determination as to grade and authenticity. This service is still currently available.

At first this certification service was greeted with universal applause. At last there would be agreement as to grade. An ANACS certificate would state for all time a coin's indisputable grade. If ANACS said a coin was MS-65, then any dealer should be willing to pay his bid MS-65 price for the coin. (Dealers are in reality market-makers who usually offer bid—what they will buy a coin for—and ask—what they will sell a coin for—prices.)

If investor interest in the field had seemed strong before, now it redoubled. With certification came certainty. A buyer could purchase today and be assured that tomorrow when he or she sold, there would not be a grading argument, or at least so everyone thought.

CERTIFICATION PROBLEMS

It hasn't worked out quite that way for several reasons, some of which we have already discussed.

ANACS looks primarily at preservation—at how well preserved the coin is. As we noted, the system's very name, "mint-state," indicates that it is based on preservation. This has come to be known as "technical" grading, or grading by "technical standards."

Any system based on preservation must of necessity give lesser attention to such things as strike and luster,

REQUEST FOR ANACS CERTIFICATION
You must use a separate form for each item. Please send coins in easy access holders.

Name _____ ANA No. _____
(Print or type)   (Last)   (First)

Address _____ Phone (____) _____

City _____ State _____ Zip _____

Issue Certificate to: _____
(Indicate personal name or company trade name)

SERVICE REQUESTED: **ITEM:**
☐ Authentication only ☐ Authentication and Grading   ☐ Coin
☐ Grading of previously authenticated coin* ☐ Reexamination*   ☐ Paper Money
☐ Duplicate* ☐ Transfer*   ☐ Medal
☐ Custom photographic service (enclose instructions).   ☐ Token
*Original ANACS certificate MUST be enclosed   ☐ Other

Issuing Country _____

Date of item _____ Mint Mark _____

Denomination _____ Variety _____
Owner's Valuation $ _____ ANACS fees and insurance are based on this value.
                                        Coins will be valued at $150 if no valuation is provided.

Comments/instructions _____

I understand and acknowledge that any opinion rendered by the ANA Certification Service on the authenticity or condition of the item submitted herewith represents a considered judgment by the examiners employed by the ANA. Authentication does NOT, however, constitute a guarantee that the item is genuine, and neither authentication nor grading by ANACS guarantees that others will not reach a different conclusion. The item will be examined with nondestructive testing techniques available to the Service and will be judged by examiners based upon information available to them, but no warranties are expressed or implied from any opinion rendered in consequence of this application. Permission is granted for ANACS to photograph and use information gained from this piece for educational purposes.

DATE _____ SIGNATURE _____

☐ Send additional ANACS forms. ☐ Send information on ANA membership.

DO NOT WRITE IN THIS SECTION
Item number _____
Diameter _____ Sp. Gr. _____
Wt. _____
Gen. _____ Alt. _____ Cft. _____ ND _____
Replica _____ Other _____
Grade-Obv. _____ Rev. _____ N/O _____
D/O Grade _____
_____
_____
_____
Date Ret. _____ RC No. _____
Reg. No. _____

FEES PER ITEM
(See reverse for fee schedule)

Authentication fee	$_____
Grading fee	_____
Duplicate fee	_____
Transfer fee	_____
Reexamination fee	_____
Custom Photography	_____
Return Postage (22¢ per oz.)	_____
Registered Mail fee	_____
TOTAL (this form only)	$_____
TOTAL PAYMENT ENCLOSED	$_____

Send this form with check payable to ANACS.
Fees are per item—postage may be grouped.

AMERICAN NUMISMATIC ASSOCIATION CERTIFICATION SERVICE

● Renders an opinion as to whether a numismatic item is genuine or otherwise.

● Renders an opinion as to grade only on United States coins submitted for authentication. U.S. coins previously authenticated by ANACS may be graded if resubmitted with the original photo certificate and payment for the grading fee.

● Issues a photo certificate with a registered number on genuine items. This certificate is returned with the item.

● Cannot determine valuations of items—values must be supplied by submittor.

● Cannot grade coins that have not been authenticated.

● Cannot be responsible for opening or returning special holders, or removing items from unusual packaging.

● Cannot grade foreign coins or paper money.

● Cannot authenticate or grade legal tender currency.

AUTHENTICATION, GRADING & REEXAMINATION FEES — BASED ON OWNER'S ESTIMATED VALUE.

Owner's Value	ANA Member Fee Auth.	ANA Member Fee Grading	Non-Member Fee Auth.	Non-Member Fee Grading
$ 0-$150	$ 7.00	$ 5.50	$ 8.00	$ 6.50
151- 300	10.00	5.50	11.50	6.50
301- 550	14.00	5.50	16.00	6.50
Over $550	2.7% of value	1% of value	3% of value	1.5% of value
Maximum Fee	$300.00	$20.00	$325.00	$25.00

All fees are per item and include photographic certificate.
Duplicate and transfer fees $7.50 per item.

REGISTERED MAIL FEES

$ 0.00 to $100 - $3.60	$4000.01 to 5000 - $5.65
100.01 to 500 - 3.90	5000.01 to 6000 - 6.00
500.01 to 1000 - 4.25	6000.01 to 7000 - 6.35
1000.01 to 2000 - 4.60	7000.01 to 8000 - 6.70
2000.01 to 3000 - 4.95	8000.01 to 9000 - 7.05
3000.01 to 4000 - 5.30	9000.01 to 10,000 - 7.40

$10,000.01 to $25,000 add 35¢ per each additional $1,000.00 evaluation.
WARNING: For your protection total value in one package should not exceed $25,000.00.

ADDITIONAL CUSTOM PHOTOGRAPHIC SERVICES
(In addition to ANACS Certificate)

Black & White Prints	ANA Mem. Fee	Non-Mem. Fee	Enlargements	ANA Mem. Fee	Non-Mem. Fee
Film developing, 1-6 coins, all orders	$ 2.50	$ 3.00	4x5 single coin image only	$ 5.00	$ 5.50
3x5 actual coin size, obv./rev.	5.00	5.50	5x7 single coin image only	5.75	6.25
4x6½ Polaroid, actual coin size, obv./rev. in double window mat	10.00	11.00	5x7 double coin image, obv./rev.	6.50	7.50
			8x10 single coin image only	6.75	7.75
Slides—(single coin image only)			8x10 double coin image, obv./rev.	7.50	8.25
24x36mm - black & white	5.00	5.50			
24x36mm - color	6.50	7.50	Quantity discounts also available.		

For additional forms or information contact.

ANACS, 818 N. Cascade, Colorado Springs, CO 80903   Phone (303) 632-2646

3/85

ANACS APPLICATION FOR COIN AUTHENTICATION AND GRADING

which along with toning and marks combine to create eye appeal. Unfortunately, eye appeal is the essence of commercial grading; it is what coin collectors and investors frequently look for in a coin.

Let's consider the elements of eye appeal.

Strike • A coin is struck when a planchet, or round cutout of metal, is placed between two dies that have images on them, and then the two dies are squeezed into the planchet under enormous pressure in a coin press.

LEFT: PLANCHETS, OR BLANK METAL DISKS, BEING STAMPED OUT. EACH OF THESE WILL LATER BECOME A COIN. BELOW: MINTING PRESSES INTO WHICH PLANCHETS ARE FED— PHILADELPHIA MINT

COINAGE PHOTO BY LARRY STEVENS

COINAGE PHOTO BY LARRY STEVENS

COINAGE PHOTO BY LARRY STEVENS

DIES THAT STRIKE THE
PLANCHETS IN THE PRESSES
TO PRODUCE COINS

Ideally, the dies will be very sharp and highly detailed, and the press will have sufficient pressure to stamp the impression on the dies clearly into the metal. That's not, however, how it always works.

Sometimes, for one reason or another, the presses do not deliver all the pressure they should. At other times the dies have been in use for a long period of time and have become worn. Whatever the reason, the coins thus created are said to be "weakly struck."

Luster • Luster refers to the way in which a coin reflects light. A variety of descriptive terms are used here, including *brilliant surface, satin velvet, cameolike,* and *chromelike.* These are explained in more detail in chapter five on grading, but for the moment, let's just understand that they refer to the different lighting aspects of a coin.

Many of these terms come under the general heading of *prooflike*. A proof coin is a coin specially struck at the mint and intended just for collectors. Among its characteristics are high refraction of light. When a business strike (intended for circulation) that's never been circulated exhibits similar qualities, it is sometimes termed prooflike.

Marks and Scratches • These come from coins scratching other coins. In many cases, particularly with silver dollars, the coins were taken from the mint and sewn into bags. When these bags were later opened by collectors, the fact that they were still mint sewn gave proof that the coins had never been put into circulation. Yet they still had scratches.

These detracting features are technically not considered wear. Rather, they are a separate category. They definitely do, however, count against eye appeal.

Toning • Toning, also called patina, is the coloration of a coin that occurs over time and is caused by chemicals

AMERICAN NUMISMATIC ASSOCIATION

LEFT: A PROOF COIN—NOTE
THE MIRRORLIKE FINISH
RIGHT: MS-63 "BUSINESS STRIKE"
COMPARE WITH PROOF COIN

coming into contact with the coin's surface. Silver coins sometimes tone beautifully, and patina often adds to their value. Copper coins tend to tone badly, and this may reduce their value.

It's the combination of strike, luster, lack of marks and scratches, as well as pleasant toning that produces what is termed eye appeal. (We'll say much more about eye appeal in the chapter on grading.)

EYE APPEAL
AND COMMERCIAL
GRADING

The affect of eye appeal on commercial grading is not to be discounted. It can make an enormous difference. What every dealer who is worth his salt quickly comes to realize is that buyers like coins that look good (have strong eye appeal).

Suppose there are two coins that both have ANACS MS-65/65 certificates. (The double 65 indicates the grade for obverse and reverse.) But one is drab and weakly struck, while the other is brilliant and highly detailed. If you, the reader, were offered both coins at the same price, I am quite confident you would without hesitation pick the coin with greater eye appeal. There's no question at all in my mind that this is what you'd do, and there shouldn't be any question in yours.

Recognizing the fact that eye appeal makes such a big difference, dealers have come to realize that two such similar coins are in reality two very different coins, regardless of what technical grading may say. Hence, they might grade the finer-looking coin as a commercial MS-67 and the poorer-looking coin as a commercial MS-63, even though both might have ANACS paper saying they are MS-65 coins.

Thus, having an ANACS certificate, while it may indicate technical grade, is *not* a statement of commercial grade.

DEALERS' CERTIFICATES

Coin dealers—aware of the confusion between technical and commercial grading (remember that technical grading considers primarily the coin's state of preservation, whereas commercial grading also considers its eye appeal)—have begun issuing their own certificates. Typically, these certificates give the dealer's version of the coin's commercial grade.

Dealers' certificates are an attempt to associate grade more closely with value. Many of these are currently on the market. (See list of certification services at the end of this chapter.)

GRADE DISAGREEMENT

If every certificate that was issued gave the same grade for a coin, there would be no problem at all with grading. However, as we've already seen, an ANACS certificate will frequently differ from a dealer's certificate because one is based on technical grading while the other uses a commercial approach.

However, there is a yet more discomforting problem. While some coins are easily graded (most professionals looking at the coin would agree as to its grade), others are more difficult to grade and any two professionals looking at them might give two different grades. These borderline coins might produce arguments depending not only on the individual grader but on the grading service.

As a solution to this problem (as noted earlier), several grading services have recently undertaken to "guarantee" their coins. This means that once that coin has been given a certain grade, whoever belongs to that grading service will honor that grade at his bid price for the coin. It remains to be seen how valuable these guarantees prove to be in the long run.

GRADING DRIFT

Yet another concern is how grading is perceived at different times in history. (These times need not be far apart, perhaps only a year or two.) This is bound to occur because the times influence how we look at things. In boom markets when there is enormous demand for coins, the pressure is to upgrade pieces. In down markets, when there is much less demand, the pressure is to downgrade coins.

In addition, regardless of the grading service, over time different people will look at coins and will come up with different opinions based on their own assessments.

As a result, grading standards from within a service will vary somewhat. For example, it is sometimes suggested among rare coin professionals that between 1981 and 1983 ANACS graded coins more leniently than it has done so since.

In response to this, early in 1986, the ANA issued a policy statement that follows:

Here's an example of what this discussion is all about.

What you see (page 62) is a coin graded as an MS-65/65 by ANACS in 1982. I sent this same coin back to ANACS for grading in 1985 with the resulting grade change of MS-63/63.

The coin hadn't changed. It was even in the same holder. What had changed was the perception of the graders.

The Results of Grading Drift • As a result of grading drift, certificates tend to be valued according to their date. For example, dealers will sometimes give two prices for the certificates of one well-known private grading service (not ANACS). The first price is for certificates with an early date. The second price (discounted by as much as 80 percent!), is for later-date certificates for which the dealers feel there was laxer grading. When you are thinking about getting your coin certified, be sure that you first check around with dealers to see if they are discounting the grading service you are considering using.

Grading is an art and not an exact science. More precisely, grading is a matter of opinion. Differences of opinion may occur among graders as to a particular coin, and any grader could conceivably change his interpretations of the grading standards over the years.

When the ANA *Official Grading Standards for United States Coins* book was published in 1978, it represented a new grading system, previously untried. As Abe Kosoff, who spearheaded the project, and others said at the time, the grading standards may change over a period of time.

The grading standards as enumerated in the book were and are not precise, with the descriptions lending themselves to different interpretations. The marketplace—composed of collectors and dealers—has tightened its interpretation in recent years and ANACS has reflected those changes. Accordingly, the ANA Grading Service, endeavoring to keep in step with current market interpretations (rather than create interpretations of its own), has in recent times graded coins more conservatively than in the past, in many instances.

Hence, it may be the situation that a coin which was graded MS-65 by the Grading Service in 1981 or 1982, for example, may, if regarded in 1985 or 1986, merit the current interpretation of MS-63 or less. Similarly, dealers and others in the commercial sector have found that coins that they graded MS-65 several years ago may merit MS-63 or lower interpretations today.

In each instance, the ANA Grading Service was endeavoring to the best of its ability to grade in conformity with prevailing interpretations at the time, as were many dealers.

Because of its imprecise nature, which admits a great deal of subjectivity and opinion, it may be the case that the interpretation of grading standards will continue to change in the future, as indeed they have done over a long period of past years.

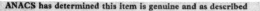

ANACS has determined this item is genuine and as described

USA 1865 TWO CENTS

No: S-3201-B   Size: 23.0mm   Grade: MS63/63
Registered to: 08-29-84

ANACS has determined this item is genuine and as described

USA 1865 TWO CENTS

No: F-6760-Y   Size: 23.0mm   Grade: MS60/60
Registered to: ROBERT WOLENIK   12-02-85

COINAGE PHOTO BY ROBERT WOLENIK

THE SAME COIN—IN 1984
IT GRADED MS-63/63. IN
1985 IT GRADED MS-65/65.

THE CERTIFICATE GAME

Perhaps the most dangerous aspect of certificates is that some investors are prone to buy the certificate instead of the coin.

This is very much like the old advertising saw about sardines. Two advertising men were discussing a brand of sardines they were promoting. The one man was saying that he had sent a can of the sardines to one public relations firm and then another, and each time he had gotten a better response than before.

The second man said, "Yes, I know what you mean. Except that yesterday I was hungry and I got hold of that very can of sardines and opened it. It was empty—there were no sardines in it!"

The first advertising man was aghast. "You shouldn't have opened it," he replied, "That can of sardines wasn't for eating. It was for selling."

With coins, sometimes the certificates become so important that the coin is secondary. And should somebody take a close look at the coin, they could be in for a nasty surprise.

It's vitally important to understand that certificates can be a very useful guide to coin grading and perhaps valuation. But the certificate should not be considered an absolute source of information for these reasons:

1. The coin could be misgraded regardless of what the certificate says.

2. There could have been grading drift since the certificate was issued.

3. The coin could have been damaged since the certificate was issued.

4. The certificate could have been tampered with. Yes, look at and consider the certificate. But also look at and consider the coin.

PLAYING WITH CERTIFICATES

I have seen some sneaky investors who have played the certificate game in reverse. They would buy a coin that already had a certificate saying it was MS-63, but that they believed to be slightly better. Then they'd send it out to a certification service seeking an MS-65 grade. (Remember, the price differential between these two grades can be as much as a factor of 10.)

If the certificate came back as MS-63, the investor would throw out the new certificate and send the coin in to another service. Eventually, given enough tries, the player might get a certified grade of MS-65. He would then find an unsuspecting investor *who looked first at the certificate instead of the coin* and sell it to him for a whopping profit as an MS-65.

This could never happen to a collector who understood grading and who would first examine the coin. But it could easily happen to an investor who relied solely on certificates for expertise.

CERTIFICATION SERVICES

Note: *Although a best effort was made to secure the latest services, prices and addresses, these may have changed by the time you read this material. Check with services FIRST before submitting any coins for evaluation.*

AMERICAN NUMISMATIC ASSOCIATION CERTIFICATION SERVICES (ANACS)

Discussed in detail in Chapter 4. Write: 818 N. Cascade, Colorado Springs, CO 80903.

PROFESSIONAL COIN
GRADING SERVICE (PCGS)

As of this writing, this is probably the most widely used grading service other than ANACS. A major force behind it is dealer David Hall of Newport Beach, California. The grading is all done by Hall and a group of six other dealers. Dealer members of the service agree to accept the grade assigned to coins and to honor that grade at their current bid price, sight unseen. Coins are sealed in plastic with the grade on the holder. The cost is currently $15 per coin. Write: PO Box 9458, Newport Beach, CA 92658.

NUMISMATIC CERTIFICATION
INSTITUTE (NCI)

This grading service is run by Heritage Capital Corp. of Dallas, Texas. It has been in existence for several years and is widely used. The principal graders are Steve Ivy and Jim Halperin. NCI offers a unique plan in which the customer suggests the grade desired for the coin. If NCI can't give that grade, the coin is returned ungraded and there is a minimum charge of $5. If the service can give the desired grade, there is a minimum fee of $10 plus an escalating fee (currently 2 percent of the coin's value) for the service. A photo of the coin appears on the certificate. Write: Heritage Bldg., 311 Market St., Dallas, TX 75202.

INTERNATIONAL NUMISMATIC
SOCIETY (INS)

This service grades both United States and world coins. It issues two certificates, one stating authenticity, the other stating grade. The fees are from $15 to $240, and discounts are offered for members and volume customers. The service takes pride in its quick turnaround time. A photo of the coin appears on the certificate. Write: PO Box 66555, Washington, DC 20035.

MARKET PRICING
CERTIFICATE

The Rare Coin Exchange offers a certificate of grading currently using three authenticators. The grading is done using the ANACS number system plus letter grades from "A" to "E." The cost is based on a sliding scale up to a maximum of 4 percent of the owner's valuation. A photo of the coin is included in a sealed certificate. Write: 1423 Fullerton Ave., Chicago IL 60614.

ACCUGRADE

This service is provided by Silver Dollars, Unlimited. The grading is done by coin dealer Alan Hager. He uses his own grading system. The system is explained in detail in a series of books (currently two volumes have been published) by Hager which are available to the public. The certificate includes a photo of the coin. The price is $22 per coin with volume discounts. Write: PO Box 632, Bedford, NY 10506.

A-MARK PRECIOUS
METALS, INC.

This service grades only "eagles" ($10) and "double eagles" ($20) gold pieces. The certificate carries a guarantee of authenticity and grade and the coins are permanently mounted in a plastic holder. The service is only available to those who buy these coins directly from A-Mark. Write: 9696 Wilshire Blvd., Beverly Hills, CA 90212.

COIN AND STAMP
GRADING INSTITUTE

Offers a digital computer printout of the coin's image. Uses ANA standards and offers a sealed certificate of grade. The service guarantees to return coins within 10 working days. The minimum fee is $15. Write: PO Box 35426, Edina, MN 55435.

AUTHENTIGRADE

A service offered by professional dealer Ronald Gillio. It is available only for "eagles" ($10) and "double eagles" ($20). Coins are permanently sealed into compact holders that include the grade and a certification number. A permanent computerized record is kept of every number, along with the denomination, type, grade and authenticator. Write: 1013 State St., Santa Barbara, CA 93101.

NATIONAL NUMISMATICS CERTIFICATION SERVICE (NNCS)

Offered by professional dealer Martin Paul. Coins are graded using extended numbers (60+, 63+, 64+, 65+ etc.). The coins are ultrasonically sealed in holders. The grading fee is 3 percent of the owner's valuation with a minimum fee of $15. Write: 221 Boston Post Rd., Suite 260, Marlboro, MA 01752.

VAN ALLEN GRADING SERVICE

Coins are graded by professional Leroy Van Allen using a 10 power microscope. A detailed certificate including a large black and white photo is issued. The price is $15 per coin with quantity discounts available. Write: PO Box 196, Sidney, OH 45365.

AMERICAN CERTIFICATION SERVICE

Coins are graded to "real world standards" without the use of "split grades." The fee is 3 percent based on the owner's valuation with a minimum of $15. Write: 1992 N. Jerusalem Rd., N. Bellmore, NY 11710.

PROFESSIONAL APPRAISAL
BY LES FOX

Les and Sue Fox do all the grading, mainly of U.S. coins. An appraisal form is used and no certificate is issued. The form includes wholesale and retail value and offers an opinion as to whether the owner should retain or sell the coin. The service is done in lots of 20 coins—$200 for the first 20, $5 for each additional. Write: Les Fox/Fortune Teller Publications, Inc. PO Box 4206, Tequesta, FL 33469.

Chapter

5

HOW TO GRADE YOUR OWN COINS

One statement that all experts would agree on is that the prime determiner of value in a coin is its grade. Unfortunately, having said this, they would undoubtedly disagree immediately on how to grade any particular coin. For, as we've seen, grading remains much more an art than a science.

Yet it is an art that every investor-collector had better learn if he or she expects to profit from the field.

This is not to say, of course, that to invest in rare coins you must immediately become an expert in grading. That takes years of time. What you must do is learn enough about grading to avoid being taken advantage of.

To put it another way, if you were investing in residential real estate, even if you were a passive investor in a limited partnership deal (syndicate), it would behoove you to know the difference between a good location and a bad one, a realistic market price and a fantasy price, good financing and bad—in other words, the difference between a good deal and a bad one.

Rare coins are similar. Even if you are dealing with an investment counselor, it pays for you yourself to know what you are buying, whether you are getting a good deal or a bad one. The way to do this, in large part, is to become at least relatively competent at grading.

That's what this chapter aims to do—to give you the rudiments of coin grading so that you'll have some idea of what you're getting into.

Don't expect to read this one chapter and instantly be a top coin grader. While you should be able to discriminate between major grades, you probably still won't be able to see subtle differences. That kind of judgment takes years of constant exposure to coins to achieve.

LIMITING THE FIELD

There are a great many coin grades from About Good (AG-3) to Perfect (MS-70), and entire books have been written just describing the differences for each U.S. coin. (We'll be introducing those books shortly.) Rather than try to cover everything, which obviously would be beyond the scope of this book, we are going to limit our grading education here to learning how to discriminate between investment-grade coins (MS-60 and above) and collector coins (AU-55) and below. For those who wish to invest in the field, understanding this distinction is mandatory.

An investment-quality coin has traditionally meant an uncirculated coin. Of course, "uncirculated" means MS-60, and in today's market this is the lowest investment grade (many consider it not to be an investment grade at all), so as we go we'll move a step forward and see how to discriminate between MS-60 and the higher-grade coins such as MS-65.

THE COIN IN QUESTION

For grading purposes we're going to pick primarily the Morgan dollar (minted between 1878 and 1904, with additional coins minted in 1921). This coin has been extremely popular. In fact, there are dealers who do nothing but make a market in Morgan (and Peace) dollars. For many investors getting started in the field, this is often the first step.

We are going to see how Morgan dollars are graded. Of course, having once seen how this coin is graded, it should be possible for you to use the same format and techniques to grade whatever coin you may have.

HOW TO HOLD THE COIN

If you own a Morgan dollar, get it and examine it as we go through this chapter. If not, look at the picture, which illustrates holding a coin in general.

To begin, it's important to hold a coin properly for ex-

HOLDING COIN FOR EXAMINATION
UNDER A MAGNIFIER. BE SURE TO HOLD
COIN FIRMLY, BUT *ONLY BY THE RIM.*

amination. This has already been discussed in an earlier chapter, but a few comments bear repeating:

1. Examine the coin, if possible, *outside* of its holder. (Be careful not to damage the coin on staples or other sharp objects when removing it from its holder.)

2. Hold the coin by its rim with your thumb and forefinger. *Never touch the surface, as immediate damage may result.* Don't be afraid to squeeze fairly hard. It is, after all, metal and won't crumble. On the other hand, don't squeeze so hard (or so softly) that it pops out of your grasp.

3. Hold the coin over a piece of velvet (black or dark blue), so that if you should drop it, it won't bang to the floor

and get scratched. (Also, the dark color of the background helps in the examination.)

4. Don't sneeze or cough on the coin. Don't even hold it up in front of your nose. Moisture, even small amounts, can be harmful.

HOW TO EXAMINE IT

Here we're talking about how to look at the coin. Again, we've discussed some of this before, but a few comments are worth reiterating:

1. Be sure you have an appropriate light source. A spotlight is usually considered best. Hold the coin at least 4 inches away from the light to get an even dispersion.

2. Use a magnifying lens. This will help to reveal scratches and other imperfections. The ideal magnification is 5X. If you go much higher, particularly up to 10X, you will see minute defects that don't really count. Also, use a magnifier with a wide lens so you can see a large portion of the coin at a single glance. With a tiny lens you might miss defects that are larger than the area covered by the lens. (You might miss the forest because of the trees.)

3. To begin, quickly look at the obverse and reverse of the coin with your naked eye to get a first impression. You don't want to begin looking at the details immediately and forget the overall picture.

4. Next, using the magnifier, focus on the obverse of the coin and examine the devices. Remember, the devices are the raised images on the coin. Wear will usually be most evident here. Then examine the fields, remember these are the background surfaces. In the next section we'll go into great detail on what to look for, but for now, let's just try to keep track of where to look.

A good method is to first look for those areas on the coin that usually show wear (we'll discuss how to know where these are in a few paragraphs). Next, go around from 12 o'clock clockwise back to 12 o'clock. In this way you can be sure you haven't forgotten to examine any portion of the surface.

Now do the same thing for the reverse.

5. Look at the rim. Rotate the coin so that you can see the entire rim.

6. Finally, rotate the coin so that the surface catches light from a variety of angles.

WHAT TO LOOK FOR

Now we get down to the nitty-gritty of it. There are five items that we are going to be looking for in grading a coin:

Wear (the state of preservation)
Marks and scratches
Strike
Luster
Toning

WEAR

Wear is frequently described as the single most important part of a coin grade. That certainly is the case for technical grading. As indicated the grade is composed of a variety of factors of which wear is only one, albeit a very important one.

Wear is generally described as any loss of surface detail that happens to a coin *after* it leaves the mint. Remember, a coin as it comes from the mint presses is said to be in "mint state." Once it leaves the presses, any time in circulation can remove or flatten particles of metal on the coin. This, then, is wear.

How to Determine Wear • In order to determine wear we must first know what the coin looked like when it came from the mint. To help us here there are two excellent resources that I recommend highly:

A Guide to the Grading of U.S. Coins, by Martin R. Brown and John W. Dunn (the "B & D" grading guide), published by General Distributors, and the *Official ANA Grading Standards for U.S. Coins,* published by Whitman.

EXTREMELY FINE   *Very light wear on only the highest points.*

BROWN AND DUNN GRADING
OF "ABOUT UNCIRCULATED"
MORGAN DOLLAR

Both of these books present written descriptions of coins as they came from the mint, supplemented by drawings that indicate high points where wear is likely to occur for each grade below MS-60. (Remember, MS-60 means un-circulated, or without wear.) For example, here is the de-scription for wear from the ANA grading guide:

Obverse: Slight trace of wear shows on hair above ear, eye, edges of cotton leaves, and high upper fold of cap. Luster fading from cheek. Reverse: Slight trace of wear shows on breast, tops of legs and talons. Most of the mint luster is still present, al-though marred by light bag marks and surface abrasions.

Note: the ANA guide describes the places to watch for wear slightly differently from the B & D guide. Which is correct?

It doesn't matter. Use both guides, and watch for wear in all places mentioned. Wear means that the lines aren't clearly defined or are smoothed out. Imagine a person rub-bing his or her finger over the coin several times. Even though the coin is metal, it is mainly a soft metal and a

ABOUT UNCIRCULATED   *Small trace of wear visible on highest points.*

ANA GRADING GUIDE FOR
AU-55 (ABOUT UNCIRCULATED)
MORGAN DOLLAR

slight abrasion will reduce the surface. Just a few rubs and the faintest lines on the highest portions of the image will be reduced. That's the kind of wear we are looking for.

If we find at least as much wear as indicated (often we will find substantially more), we can be fairly sure that the coin is AU-55 or lower. On the other hand, if there is no wear present, if all the details are there as struck, then we can be fairly sure the coin is MS-60 or higher.

Remember, the wear spots will be different for each type of coin. The B & D and the ANA grading books list wear indicators for all U.S. coins. Therefore, when you are starting out, these books are essential.

Note also that all that we've done here is determine whether the coin has no wear or some wear. If it has some wear, then it could be anything from an AU-55 to an AG-3 (About Good) coin. *If it has no wear, then it is a MS-60 or higher, an investment-grade coin.*

These two guides will be very useful in helping you to determine grades below MS-60. However, they will not be of much use with grades above MS-60. The reason is that grades above MS-60 *all* show no wear. MS-60 means un-circulated, untouched. Diagrams, therefore, are not particularly useful in the investment-grade coins. We have, however, learned to make a first and vital distinction.

MARKS AND SCRATCHES

Normally at this point the next item to consider under grading would be strike. We'll get to it shortly; however, in terms of the Morgan dollars a different area has to be considered first, and that is marks and scratches.

Every type of coin has its own peculiarities. In terms of the Morgan dollars, it is that virtually all of them have some marks and scratches. The reason is that all the nonproof coins were placed into bags of 1,000 immediately after striking. Bouncing around in the mint-sewn canvas bags meant that the coins rubbed against one another, thus producing abrasions.

It's important to understand the difference between wear and marks and scratches. "Wear" means the rubbing off of the coin's surface that comes when it is placed into circulation, and it includes finger handling. "Marks and scratches" means coins banging against one another in mint bags, yet untouched by hands. It's a subtle but important difference.

MORGAN DOLLAR WITH
SCRATCHES CLEARLY
VISIBLE ON CHIN AREA

AMERICAN NUMISMATIC ASSOCIATION

LEFT: MS-60 MORGAN DOLLAR REVERSE
RIGHT: MS-65 MORGAN DOLLAR REVERSE

Wear typically appears in the high points previously described. Marks and scratches can appear on any surface area of the coin, including the field.

Marks and scratches are one distinction between the MS-60 coin and the MS-65 and other higher grades. An MS-60 may have no wear, but it will typically have obvious small marks and scratches.

An MS-65 coin, on the other hand, will have *no obvious* scratches or bag marks.

In-between Grades • Scratches and marks also play a role in determining the in-between grades. An MS-67 coin will normally have no scratches or bag marks at all, not even minute ones visible to the naked eye. (Of course, some will appear with magnification.) An MS-63, on the other hand, will have noticeable scratches and bag marks, but they won't be as unsightly as those found on the MS-60 coin.

Rim Marks • Thus far we've only dealt with abrasions to the obverse and reverse of the coin. It is possible, however, for the coin to have an impairment of the rim. This typically will come about because the coin has been dropped on its rim and hit a hard object. As a result the rim will be nicked or dented.

Any such rim damage will detract from the value of the coin and counts against almost (although not quite) as much as do surface marks and scratches.

Using Judgment • If this all seems rather unscientific, rest assured it is. It is a matter of judgment. Marks and scratches definitely detract from a coin's value. In addition, the *location* of the marks or scratches may be important. If the damage is overshadowed by an edge, it may actually not detract that much from the coin. On the other hand, if the scratch is right across the device, even though it's slight, it may significantly drop a coin's value.

You will have to see at least a dozen Morgan dollars in both MS-65 and MS-60 grades before you can easily evaluate the differences in scratches and marks. You may have to see hundreds of such coins before you can easily discriminate between MS-63 and MS-65 or MS-65 and MS-67. This is one of the reasons that many collectors *specialize.* It's hard to know everything about every coin, but it's possible to know nearly everything about one specific type of coin.

STRIKE

The strike refers to the sharpness of details on a coin. In a series that isn't noted for its bag marks and scratches (unlike the Morgan dollars, which are), strike would normally come after wear as a determiner of grade.

The Morgan dollars are in general weakly struck. This probably has a great deal to do with the era in which they were minted. The Morgans were really the first mass-produced large coins from the U.S. Mint. True, the mint had been producing dollars as early as 1794. However, with the exception of trade dollars (1873–1885), these were rarely

LEFT: A WELL-STRUCK WALKING LIBERTY
RIGHT: A WEAKLY STRUCK WALKING LIBERTY.
COMPARE WITH THE WELL-STRUCK COIN.

produced in large quantities. The typical mintage had been half a million coins per year per mint or less.

The Morgan dollars, however, were produced in the multimillions. The 1889 Philadelphia mint issue was over 21 million. The 1921 Philadelphia issue was over 44 million! It only stands to reason that in such quantities, quality will suffer.

Typically, a weak strike occurs because of worn dies. It's important to remember that on a coin there are raised devices opposite each other on both sides. The metal has to flow away from two raised areas. As a result, if there is not enough pressure from the press or the die is even slightly worn, the details in part of the raised image may not be deep and sharp.

Note that a weak strike typically does *not* involve the *entire* coin. Rather, it affects only certain parts of it. Also, a weak strike *occurs at the mint*—it may appear similar to wear to an unsophisticated viewer, but it is quite different.

With all coins, strike is an important consideration in determining grade. Of course, we're now talking about "commercial grading," which affects value, not "technical grading," which is primarily a statement of preservation.

In an MS-60 coin there typically will be weakly struck *areas.* This means that while the coin on the whole may have a fairly good strike, certain parts of the device may be weak. It is for this reason (as well as to check for marks and scratches) that when we examine the coin, we carefully look over its entire surface. We are looking for weakly struck areas.

The appearance of a weakly struck area is like that of a photo that wasn't fully developed. The image is not quite there. The lines simply aren't fully developed. This is opposed to wear. Wear has a characteristic dull and rubbed-off appearance. A wear strike, on the other hand, can be bright, just not all there.

In MS-65 coins there should be no weak areas. This is not to say that under a magnifying lens weak areas won't show up. They may. But to the naked eye, no weak areas should detract from the appearance of the coin.

Obviously, in an MS-63, we will have fewer weakly struck areas, yet the coin will not be a near-perfect strike as will the MS-65.

For the MS-67 coin, we are looking for something different. This coin requires not only that there be no weakly struck areas, but that the coin overall have the exact opposite, an exceptionally strong strike. The following scale may prove helpful in understanding this.

Weak Strike	Good Strike	Strong Strike

MS-60	MS-63	MS-65	MS-66	MS-67

Judgment • As before, a great deal comes down to personal judgment. Were you to hold an MS-65 and an MS-60 in your hand (not photos now, which really can't illustrate this, but the two coins), you would immediately see the difference.

On the other hand, were you to hold an MS-65 and an MS-67 in your hands, you might have a tough time seeing the difference. The reason is that the difference between an MS-65 and an MS-67 is very subtle, while that between an MS-65 and an MS-60 is very great.

Die Cracks vs. Scratches • In the early days of minting, dies were produced entirely by hand. As a result they sometimes had defects in the metal or areas that were weaker than others. Sometimes the result was minute cracks. These cracks can frequently be seen on coins minted up to about 1850. Typically, they are evidence of the authenticity of the coin and do not detract from the value.

In other circumstances, well into the 20th century, dies were used so much that they actually wore down. Sometimes, if a crack or weakness occurred, they were removed, polished, and replaced in the press. This in some circumstances actually removed portions of the image!

It's important to distinguish between a die crack and a scratch on the coin, since they have a similar appearance. In a die crack the metal is usually raised to a higher level

AMERICAN NUMISMATIC ASSOCIATION

NOTICE THE CIRCULAR DIE CRACK JUST INSIDE THE RIM OF THIS 1820 LARGE CENT

on one side of the crack. In other words, there are two planes on the coin's surface. In a scratch, on the other hand, magnification will usually reveal a single plane with a groove running through it. Scratches detract from a coin's value, die cracks usually don't.

Die cracks are considered coin varieties. These are well documented in coin books that list types and mintages (such as *A Guidebook of U.S. Coins,* by R. S. Yeoman, published by Whitman, also known as the Red Book). If you are handling early coins, be sure you check to see that the apparent defect in the coin you are looking at isn't, in fact, a valuable rarity.

LUSTER

Luster refers to the way a coin reflects light. There are many descriptive terms that fit under luster, including the following: brilliant surface; frosted surface; satin-velvet surface; chromelike (usually comes from polished dies; the coin looks as though it has been cleaned, but it hasn't); cameo effect (high contrast between field and devices).

When coins exhibit many of these qualities, such as cameo, they are said to be "prooflike." They look like proof coins but aren't.

Luster is a greater or lesser factor in evaluating coins, depending on the type. Some coin series all reflect light pretty much the same, in which case luster may not have a major effect on the coin's value. Other series, however, reflect light in dramatically different ways. This is nowhere more evident than with the Morgan dollars we are considering. Here luster represents an important aspect of evaluation.

Depending on the pressure with which they were struck and the condition of the dies and planchet, *some* Morgan dollars have surfaces that approach the reflective qualities of proof coins. These business strikes are often called prooflike. ("Proof" refers to a specific method of minting in which the coin is struck at least twice. The coins we are describing here are *not* proof, but because of chance in the minting process, have a prooflike surface.)

A coin that has high luster will typically have a mirror-like finish. This means that the metal will be "brilliant"—will reflect a bright light in all directions. Thus, if you swivel the coin in your hands, the reflected light will be of equal intensity from any side.

In contrast to this brilliant surface, some prooflike coins will have a "frosted" finish. This comes about when tiny metal crystals are created at the time of striking. These coins also reflect a great deal of light; however, the crystals on the surface tend to diffuse the light instead of making it harsh. It's much the same difference between the soft light of a frosted light bulb and the harsh light of a clear light bulb. A frosted, prooflike surface on a business strike coin is much rarer than a brilliant surface.

Difference Between Proof and Prooflike • In a true proof coin there will be a highly reflective surface visible both in the field and in the devices. The field will typically be a mirrorlike surface while the devices will be frosted. The contrast between the mirrorlike field and the frosted devices will produce a high contrast called a "cameo" effect (noted earlier).

In a proof*like* coin, however, typically only the field will have this proof*like* surface. The device or a portion of it may have a much duller finish. This is because the device gets its high reflective appearance from the second strike in a press, yet a business strike is hit only once.

The difference between a brilliant field and a common or dull device (dull here does not mean that the device lacks appeal, it only means that it doesn't have the brilliance of the field) results in a coin that has strongly contrasting field and device. This tends to make the device stand out, to highlight it, and is considered a desirable feature. This is called a "prooflike cameo."

COINAGE PHOTO BY LARRY STEVENS

PROOF CAMEO KENNEDY HALF-DOLLAR

In coin grading from a technical aspect, little-to-no consideration is given to luster. From a commercial viewpoint, however, luster is vital. The following scale will help to explain luster with regard to commercial grading:

LUSTER

MS-60	MS-63	MS-65	MS-67
Plain	Some Brilliance in Field	Brilliant Overall	Brilliant Field Contrasting Device

TONING

Toning refers to a change in color that occurs in coins over a period of time. Normally this is the result of oxidation or of contact with moisture in the atmosphere. Coins of different metals tone differently.

Copper coins, for example, oxidize rapidly, and they may quickly loose their mint brilliance turning a dull brown color.

Nickel coins tend to go gray and to loose their brilliance. Silver coins will develop a black, blue, and/or brownish tinge that can be quite attractive. Gold coins seldom tone, but they can get more orangy in color over time (as the copper alloy in them oxidizes).

In the past this toning, when it was attractive, was prized and added to the value of coins. In copper and silver coins it was frequently referred to as a patina. Today *patina* and *toning* are virtually synonymous terms.

In the Morgan dollars toning is common. Interestingly, however, although toning occurs over the surface of the coin, it rarely occurs evenly. Typically a corner or half of a coin will be affected. Mint luster will often be visible behind a toned coin.

Investors tend to shy away from toned coins regardless of what experts say. There are several reasons. Because of the toning it can be more difficult to evaluate a coin. For a beginner especially, wear (in particular, rub marks from slight circulation) can be concealed by toning. Also, for the uninitiated a toned coin can simply look bad.

AMERICAN NUMISMATIC ASSOCIATION

BAD TONING IS CLEARLY
VISIBLE EVEN IN THIS
BLACK-AND-WHITE PHOTO

Of course, as we've seen, things are never really black or white in rare coins. In cases where there are only a few dozen or less coins in existence, toning tends to work the other way! These extreme rarities are usually bought by investors who have strong collector tendencies and who go for the beauty of high toning. Thus patina (as it is usually described when talking about extreme rarities) here actually adds to value rather than detracts from it.

Defective Coloration • It's important to understand the difference between toning and defective coloration. Sometimes coins will be placed in contact with chemically active paper or other substances. When this results in black spots, dark "pits," or other blemishes it is called discoloration. On the other hand, the same chemical agents can produce an attractive coloration on the coin. This is called toning.

Normally, a coin with any serious blemish could not be considered an MS-65. Minor blemishes might qualify for MS-63. Significant blemishes could still be an MS-60 coin.

THE BOTTOM LINE

What should be obvious from this discussion of grading is that there are two kinds of grading—"rough" and "final." For the Morgan dollar series (and most other series as well), it's relatively easy with experience to tell whether a coin is better or worse than MS-60. MS-60, after all, is the grade that defines Uncirculated, having no wear. This is called "rough" grading.

However, it's one thing to know a coin is MS-60 or better and quite another to be able to tell whether it is MS-63, MS-65, or MS-67. This is called "final" grading. When we add in the grades of MS-64 and MS-66 we get into even more difficult distinctions.

Yet, if you have a good eye and see enough coins, you, too, will eventually be able to see most of these grades as distinct. However, that wasn't our goal here. Our primary goal as stated at the beginning of this chapter was to be able to determine whether a coin was investment grade (MS-60) or better.

That's a vital first step. Once you have taken it, you can move forward into more subtle distinctions. But keep in mind that, quite frankly, there are no shortcuts after this. You simply need to be looking continually at great numbers of coins.

Chapter

6

WHIZZED COINS, FAKES, AND OTHER PROBLEMS TO AVOID

R are coins are so valuable that the temptation always exists to take a less valuable coin and try to turn it into its more valuable cousin. This can involve something no more simple than attompting to clean the surface. Or it can involve fraudulently creating counterfeit dies and then striking counterfeit coins.

In this chapter we'll look at the whole spectrum of suspect coins, from the relatively innocuous and obvious whizzing to the criminal activity of deliberate faking.

WHIZZING

As we've seen, the quality of a coin's surface in large part determines its value (popularity, scarcity, trends, and so on are also factors). Unfortunately, sometimes that surface can be changed either intentionally or accidentally. Since any change will affect value (frequently for the worse), it's important to be aware of the more common problems likely to occur in this area.

Whizzing is a term used to describe the cleaning of a coin's surface, usually by means of a fine wire brush. The brush is attached to a drill and moved across the surface, making a "whizzing" sound. The term generically also refers to any kind of cleaning that abrades or changes a coin's surface.

Whizzed coins are usually "sucker" coins. They are aimed at amateurs who really don't know much about the field. Since they are well known to experienced investors and can be spotted fairly easily, they don't make many inroads into investor coins. Nevertheless, one has to be on the watch for them.

Typically, a whizzed coin would be an AU-55 or slightly lower grade. In its natural state the coin would be somewhat dull from having been in circulation. Once it is whizzed, however, it will give off a very bright reflective appearance.

To an unsuspecting buyer, one who looks for shine and doesn't really understand grading, this coin might appear to be investment grade. Thus the seller tries to sell the whizzed coin for one or more grades higher than it really is.

How to Tell a Whizzed Coin • In a true whizzed coin a rotary wire brush is spun on the coin's surface for a few moments. The result is a series of minute concentric circles, or scratches, which reflect light in a manner similar to that of a true brilliant coin.

However, in a true brilliant coin, the brilliance comes from the metal having been flattened in a press. As a result it will have two characteristics:

1. The devices will generally have different brilliance from the fields. (See the previous chapter for a further explanation.)

2. The brilliance in the field will be caused by a uniformly *flat* and polished surface.

In a whizzed coin the following traits will be visible:

1. The devices and the field will have identical brilliance (since the wire brush made no discrimination when it passed over the coin's surface).

2. Examination under a microscope will reveal circular scratches running from field to device, where the wire hit the surface metal.

3. Close examination will reveal unusual wear or rub spots since, after all, the wire brush did remove some of the coin's surface.

Whizzing a coin destroys its value, since no collector will want it. This is an important point. Whizzing doesn't simply lower the grade or reduce the value. It *destroys* a coin's value.

You undoubtedly won't find whizzed coins coming from

AMERICAN NUMISMATIC ASSOCIATION

"WHIZZED" COIN HAS
THE IMPOSSIBLE—BOTH
WEAR AND BRILLIANCE

any major dealer. You are more likely to find them at traveling vendors who inhabit carnivals and flea markets and who may additionally be selling jewelry and trinkets, whose value may also be suspect.

PROCESSED COINS

A bit more difficult to spot are coins that have been "processed," or subjected to chemical treatment. There are all kinds of processes from acid washes to abrasive powders (similar to cleansers). The idea here is the same as whizzing. However, to avoid the telltale marks of whizzing, chemicals are used.

Processed coins can usually be spotted by examining the coin under a microscope. While to the naked eye the coin may appear brilliant, under a microscope the following may be observed:

1. The fields will have a dull, pitted look. This comes from the surface having been unevenly worn away by the chemical or abrasive.

2. Minute amounts of the coin's detail will be lost. This only stands to reason, since any processing will remove some of the coin's surface.

"PROCESSED" COINS
HAVE UNEVEN SURFACE
WEAR AND LOST DETAIL

AMERICAN NUMISMATIC ASSOCIATION

ARTIFICIAL TONING

We noted in the last chapter that toning was an important consideration with coins. Toning is a natural process that occurs over a period of years and is usually associated with oxidation.

However, inventive schemers have developed methods of quickening the process. A variety of techniques can be used, including everything from blowing cigar smoke at coins to baking them inside potatoes. In fact, a truly clever chemist can in a few hours produce a wide variety of toning colors on almost any coin.

The trick, of course, is to make the artificial toning look like the natural toning that occurs over years. This is far more difficult. An experienced collector looking at the toning color on a coin can usually spot artificial traits in a moment. The giveaways are a lack of development (movement of the toning across the coin) and unusual shades.

Since toning, as we noted, is not that critical an element with investment-grade coins (the better grades tend to have less, not more, toning), artificial toning by itself is not usually a serious problem.

COMBINED TECHNIQUES

Real problems occur when a clever schemer uses a variety of techniques to artificially change a coin's surface. Abrasives, acid dips, and then toning to cover it all up can sometimes produce a rather convincing coin.

Nevertheless, a close examination regardless of toning should reveal etching marks in a processed coin or telltale scratches in a whizzed coin.

Regardless of how it's done, remember that all of these techniques *lower* a coin's value. They don't raise it.

NATURAL BLEMISHES

Thus far we have discussed changing the coin's surface by artificial means. However, nature itself can sometimes produce undesirable and value-reducing changes.

Pit Marks • These are tiny black marks that sometimes pit the surface of a coin. They occur on copper coins more than on any other metal. Also called "carbon spots," these

"PIT MARKS" CAN DESTROY A COIN'S
BEAUTY AND VALUE, AS HAPPENED IN
THE CASE OF THIS SHIELD NICKEL

tiny black marks occur because of a coin's coming in contact with some chemical to which it has a reaction.

Sulfur, commonly found in paper, is sometimes the culprit. Tiny droplets of acidic moisture from the atmosphere can also sometimes produce this effect. Copper is a fast reactor, and it quickly changes tone when thus exposed.

Pit marks produce an unsightly appearance, and they distinctly detract from a coin's value. It's hard to imagine an MS-65 coin having such marks, although they might be there on an MS-60 coin.

Paper Stains • Sometimes older coins were stored by placing them in paper envelopes. The paper might contain sulfur or other chemicals. As a result an unusual toning effect could take place. The most visual example is where a coin was laid across a piece of chemically active paper. One side of the coin is natural, the other is darkly toned. This sort of "staining" adversely affects value.

Plastic Leaching • This is a very common problem today, when most coins are stored in plastic containers. It comes about because many plastics are not inert. Rather, they leach out chemicals that then affect the coins.

This process usually takes years and, consequently, seldom affects coin dealers who are regularly turning over coins. Those it affects most are investors who buy coins and then dump them into safety deposit boxes *in the same holders in which they were purchased,* often leaving them there for years without examining them.

Over a period of time the chemicals in the plastic holders can leach out and actually begin to dissolve areas of a coin, thus making it virtually worthless.

HOW TO AVOID
NATURAL BLEMISHES

To begin with, beware of coins that already contain blemishes when you buy them. Pit marks tend to get worse, not better. Stains don't go away.

When you store coins, avoid chemically active plastics and paper. This includes paper that contains sulfur and plastic that might have polyvinyl chloride (PVC) in it. You'll have to do your own investigating here, as brands and composition change all the time.

Finally, check your coins frequently. Should you have a bad container, it's better to find out early, when only minimal damage has been done, than later, when a coin has been destroyed.

CLEANING

Can coins be legitimately cleaned? Thus far we've been talking about the damage that can be done to a coin by changing its surface. Now let's consider the question, Can a coin's surface be *improved* by cleaning?

We might especially wonder this with regard to copper coins that have browned and some silver coins that might have developed uneven and unattractive toning.

Cleaning is often done and usually consists of dipping a coin in a mildly acid solution for a second or two. Most coin shops can recommend several different commercial cleaning products. However, be aware that cleaning remains controversial. The ANA in its official grading guide states:

> All types of cleaning, "good" and "bad," result in the coin's surface being changed, even if only slightly. . . . Generally, experienced numismatists agree that a coin should not be cleaned unless there are spots of oxidation, pitting which might worsen in time, or unsightly streaking or discoloration.

My own opinion is that you should stay away from cleaning. Cleaning implies that the coin is "dirty," that there's something wrong with it. If that's the case, then you shouldn't have bought it in the first place. If you already own it, then cleaning may, if done improperly (there's always an element of luck when cleaning, since there's no real way to tell beforehand how it will come out), actually make the coin less valuable.

THE BOTTOM LINE
WITH WHIZZED AND
PROCESSED COINS

Ultimately the question has to be asked, What are my chances of being cheated by being offered a whizzed or otherwise processed coin?

Overall, major dealers, those with good reputations to uphold, will not be caught dead with whizzed or processed coins. The blemish to their reputation should they try to sell such merchandise would far outweigh any profit they were likely to get. Nevertheless, you as a coin buyer are the ultimate discriminator.

As we've already seen in other areas in this book, a lot depends on your own expertise. If you take the time to examine a large number of coins yourself, if you learn what to watch for, in other words, if you educate yourself with regard to the field, then the chances are extremely slim that you'll get cheated. Then again, if you have to trust in the good faith of every person you meet who happens to be selling coins, then maybe you will run into one or more of these problems.

FAKES

At one time fake coins were a serious threat to the rare coin field. However, with the institution in the mid-1970s of the American Numismatic Association Certification Service (ANACS), which authenticated coins (ANACS authenticated coins long before it began grading them), much of the problem disappeared. The ANACS graders have been generally praised for their ability to spot fake coins.

Since most valuable coins are sent to ANACS for authentication, the chances of being sold a fake are far less serious today than they were in the past. Nevertheless, fakes do crop up, and as an investor in rare coins you must be wary of them.

Changed Date or Mint Mark • The most common fake coin an investor is likely to encounter is one in which a mint mark or date has been altered. For example, the 1909 VDB coin (on which designer Victor David Brenner's initials appeared) is a popular Lincoln cent. However, nearly 28 million were minted at Philadelphia, meaning that they simply don't command a very high price. (A recent price for the coin was under forty dollars in MS-65 condition.)

On the other hand, only about half a million were minted at San Francisco. Thus the 1909-S VDB in MS-65 condition recently commanded prices in excess of $325.

AN ALTERED MINT MARK—LOOK
CLOSELY AT THE IRREGULAR
PATTERN AROUND THE D ON
THIS MERCURY DIME

LEFT: 1909 LINCOLN CENT WITHOUT MINT
MARK (PHILADELPHIA MINT DOES
NOT PUT MINT MARKS ON COINS)
RIGHT: MORE VALUABLE 1909 LINCOLN CENT
WITH S (SAN FRANCISCO) MINT MARKS

The only difference between the two coins is that the Philadelphia-struck piece has no mint mark on it. (Coins struck at Philadelphia have traditionally been recognized by a lack of a mint mark.) The San Francisco piece, however, has the traditional S under the date.

Therefore, some schemers have taken a legitimate 1909 Philadelphia Lincoln VDB coin and have soldered or otherwise adhered an S stolen from some inexpensive San Francisco cent to it. The result is a fake coin that its creators then try to pass off as authentic.

Adding a mint mark is only one way of changing a coin and making a fake. In other cases mint marks have been removed or dates have been altered (an 8 made into a 9 or vice versa). In *every case* of an altered mint mark a far-less-expensive coin has been altered to look like its more expensive cousin.

Detecting the Fakes • Coins are struck under enormous pressure in mint presses. At the time of striking *all* the characteristics of the coins are created, including date and mint mark. A single piece of round metal (a planchet) is made to flow into a design.

On the other hand, in any changed coin such as we've described here, something has been added, taken away, or altered. In the process of doing this telltale signs always appear. Under strong magnification even an untrained eye can usually spot soldered, glued, filed, or otherwise changed characteristics.

Therefore, whenever buying an unauthenticated rare coin whose price depends solely on a date or mint mark or other single characteristic, *examine that characteristic very carefully.* If you're not sure, take it to an expert. If an 1885 sells for $100 and an 1895 sells for $5,000, examine the 9 in the date very closely.

Of course, to be even safer you could always send the coin to ANACS for authentication.

Cast Fakes • Another, though usually more obvious, fake is a cast coin. This is made when an impression, or cast, is made of an authentic coin. Then, much like casting a bronze statue, hot metal is poured into the cast and a fake coin is created.

Cast fakes are normally easy to spot. They have certain characteristics, which include:

1. less-distinct designs (after all, they are copies, like Xeroxes);

2. sometimes a seam on the edge of the coin where the two halves of the cast were placed together (this is the same sort of thing that happens when the two halves of a cheap glass are melded together); and

3. a distinct hollow ring. (Although this is *not* recommended, if you were to drop a true coin on its edge on a countertop, it would give a solid tone much like a bell. If you drop a cast fake, it tends to give a much hollower tone.

Of course, unless you're sure you're dealing with a fake, you wouldn't want to drop the coin for fear of damaging a true and valuable piece.)

Fake Dies • This usually involves only very rare and valuable coins for a simple reason—the process of making this kind of fake is time-consuming and costly. Here the schemers actually create a new set of dies. Once the dies are created, they strike off new coins on presses similar to the ones the mint uses.

If the dies are cleverly constructed and if the press is of sufficient quality, the counterfeiters will have produced a virtually perfect fake.

The untrained investor will very likely be unable to detect this fake, and many experienced dealers and collectors could not detect it either.

However, fake-die coins are detectable simply because each die has its own characteristics. The dies used to strike rare and valuable coins at the mint have all been catalogued in terms of the characteristics on the coins. Thus, when a coin with unusual characteristics suddenly appears, experts are very quickly able to identify it as having come from a fake die.

Coins from fake dies are rare, and the best protection against them is authentication by ANACS.

Stolen Dies • Finally there is the matter of stolen dies. Although the mint destroys each die after its lifespan is over and denies that any dies have been stolen, occasionally suspicious coins do appear. These are coins that seem to come from true mint dies yet often have some unusual characteristics.

Note how mint dies are destroyed. A portion of the surface of the die is gouged out. The die itself is then, eventually, melted down.

However—and this is pure speculation—if a die were only damaged in a minor way by gouging and then were

COINAGE MAGAZINE

DESTROYED DIES—THE
GOUGED X MAKES THEM
USELESS TO COUNTERFEITERS

stolen, an expert craftsman might be able to repair it and then virtually perfect fake coins could be created. If a die were stolen before it was gouged it would be virtually impossible to detect coins struck from it from true coins.

Detecting fakes from stolen dies is usually fairly easy, however, for two reasons. First, the only dies that are generally available are those for recent coins, and there are relatively few rare and valuable coins in these. (Dies from old coins are still kept at the mint, but usually they are under lock and key in tight security.)

Second, while it might be possible to steal a single intact die, it would be virtually impossible to steal two intact dies—both an obverse and a reverse for the same coin. Thus coins produced from fake dies typically will have one side perfect, while the other will be cast or created from a fake die and thus identifiable.

AVOIDING FAKES

As noted, fakes are rare in this field. All reputable dealers will guarantee that the coins they sell are true, and most will put this in writing. If a coin should turn out to be a fake, nearly all dealers will take it back *virtually at any time* and refund the money paid or exchange it for a true coin. The dealers' reputations depend on selling authentic coins.

Additionally, any knowledgeable investor or collector will look closely at coins to see if they have been changed, cast, or otherwise counterfeited. After a little experience in the field, this will come naturally.

Finally, there is ANACS. Its authentication service has proved invaluable in ridding the field of fake coins.

Chapter

7

HOW TO GET STARTED

One of the first questions that a person starting out collecting or investing in rare coins always asks is, What should I buy?

Since the field is enormous, it's a very hard question to answer. There are foreign coins (from every country in the world), there are ancient coins, and there are good old U.S. coins. For most of us it's really hard to pick and choose.

But we can't start everywhere, so the first order of business is limiting our field of interest. Of course, we may want to see our coin dealer and ask him what he thinks we should buy. But most of the time the response to such a question is, What are you interested in? This puts us back to square one.

If we are primarily interested in collecting rare coins (as opposed to investment as our primary motive), then we may want to begin by purchasing one coin of every denomination. Historically, that's how great collections were started.

Later those acquirers of the great collections purchased one of each date for each denomination and then one of each mint mark for each date. Since this can amount to thousands of different coins and millions of dollars in the better grades, it's easy to see how coin collecting could develop into a life's work.

INVESTOR BEGINNINGS

Most investors today, however, aren't interested in such a time-consuming labor of love. Most would rather go after a specific denomination or perhaps even a specific type (such as only Mercury dimes or commemorative half-dollars) within a denomination.

By limiting themselves in this manner, many investors are able to learn a great deal about their specialty and in short order to become expert in it. Having done that, they are well able to recognize and take advantage of bargains.

For example, a friend specializes in Hawaiian coins. Most people aren't even aware that there were Hawaiian pieces. But there is a small but dedicated group of collectors.

Every so often, when the regular coin market gets hot, Hawaiian pieces for some unknown reason become momentarily popular. My friend is then able to sell at great profit those coins he previously bought for very low prices. He makes a handsome income from his Hawaiian collection-investment.

BUY U.S.

Besides limiting oneself to a particular type of coin, my suggestion is that when starting out we also limit ourselves to U.S. coinage only. Don't start with Mexican, Canadian, British, ancients, and so on (I suspect most experts would agree here). Here are three good reasons why:

1. We are already familiar with most U.S. coins.

2. They have the biggest market worldwide and the greatest liquidity.

3. We'll have no trouble getting detailed information on them.

PICKING THE
SPECIFIC DENOMINATION

If we've decided on U.S. coins, the next decision is which denomination to collect. Remember, we're not going to collect them all. Just within the field of U.S. coins there is great diversity, and finding a place to begin can be troublesome. My suggestion is to consider two avenues. First, find out if we have a favorite coin. Many of us collected Lincoln cents as children, and we still have fond memories of that. This might be an excellent place to start. We're already familiar with the coin, and we have an attachment to it. It could be the beginning of a strong collection-investment.

Second, if we don't have a favorite coin (or if we have several), consider which coin series have done the best financially over the past few years. Very few people who collect coins today aren't also interested in making a profit. So, why not collect something that's more likely to show a strong profit than something that's likely to be stagnant?

COIN TRENDS

Over the past twenty years *all* rare U.S. coinage has gone up substantially in price. However, some issues have done especially well. In my opinion this latter group includes:

Early U.S. coinage
Peace and Morgan dollars
U.S. commemorative half-dollars
Mercury dimes
U.S. gold coins

Those coins that have not done particularly well include:

Lincoln cents
Liberty and Jefferson nickels
Anthony dollars
Eisenhower dollars
Washington quarters

The above list should not be taken as a recommendation since the field is constantly changing. However, any one of those listed might be a good starting place. (Note that the current issues, those of the last fifty years, in general have not done well. That tends to be true throughout the field. The older coins, those at least 50 years old, are the scarcer and more highly prized.)

LIQUIDITY

Another consideration is liquidity: How hard or difficult is it to resell the denomination we pick? The answer here is that the more unique the coin, generally speaking, the more difficult it may be to resell *for top dollar.* Some coins have ready markets. Dealers all over the country regularly make a market in U.S. silver dollars. Many make a similar market in U.S. twenty and ten-dollar gold pieces as well as commemorative halves. If you want to sell, just pop into any dealer's showroom. He can quickly give you the going price.

On the other hand, if you're collecting early American cents, it's not quite so easy. You may have to search for a while to find a dealer who specializes in these. More to the point, if the dealer doesn't have a buyer for the particular coin you want to sell, you may find you'll either have to wait or accept a much lower offer. Some coins just aren't as liquid as others.

CHOOSING WITHIN
A SERIES

Assuming you've decided on a denomination, for example, U.S. Morgan dollars, which dates and which mint marks in the denomination should you buy? What about special coins that have such things as "double dies" or unusual characteristics—should you go after these? What about price? Prices differ depending on the date, the mint mark, and the special characteristics of a coin. Should you opt for the most expensive, the least expensive, or somewhere in between?

RARITY

The reason that different dates and mint marks in a series sell for different prices is simply rarity. (Rarity is always understood in coin investing, but for some reason seldom discussed.) Rarity is another great determiner of coin value (grade and popularity being the other two). Some would say that rarity is the principle determiner of value.

It stands to reason that if a million of a coin exist, the very supply is going to keep the price down. On the other hand, if there are only a few thousand in existence in all grades, then their very scarcity is going to drive prices up.

However, determining true rarity is really quite difficult. While accurate statistics for the number of coins actually minted for virtually every denomination and year are readily available (check the Red Book—see Chapter 11), accurate statistics that show how many are actually left are not. Just because half a million coins were minted in 1839 doesn't mean that half a million are left today. Indeed, perhaps less than 1 percent have survived being melted down or otherwise destroyed over the intervening years, and perhaps less than 1 percent of those are in uncirculated condition.

Scholars in the field of numismatics devote a great deal of their time to guesstimating rarity. They check such things as the number of times a particular coin comes up for sale at an auction, how often it's traded by dealers, and so forth.

For the great rarities (for example, the 1804 silver dollar) they are able to pinpoint pretty exactly how many are left and even who owns them! (The risk in buying very great rarities, those coins where only a handful are thought to exist, is that at any time a buried pot full of them could turn up, dramatically cutting their value.)

ASSUMED RARITY

The guessing gets more intense, however, with lesser rarity. There were 14,070,875 1884-P (Philadelphia mint) silver dollars minted. How many are left today? One percent would be 14,070. Are there 1 percent left? Maybe there are 5 percent or .5 percent. Without being able to count heads, it's really anybody's guess.

What usually happens is that rarity becomes relative. As noted above, there were about 14 million 1884-P silver dollars minted. However, there were only 3,200,000 1884-S (San Francisco mint) silver dollars minted. If the same percentage from each year were saved (a big assumption), then it stands to reason that the 1884-S with one-third the mintage is going to be three times rarer today than its more ubiquitous 1884-P cousin. Additionally, because of this, it should be worth about three times more.

This is in fact what has happened with these two coins. In MS-65 condition the 1884-P recently brought about $650 and the 1884-S about $1,800. The guesstimate of survivability is apparently being made by collectors and investors on the basis of original mintage.

(Readers are cautioned not to jump to the conclusion that the above relationship works for *all* coins. It does not. However, it is a useful generalization.)

A CLUE
FOR INVESTORS

If you find a series where the above relationship (mintage to rarity) works, then it doesn't matter which coin in the series you buy!

Assuming all coins in a series go up by an equal percentage (which is roughly what sometimes happens), either the 1884-S or the 1884-P will give an investor the same percentage of return. Thus, for such an investor, either coin would have equal potential, depending on which was actually available.

The advantage of knowing this is that the investor who has limited funds can invest in a series and, if the market rises, presumably take advantage whether he or she bought greater or lesser rarity (of the same grade). In the above example, if the market goes up 20 percent, the 1884-P will go up by $130 and the 1884-S should go up by $360. The profit *percentage* should be very close.

THE REAL WORLD

The conclusion I am aiming toward is that in many cases it really doesn't matter what you buy in a series, say the

Morgan dollars. What counts is finding something in top grade for the amount of money you have to invest.

Be aware, however, that just throwing a dart at a series of coins to pick the date and mint mark you want does have its drawbacks. For example, in the 1970s the U.S. Mint began selling off Morgan dollars of the 1880 period that had CC (Carson City) mint marks. (A hoard had been found, and the government in its infinite wisdom decided to have a chaotic national sale to the public rather than dispose of the coins in an orderly fashion through the established coin dealers.) The name recognition of Carson City dollars soared during this period, and for a time (until the vast number of coins to be sold became apparent) all CC dollars regardless of date or denomination did especially well.

Thus if you had bought only P Morgans you would not have been able to take advantage of the CC Morgan price rise. Only the CC coins rose significantly in value (temporarily). The other mint marks did not rise as much.

Thus, while it may be true in general to say that you can buy any coin in a series and expect equal appreciation, it doesn't always work out that way.

WHAT'S AVAILABLE

Having thus generally explored what to look for when getting started in U.S. coins, we come now to asking what's available? What, in fact, are the collectible U.S. coins?

To find out what's available, all that's needed is a copy of the Red Book or the Blue Book. They list all U.S. denominations. The *Gray Sheet* will give up-to-the-minute values for most of these.

Simple, right? Unfortunately, we will quickly find that what we have are thousands of coins to choose from in dozens of different categories. Trying to make an investment selection from those sources can still be overwhelming. Therefore, to help get you started, here is a very brief description of the more popular U.S. coins.

AMERICAN NUMISMATIC ASSOCIATION

CLASSIC HEAD HALF-CENT
1809–1836

HALF-CENTS 1793–1857

These are typically collector, not investor, coins. Generally, the later dates are more frequently collected. The classic head type issued between 1809 and 1839 offers many dates in MS-60 for $300 or less as of this writing. (The scarce 1810 is an exception, selling for perhaps three times this amount.) The coins issued between 1849 and 1857 were all proof and normally command prices above the $2,000 level.

LARGE CENTS 1793–1857

Again, these tend to be collector, not investor, coins. The early large cents are not generally available in grades above EF-40, although small numbers do exist all the way up to MS-60. (These are considered great rarities.)

Many collectors concentrate on the coronet type issued between 1816 and 1857. Virtually any of these coins in MS-60 can be purchased for under $300 as of this writing, some for substantially less.

INDIAN HEAD CENT
1859–1909

SMALL CENTS 1856
TO PRESENT

Investors have dabbled in these coins somewhat, but more as a sidelight than as a determined investment. The fact that everyone wants an Indian head cent or two seems to account for the interest.

The Indian head cents were issued between 1859 and 1909. As of this writing, the cost in MS-60 is rarely over $200 and for dates after 1880 is frequently under $50. The sole exception is the rare 1877, of which only about 500 are believed to be in existence. This coin regularly brings over a thousand dollars in MS-60 condition.

The Lincoln cents, issued since 1909, have been the great disappointment in recent years for many would-be investors. Copper coins in general and Lincolns in particular have not matched the records set by other denominations. As of this writing, they are still considered to be stagnant by most investors.

The Lincoln coins that have come out since World War II can usually be purchased for no more than a quarter

AMERICAN NUMISMATIC ASSOCIATION

FAMOUS 1955 DOUBLED
DIE ERROR CENT

apiece in MS-65 condition with the following exceptions: (1) the 1944 D over S, in which the D (for the Denver mint) was stamped over the S (for the San Francisco mint), and which may go for $200 in MS-65 condition; and (2) the 1955 double die—a classic error coin that became an instant rarity. The die became damaged, and before it was corrected a doubled image of the date was stamped on thousands of coins. They entered circulation and today are highly prized commanding ever increasing prices.

Lincolns dated prior to World War II are substantially higher in price, although many can still be obtained for substantially under $100 in MS-65 grade.

Of particular interest to many collectors are the 1909 VDB coins. The designer of the Lincoln cent, Victor David Brenner, had his initials put on the coin. This caused an immediate uproar by people who were opposed to it. The mintage was stopped and the initials removed, never to appear again.

However, this instantly made some of the 1909 coins highly prized rarities. In particular, the 1909-S VDB—of which only 484,000 were minted—has been extremely popular (nearly 28 million of the Philadelphia mint coins were struck).

The 1909-S VDB often commands prices of over $300 in MS-65 condition.

TWO-CENT PIECES
1864–1873

Another collector coin, this was issued immediately after the Civil War to provide coinage during a period of drastic inflation. (Requests for a two-cent piece were heard in this country around 1980, when inflation was also very high!) It tends to be high-priced, with values in the thousands of dollars.

AMERICAN NUMISMATIC ASSOCIATION

TWO-CENT PIECE
1864–1873

THREE-CENT PIECES
1851–1889

Favored by collectors, these coins were issued in silver (1851–1873) and nickel (1865–1889). Relatively few remain, probably because of the odd denomination, and they

AMERICAN NUMISMATIC ASSOCIATION

THREE-CENT PIECE
1865–1889

are considered quite rare. A typical piece such as the silver 1866 may easily cost upwards of $4,000 as of this writing.

NICKEL FIVE-CENT PIECE
1866 TO PRESENT

Nickels just don't turn investors on. They have been at the bottom of the investment heap for a long time, and there aren't many signs indicating change. The lack of popularity may simply be because the coins are nickel (a base metal), while the other coinage was silver or gold. Whatever the reason, these coins have not really been as popular as other series.

There have been four different designs: shield, Liberty head, buffalo (Indian), and Jefferson. Even today the most popular of the series is the buffalo–Indian head. Be they collector or investor, everyone seems to want to have at least one of these in their collection. Unfortunately, prices have escalated to the point where a coin in true MS-65 condition can cost anywhere from $300 to $3,000 to $4,000.

BUFFALO (INDIAN HEAD)
NICKEL—1913–1938

SHIELD NICKEL
1866–1883

Of particular interest in this series was the 1916-P double die and the 1918 over 1917. In the latter case the 8 in the date was struck over a 7 in some coins issued by the Philadelphia mint. Additionally, in 1937 the Denver mint, using a weak die, struck a number of the coins on which the buffalo appears to have only three legs. All of these varieties are quite expensive, with the 1918/7-D selling for as high as $25,000.

AMERICAN NUMISMATIC ASSOCIATION

LIBERTY SEATED
HALF-DIME—1837–1873

HALF-DIMES 1794–1873

Few outside numismatics realize that parallel to the nickel, the government also issued a "half-dime." This tends to be strictly a collector rather than investor coin. Almost any date in uncirculated condition is going to cost $300 or more.

DIMES 1796 TO PRESENT

Dimes are definitely investor coins. Their performance in recent years has buoyed even the most pessimistic of buyers. They have continued to be among the market leaders, setting new price highs time and time again.

Dimes are particularly popular among those new to the field. While the coin has had many different designs

MERCURY DIME
1916–1945

including "draped bust," Liberty seated, and Barber (Liberty head), because of its beauty the Mercury is usually considered the most popular. Mercs were minted from 1916 to 1945.

The Barber design that preceded it has also been popular, but probably more so with collectors than investors. The Barber coins are generally considered quite rare, and in MS-65 grade they usually bring well over $2,000. Many of the Philadelphia-minted Mercuries, however, particularly the common dates, in MS-65 condition are still available for under $400. The scarcer Denver and San Francisco mint marks usually command prices well over $1,000.

During World War II the government struck a number of the coins dated 1942 over 1941 (the 2 was struck over the 1). This occurred in both issues of Philadelphia and Denver and is today highly prized.

QUARTERS 1796 TO PRESENT

There have been numerous quarter designs, including the bust (1796–1838), Liberty seated (1838–1891), and Lib-

STANDING LIBERTY
QUARTER—1916–1930

erty head (1892–1916). However, the coin that both collectors and investors love seems to be the Standing Liberty (1916–1930). These have shown strong advances over the past few years.

The Standing Liberty coins are amongst the highest-priced series. A coin in MS-65 can easily run $5,000 by recent bids, and the cheapest in the series, which is probably the 1917-P, still costs well over $1,000 as of this writing.

The Washington quarters issued from 1932 to the present have been a sort of joke amongst investors. These recent coins simply have had no real market. Although the dates in the 1930s were highly prized, most of the rest of the issue has been lackluster.

However, with the surge in investor interest in the field overall, these coins appear to be advancing. It could very well be that late-date Washington quarters could be "sleepers"—coins that are cheap now but that could show dramatic interest in the future.

HALF-DOLLARS 1794 TO PRESENT

There have probably been more types of half-dollars than there have been types of any other denomination. These include the original "flowing hair" design (1794–1795), bust types (1796–1838), the Liberty seated (1839–1891), Liberty head (1892–1915), Walking Liberty (1916–1947), Franklin/Liberty Bell (1848–1963), and the Kennedy half (1964 to date).

In addition there have also been numerous "commemorative" half-dollars, which we'll get to in a few paragraphs.

While the early half-dollars are primarily collector coins, three series—the Walking Liberty (called "walkers" for short), the Franklins, and the early Kennedy coins (silver in 1964 and silver clad from 1965 to 1970) have been the realm of the investor.

Of particular interest have been the Franklins. This is not to say that the walkers have not shown strong price increases. They have. But for some reason the Franklin coins have been amongst the strongest in the entire field.

With the Franklin series something unusual has happened. Dealers have begun quoting prices not by grade

AMERICAN NUMISMATIC ASSOCIATION

CAPPED BUST HALF-DOLLAR
1807–1836

LEFT: FRANKLIN HALF-DOLLAR—1948–1963
RIGHT: BELL LINES (SEE BELL RIM) ON REVERSE

but by "bell lines." The assumption is that the coin is already an MS-65. Thus the more important distinction has become the lines on the Liberty Bell on the back of the coin. The lines are either "full," meaning they are all there, and clear or not. Full-bell-line coins have been selling for twice the price of those that aren't.

Franklin halves are still available in many dates for under $100 with full bell lines (MS-65). It may be their low price that has attracted so much attention.

COMMEMORATIVE HALVES

The U.S. government issued commemorative half dollars in limited mintages between 1921 and 1939. Over forty-five different designs were minted. Between 1946 and 1951 the Booker T. Washington half was issued, and between 1951 and 1954 the Washington-Carver half was issued. And then again in 1982 interest in the commemoratives was rekindled when the government began issuing a new Washington commemorative half.

AMERICAN NUMISMATIC ASSOCIATION

BOOKER T. WASHINGTON
COMMEMORATIVE HALF

The commemorative halves are considered a series unto themselves by most collectors and investors. They are extremely popular and are often the starting point for many collections.

Prices for the coins vary greatly. A 1939 Arkansas commemorative set (all three mints—Philadelphia, Denver, and San Francisco) recently was selling for over $6,500. On the other hand, the 1982 Washington quarters were selling for under $15 (all in MS-65 grade, of course).

It's hard to find any expert in the field who has anything bad to say about the commemoratives. In fact, most continue to be amazed at how well these coins have repeatedly performed.

DOLLARS

These are the super coins as far as investors are concerned. Issued since 1794, designs have included bust (1794–1804), Seated Liberty (1836–1873), trade (1873–1885), Morgan (Liberty head, 1878–1921), Peace (1921–

1935), Eisenhower (1971–1978), and Susan B. Anthony (smaller size, 1979–1981).

The recent Susan B. Anthony coin has been probably one of the *least*-desired numismatic pieces. The Eisenhower dollar has generally been too recent to be of great interest, although prices within the last year have shown signs of awakening. The "Ike" coin could be a real sleeper.

What's stimulated the greatest interest, however, are the Peace and Morgan dollars. They have been the hottest of the hot for nearly a decade now, and there seems to be no letup in sight.

The problem with many of these coins, however, is the difficulty in grading them. Even dealers often disagree as to whether a coin is MS-64, MS-65, or MS-66. Thus, many investors have recently been taking to buying these coins in less than MS-65 grade.

The reasoning here appears to be that if the coin is bought in MS-63 (or possibly even MS-64), the buyer stands a better chance of getting the right grade. Buy the MS-65 and find it's graded wrong, and you've lost more than half your investment. Buy an MS-63 and find it's graded wrong, and you might have lost a few bucks.

Of course, the great price increases have occurred in the MS-65 grades. Over the last ten years I've seen these wonder coins double in price and then double again. Just about the time that everyone is wondering if they've hit their ceiling, they quadruple in price! In the past, even during slow periods of recession in the coin field, the dollars have pretty well held their value.

Of course, the question that everyone continually asks is, When will the race be over? Quite frankly, no one knows. These coins are really too scary to make any prediction on.

GOLD

The U.S. has minted a variety of gold pieces over the years between 1795 and 1933 (when gold ownership in the U.S. was delegalized—it was legalized again in 1975). Recent legislation authorizing a new bullion U.S. gold eagle ($50) has sparked interest in this area. But even so, gold coins have long been both investor and collector favorites. (Note: the new U.S. Eagle coins are bullion. They are sold for their gold content only. Strictly speaking, except in proof versions, they have no numismatic value.)

The major gold coins that are sought after by collectors include:

> twenty dollars (double eagle, 1850–1933)
> ten dollars (eagle, 1795–1933)
> five dollars (half-eagle, 1795-1929)

The U.S. also minted a $4.00 gold piece as well as a $2.50 (quarter eagle) and $1.00 coin, but these have largely remained in the domain of the collector.

Investors in gold coins are largely divided into two groups. The smaller group is those who buy gold coins just as they would any other coins, for rarity and top grade. The much larger group is those who buy common-date gold coins, blending an investment in bullion with one in rare coins.

For collectors the ultimate coin may well be the Saint-Gaudens design (1907–1933). A few proof coins struck in very high relief in 1907 are considered priceless. Even the common dates in MS-65 are hard to find recently for under $4,000.

The Bullion Connection • Gold has been an investment medium since it was relegalized in the U.S. in 1975. Investors buy gold commodity futures, gold mining stocks, gold bullion in bars, and rare gold coins. The latter has become one of the better ways of investing in gold for two reasons.

First, the rare coins belong to the numismatic market. Thus, when the market goes up, they go up because of their *numismatic* value.

Second, these same coins are also .900 pure gold. Thus, when the price of gold goes up, they have a second reason to advance. Hence gold coins are boosted by two separate fields.

Interestingly, when prices go down in one or the other of the two fields, gold coin prices tend to stabilize rather than fall. Perhaps it is the influence of the "other" field that keeps them up there.

Most popular with bullion investors are the later-date twenty-dollar gold pieces. These are frequently sold in common dates for a numismatic "premium" above bullion value. The premium varies depending on the demand for the coins.

Next in popularity with bullion buyers are the ten-dollar gold pieces. They are smaller, yet their premium is frequently double that of the larger twenty-dollar pieces.

ROLLS

Finally, rather than invest in single coins, some investors opt to invest in rolls of coins. There are investors' rolls of cents, nickels, dimes, quarters, halves, and even dollars. A roll consists of a number of coins, depending on the denomination, rolled in bank paper (now in plastic keepers).

The roll market tends to get very strong when the price of metals goes up. During the last great boom period in the 1980s, when silver momentarily hit fifty dollars an ounce, rolls were in great demand. Recently, with silver and copper in the depths, they are not that popular.

One has to be extremely careful when trading rolls and use an entirely new set of criteria. To understand this, one has to know how investing in rolls came about.

In years past, in the 1920s and 1930s, some collectors put aside bankrolls of coins. These originally wrapped rolls contained both common-date, common-grade coins as well as some true rarities.

In about the 1960s, some dealers and investors began to discover that these rolls were a true treasure trove. Buy a roll for its common-date value and find just one true rarity, and you could make ten times your initial investment. Buying and selling of rolls soared.

COINAGE PHOTO BY LARRY STEVENS

MANY COLLECTORS AND INVESTORS
SPECIALIZE IN COLLECTING ROLLS OF
UNCIRCULATED COINS

That was a long time ago, however, and the chances of there being any originally wrapped coin rolls is minute. Today, most rolls are actually "rerolls." The original rolls were broken open, the true rarities taken out, and the common coins rerolled. What the investor is buying, therefore, is a stack of silver dollar, or half-dollar, or whatever coins. These rolls sell for a premium above their bullion value.

In addition there are uncirculated rolls available. These are rolls of coins all supposedly in uncirculated condition (MS-60 or higher). The rolls are bought and sold (without being opened) for rare coin prices.

My personal feeling is that this is risky business. I can recall one roll that I examined. I opened the end and saw what was truly a brilliant uncirculated coin. Then I fudged. I massaged that coin out so I could see the one underneath. It was a well-worn common date. I had to assume that the roll wasn't worth a tenth of its asking price.

Unless you're very sure of the seller, my suggestion is to stay away from rolls of uncirculated coins. The chances of getting hurt are just too high to warrant the risk.

OTHER COINS

There are a number of other series that we haven't covered including gold commemorative coins, private issues (territorial) coins, and colonial coins. These tend, however, to be exclusively collectors' items not sought after by investors.

My suggestion is that if you're seriously looking at investing in coins you consider those denominations mentioned in this chapter. This is not to say that I'm recommending one coin over another; I'm not. It's also not to say that just because a coin's been popular in the past that it will continue to be popular in the future. It's only to say that this is the area where most investors are currently spending their money. It's the area that bears investigating.

Chapter

8

WHERE TO
BUY AND
SELL COINS

Unlike the stock market, bond market, or even the commodities market, there is no central "exchange" or hall in New York or anywhere else where coins are regularly bought and sold. Rather, coins are traded directly by market makers (dealers), at auctions or through private sales. We'll cover the benefits and drawbacks of each in this chapter, giving suggestions on how to get started.

AUCTIONS

Nearly everyone has attended an auction at one time or another, and coin auctions are not much different from other types. An auctioneer presents different "lots" (which may be one or more coins) for sale. Bidders may then compete for the prize.

Coin auctions do have one somewhat unusual aspect, in that in many cases mail bids are allowed and encouraged. In a mail bid you send the auction house instructions as to your minimum and maximum bids, and the house will then bid for you at the sale.

BENEFITS

Auctions offer individuals the opportunity to bid on a wide selection of rare coins that otherwise might not be available to them. If the market is not too strong and there aren't too many other bidders, it is sometimes possible to get those coins at very hefty savings. In a weak market when buying at auction, it is sometimes possible to get a rarity at a fraction, perhaps half (depending on the bidding), of its listings in pricing guides!

COINAGE MAGAZINE

A TYPICAL COIN AUCTION

Similarly, when it's time to sell, in a strong market because of competitive bidding, it's sometimes possible to get significantly more for coins than their listed value in pricing guides.

In general, for the experienced investor and collector, auctions can be an excellent resource for both buying and selling rare coins. They are not, however, always the first choice for the beginner.

DRAWBACKS

The best way to illustrate the drawbacks of auctions is to relate what happened at an actual auction I attended not long ago in Beverly Hills, California.

The auction was held by a firm with which I was not familiar in a swank ballroom of one of the big hotels. Refreshments were available. Hundreds of chairs had been placed for the bidders, and the coins were on display on a long table at the front of the room for four hours prior to the auction.

I and a friend whom I consider to be an excellent grader arrived four hours early to examine the coins. We were the only ones there (which turned out be good, since the auction firm only had two Tensor lights available for viewing).

The coins represented a broad cross section of U.S. coinage from cents to gold. All were in holders and each holder marked the coin grade. They were all graded from MS-60 to MS-65.

My grading friend very quickly pointed out that virtually every coin on exhibit showed some wear. He couldn't find a single coin out of the hundreds displayed that was better than an AU-55! In addition, many of the coins had been whizzed or otherwise brightened.

It didn't take long to examine all the coins, but we decided to wait and see how the auction went. There might be some bargains even in AU-55 or lower if the prices were right.

Significantly, the crowd didn't show up until half an hour before the auction. A few people casually examined the coins, but most simply came in and sat down.

The auction started promptly. The auctioneer explained the rules, which were those uniformly accepted at all legal auctions. He then went on to explain that these were not his coins but rather had been consigned to him by a single individual who wished to remain anonymous. (I later learned that this individual was an out-of-state coin dealer.) He explained that the seller had placed the grades on the coins and that the auctioneer had nothing to do with grading them. He encouraged bidders to examine the coins and make up their own minds about the grades. He produced copies of the *Gray Sheet* and encouraged those attending to check prices with the sheet. He noted that because this was an auction, he fully expected that there would be bargains, rare coins that would sell for a fraction of their value in the pricing guide.

Then the auction started. "I have a 1917-D Mercury dime listed as MS-65. The *Gray Sheet* lists its price in this grade at a bid of three-twenty and an ask of three-fifty. Who'll start off the bidding at two-fifty?"

No one would, so the bidding started at $50 and worked its way up. The final purchaser bought the coin for $160. The auctioneer commented, "See, he got that coin for half the price listed for an MS-65 in the *Gray Sheet.* I told you we had bargains here today!"

My friend leaned over and said, "I wouldn't grade that coin higher than an AU-55. He just bought a fifty-dollar coin for one hundred sixty dollars."

So it went, with the rich and famous from Beverly Hills strolling in to "invest" their money in rare coins. After an hour or so we couldn't stand it any longer and left.

What was wrong here?

The auctioneer was being perfectly straightforward (although I'm sure he knew what was going on). He stated that he had not graded the coins. He repeated the seller's grade and encouraged bidders to make up their own minds.

The bidders were sophisticated people, but not in coins. They thought they knew a bargain when they saw one. The coins were being sold for half their listed price or less. Even if they were misgraded by a grade or two, it still had to be a bargain, didn't it?

AUCTION CAUTIONS

If you've read this book this far, you know what the value of proper grading is. In an auction you are on your own. In the above illustration we saw what can happen when a scheming seller in cahoots with an auctioneer takes advantage of unsuspecting investors. Overgraded coins are sold for unrealistically high prices. Admittedly, it's an extreme example that I'm certain happens very rarely. But it's important to point out the extreme in order to be fully aware of it.

Even reputable auction houses face an ethical dilemma. Do they accept the grade put on the coin by the seller, or do they regrade the coin themselves? If they regrade lower as a regular practice, sellers won't be inclined to use them. If they accept the seller's grading, they may be selling overgraded coins to buyers. Most major auction houses try to be fair to both buyer and seller.

However, there are only two ways that I know of that a buyer can be sure when it comes to buying rare coins at an auction. The first is to know the coins well enough yourself to be able to go there and make your own determination of grade. The more you know, the better off you are.

If you really don't know, then an alternative is to hire a dealer or someone knowledgeable to come and advise you. Such arrangements are typically that you will pay the advisor 10 percent over and above the price of any coin he or she advises you to buy and that you actually purchase. (Note that at most auctions today the *buyer* pays a fee of between 10 and 20 percent to the auctioneer. This is in addition to the seller's fee.)

You don't need a lot of money to get an advisor, since advisors are very often anxious to attend auctions anyway to make their own bids.

MAIL BIDS

In a mail bid you would normally receive a catalog. These are frequently printed on high-gloss paper, with many of the coins presented in full color. The idea is that you look at the picture, make up your mind, and mail in your bid. (There is usually a nominal fee until you become an established customer; then the catalogs are normally mailed to you free.)

Some auction houses suggest grades but do not grade the coins in the catalog. Others, as noted earlier, grade the coins themselves or list the seller's grade.

Just as with in-person bidding, with auction bidding it's up to you to verify the grade of the coins. There are a variety of ways to do this.

First, you can have someone, a friend or dealer in whom you have confidence, go to the auction house and actually examine the coins for you. (At any reputable house, the coins are almost always on display for a few weeks prior to the auction.)

Next, you can make arrangements with one of the representatives of the auction house to give you the grades of the coins you are interested in. Typically, such an arrangement is that you will make a bid based on the representative's statement of grade. If you get the coin, you will have a short period of time, usually under ten days, to examine it. If it's up to grade, you will buy it. If not, you will be able to return it.

Most auction houses will give this privilege to their regular customers but not to new or untried customers. Thus, to get a return privilege, you may need to agree to pay a certain "return fee," perhaps 10 percent, in the event you don't want the coins.

If you mail bid and don't accept the coins a few times, you can forget about dealing with that auction house. They won't want to be bothered with your nonbusiness. On the other hand, if you've rejected the coins because they were overgraded, you're probably better off not dealing with that auction house anyhow!

SELLING AT AUCTION

It's difficult to get an auction house to handle the sale of a single coin unless it's a great and valuable rarity. They will frequently undertake to sell collections, however.

A reputable auction house will refuse to handle a collection that has been grossly misgraded. Such houses will often regrade coins up or down to their own standards, feeling that their reputation is more important than any momentary monetary gain. Or they may refuse to state grade and leave that up to the buyers. Such attitudes are admirable and are to be encouraged. Nevertheless, if you're selling and the auction house says that your MS-65 is an AU-55 worth a tenth of what you paid for it, you're not going to be pleased and you're not going to use that auction house.

Before you panic, get another opinion.

The fee for auctioning is negotiable, anywhere from 5 to 20 percent for the seller, depending on estimated demand for the collection. Some auction houses will advance cash on a collection. Others will sometimes buy the collection outright and then resell it as their own at auction. Be careful here; occasionally, if the auction house realizes the seller is a novice, he or she may receive a low offer.

When the market is strong, selling at auction is an excellent way to get a high price. In a hot market, bidders compete frantically for coins, particularly those of investment grade. In the heat of an auction, they may bid higher than they intend.

In a weak market, selling at auction is spotty at best. There may be only a few bidders, which could mean that your coins will be sold for a fraction of their value. (You could always buy your own coins back in such a situation, but you'd be liable for the commission, in this case to the auction house.) On the other hand, all it takes to bid the price up are two investors who want your coin and go head-to-head to get it.

If there is no action on a coin, some auction houses will either try to resell it at their next auction or return it to the seller for a nominal fee.

FINDING AUCTION HOUSES

This book does not intend to recommend auction houses. Rather, it is suggested that the reader obtain several of the various numismatic publications listed in the last chapter. Auction houses regularly advertise here. Write or call; they will send you information and, usually for a small fee, their current catalog. Then make up your own mind.

COINAGE PHOTO BY ROBERT WOLENIK

RON SWINEY'S BIDDING BOARD

BIDDING BOARDS

A bidding board is an excellent way for a beginner to buy and/or sell coins. A bidding board is usually placed on a wall in a dealer's store. Subject to certain guidelines, a collector-investor can clip his or her coins to the board and offer them for sale. Similarly, you can buy directly from the board.

The bidding board is a sort of poor man's auction. But when it works, it offers great possibilities for those getting started in the field.

Ron Swiney of Mid-Valley Coins in the San Fernando Valley in Southern California runs a very active bidding board. Although his shop is tiny, the board covers two long walls, and on a Friday evening when the bidding is up, anywhere up to 150 bidders and sellers are crowded in.

One Friday night not long ago I paid a visit to Swiney's shop. I arrived early and had to wedge myself inside a shop that couldn't be more than 20 feet wide by 40 feet long. Hundreds and hundreds of coins had been hung in plastic containers on both long walls of the shop. The sellers were primarily customers who had presented the coins to Swiney for sale during the week.

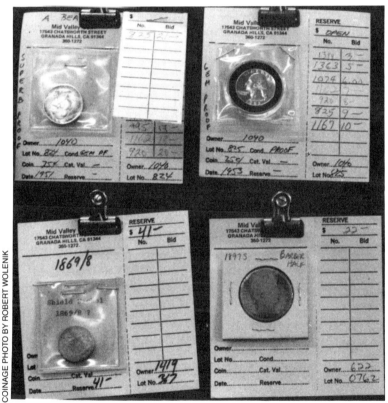

HOW COINS ARE DISPLAYED
ON A BIDDING BOARD

To bid on any of the coins it was first necessary to register. I paid a dollar, gave some identifying information, and received a number. Now I could bid.

Bidding was simple. Attached to each coin package was a sheet of paper with pricing lines. To bid, a person simply wrote in the price that he or she was willing to pay for the coin and their ID number. Most coins had a minimum bid. If someone had already made a bid on a coin, then the next bid had to be a certain amount higher. For bids under $5, the new bids had to be 10 cents over previous bids. Between $5 and $10, the increase had to be a quarter. Over $100 the increase had to be over $5. Looking over the coins displayed, I guessed that the median price was somewhere in the $200 range, although numerous coins were available for under $10.

Bidding was due to start at 8 o'clock, and the excitement began building as the hour approached. Swiney added to it by calling out bidders' numbers and giving away a free pizza and other prizes.

Between 7:50 and 8:10 (Swiney would pick a different exact time each week), a bell went off, and everyone who had been marking their bids on the cards had to step back. The bidding board was closed.

The tension went out of the air and people drifted off. Now Swiney would take down the cards and determine who was the highest bidder. That person had a week to come in and claim his or her coins.

I talked with Swiney and asked him about his success with the bidding board. He replied that the key to it was that it had to be honest. He pointed out that when he started, he lost money.

"It wasn't until three years ago that things started to roll. I put a twenty-dollar gold piece out on the board without a reserve. [A reserve is a minimum bid.] At the time the coin was a three-fifty value. Someone put a bid on it for one twenty-five, and that's what the coin sold for.

"I was really depressed. I knew the coin was worth much

more. I offered the buyer three-hundred on the spot for the coin, and he took it. He had made one-seventy-five profit in just a few minutes.

"I was really depressed that night. I had kept the store open late on a Friday, and I had lost money. But things were ready to turn around.

"The next morning the phone started ringing. I got calls from as far as a hundred miles away. People had heard about what had happened. They realized it was an honest board. I wasn't just putting up coins at high prices. There were real bargains there."

Swiney's success story has been repeated by other dealers around the country. (Note that the author does not make any recommendations on coin dealers, including Swiney. Investigate dealers on your own and make up your own mind.) However, Swiney's comments point out the downside of the bidding board.

DRAWBACKS

In the above example the coins on the bidding board were put up by customers who wanted to sell. In some few coin stores, however, the coins may be put up by the dealer, hoping to trick the customer into thinking that other sellers have put them there. Frequently, this sort of dealer will also put up phony bid prices, trying to get the real customers to think that active bidding is going on.

Stay away from this kind of bidding board. Chances are you won't find any bargains there, and you won't be able to do very well trying to sell your coins on it.

The way to tell a good bidding board from a bad one is the crowd. With a good bidding board, where there's real money to be made, there will always be a large crowd anxiously bidding on coins as well as asking to have them put up for sale. (The dealer *always* charges a fee for handling the sale of coins through a bidding board. In the above example, Swiney charged 10 percent of the sales price.)

DIRECT-TO-DEALER
BUY-SELL

Probably most buyers and sellers deal over-the-counter with coin dealers. They buy their rare coins from the dealers and they sell to them. This is usually the most convenient method. However, as with the other methods, there are both advantages and drawbacks.

ADVANTAGES

The biggest advantage usually cited for over-the-counter buying and selling to dealers is *advice.* The dealer gives the investor advice on what to buy and on when to sell.

Some readers may immediately think of a similarity here with stockbrokers. Stock investors usually pick their brokers on the basis of their ability to come up with good stocks.

Although the two are similar, the analogy really isn't correct and it's important to see why. The stockbroker merely selects stocks that should be winners. The coin dealer not only selects coins that should go up in value *but also advises on the grading of those coins.* Thus, the coin dealer's opinion is far more critical than the stockbroker's. (It's as if the broker were asked not only to pick a stock but also to render a judgment on the reliability of the stock certificate itself.)

Nothing will enhance an investor's career in rare coins more than to find a coin dealer who will grade fairly and buy and sell at reasonable prices. When you find such a dealer, go no farther. Stick with that dealer, and your rare coin fortune could be made.

Ideally, you will strike up a relationship with a dealer through a series of transactions. Perhaps at first you may purchase a few coins for $100 or less. After a period of time you'll sell them back, hopefully at a profit.

Soon, as your confidence in your dealer and your pocketbook grows, you'll be making ever-larger purchases and sales. The dealer will be handling these for you.

Typically, investors who have found the right dealer will tell him or her to locate certain coins for them. All major dealers are connected via a teletype system and thus can contact one another instantly for wholesale prices on various coins.

In addition, the large dealers all know each other and know how each grades. They automatically make allowances for dealers who grade high and those who grade low. Thus, if you have a good dealer working for you and you ask him to locate a 1914-D Lincoln cent in MS-63 condition (a fairly rare coin worth about $1,200 in this grade at this writing) and he doesn't make a market in these coins, he should be able to locate the right coin for you in a few days.

Thus, the right dealer can not only advise you but can also supply you with the coins you want.

TEN WAYS TO PICK
A GOOD COIN DEALER

The following suggestions are not foolproof, but they should help.

1. Be sure the dealer has a *professional affiliation.* Those to look for are: ANA—American Numismatic Association (a must); PNG—Professional Numismatic Guild; and ANS—American Numismatic Society.

2. Does the dealer have a *place of business?* I can remember a conversation with a coin dealer in a flea market that was set up every Sunday in a drive-in theater lot. He said, "Look, if the coin isn't as I say, come back and see me. I'm here every Sunday."

Indeed. And if the one Sunday I come back, what if he's not there? Where do I go to complain?

Vest-pocket dealers (those who don't have a place of business) may ultimately have some bargains (although I personally doubt it), but my suggestion is to buy and sell from a dealer who has a shop.

3. Find out *how long the dealer's been in business.* Most dealers are happy to tell you. Ask to see their business license. In many communities, it will state when it was first issued. Rare coins is a boom-and-bust field. Any dealer who's weathered both for a considerable length of time must be doing something right.

4. *Ask around.* When you go into a coin dealer's store, ask the dealer's opinion of two or three other dealers in town. After you try this a few times, you may find that there is one dealer that all the others dislike.

But who's honest—all the dealers or the one black sheep? I knew of one dealer in a particular city that the other dealers couldn't stand. The reason was that he consistently undersold them and took away their customers.

The only answer I have is to establish a long-term relationship with a dealer. It's the only way you can really know what kind of person you are dealing with.

5. Does the dealer *belong to a network?* As we've seen, no one dealer makes a market in every coin. Therefore, it's important that the dealer you suggest be able to obtain coins out of his or her specialty. The fastest way this can be done is by belonging to one of the dealer teletype networks.

6. Does the dealer *go to coin shows?* Coin dealers go to coin shows to buy material for their investors from other dealers. Yes, one way to get it is on the networks. That works well for easy-to-find coins. But for the scarcer pieces, it can be more difficult. An active dealer will attend at least one coin show every month including the largest, the American Numismatic Association coin show held every August. (You might want to attend as well—it's held in a different city every year.)

7. Does the dealer *have time for you?* Being busy isn't necessarily a sign of honesty. But it does show that a dealer is being trusted by a large number of people.

The problem is that when a dealer is too busy, it can get in the way of giving good service to clients. As a result, a too-busy dealer can sometimes be a poor choice for you.

There are essentially two kinds of dealers in the coin business—major companies that trade millions of dollars monthly and "mom-and-pop" shops.

Both of these have their pros and cons. For example, the big dealers have a wide variety of merchandise on hand. The small dealers don't.

On the other hand, something that can make up for this is the fact that the mom-and-pop dealers will often have the time to explain things to you.

8. Beware of fancy storefronts. I can't stress this enough. There is a kind of conman who operates In this field by setting up an office in a high-rent area, outfitting that office with a plush interior, hiring a secretarial staff, dressing like a millionaire, spending money on lavish meals, trips, and other entertainment, and in general trying too hard to impress you with how well he's doing.

Watch out for this person. Anytime someone tries too hard to impress me, I have to ask, why? Remember, the truly successful people on this planet rarely show off; they don't have to.

9. Does the dealer's stock-on-hand suddenly drop? This is just a personal note on your author's part. Here's the story. I was once doing an article on a dealer who had quickly grown to be one of the largest in the area. He had a large store with a big staff and enormous stock on hand. One day I came in and noticed the stock was virtually gone.

No, the shelves weren't empty. They were just as full as ever. However, instead of expensive rarities, they were filled with inexpensive common-date material. He had had perhaps a million dollars in coins before. Now his stock was perhaps $25,000 or less.

I noticed, but didn't say anything. Two months later this dealer was forced into bankruptcy. He had seen it coming and had sold off his stock to try to satisfy his creditors. That hadn't worked, however.

The worst part was that while he was going downhill, to try to save himself he started ripping off his regular customers. He tried to lowball material he was buying, at the same time overgrading and charging too much for material he was selling. Because his customers had absolute faith in him, they continued to deal . . . at their loss.

Thus, for what it's worth, watch out for any change in a dealer's stock-in-hand. It could portend bad things in the offing.

10. Check with the post office, the Better Business Bureau, and the district attorney's office. Some may think this advice is a bit harsh, but believe me, it's a lot better to check first than to learn the bad news later on. The truth of the matter is that a dealer who has been selling bad coins through the mails and has had numerous complaints about it, who has had former clients write letters of protest to the Better Business Bureau, who has been cited for dozens of violations by the district attorney's office, may still be in business!

It may sound impossible, but I've seen it happen too often to know that it is only too possible. Yes, things may eventually catch up with such a person, but it could take years. In the meantime, he could be operating a storefront that looks perfectly respectable.

Check with your local postmaster, DA, or Better Business Bureau. They'll quickly tell you if they've had complaints and had to take action. It's only a matter of a few phone calls, and it could put your mind at rest knowing that your prospective dealer is a solid citizen, or it could give you early warning of a shyster about to strike.

COIN SHOWS

Finally, an excellent place to buy and sell coins is on the bourse floor of a coin show. The word *bourse* means a kind of exchange. In Europe, it means a stock exchange. But in America it means the trading floor where rare coins are bought and sold.

The granddaddy of all coin shows is the ANA show held each year. In addition, there are large regional shows, city-wide shows, and even local coin club shows. Expect to see upwards of 500 separate dealers at a larger show, and as few as a couple of dozen at the smaller shows.

You can take your rare coins into a coin show and sell them on the bourse floor to dealers. Similarly, you can go into such a show and buy coins there. The price of admission is usually negligible (a few dollars). In addition, there are often educational seminars or shows being run concurrently that can help you to learn more about rare coins.

BEHAVIOR

There aren't many specific rules of behavior on a bourse floor, but those few that exist are strictly adhered to. You may wear virtually any style of clothing you like, but the more conservative choices are preferred. A suit is definitely not necessary for men nor are dresses required for women. Typical outfits are slacks and casual tops.

1. Food is usually available. *Don't eat food near coins.* The dealers will shoo you away. They don't want their inventory damaged.

2. *Don't bring a camera* unless you *first* get permission from those running the show. There's lots of cash on a bourse floor, and people get very nervous if they think they are being photographed spending it.

3. *Don't pick up any rare coin until you've first asked and secured the approval of the owner.* In most cases this isn't a possibility anyway, since the coins are locked away under glass counters. However, a dealer may have a dozen or more coins out showing them to a prospective buyer. You might saunter up and take a liking to one of them. It would be a simple matter to reach down and pick it up to get a closer look.

Don't do it unless you ask first. It could make the dealer very nervous, and nervous dealers tend to call security.

4. *Hold the coin in the approved manner, by the edge.* If you want to see a dealer have apoplexy, ask to see one of his rare coins, then take it out of the holder, and put your thumb on it.

5. You may ask to "borrow" a coin for a few moments. Dealers frequently borrow among themselves. If they know you, they will undoubtedly agree. You may then take that coin and try to sell it to another dealer for a higher price than the first dealer is asking. This is called "arbitraging" and goes on all the time. But it is considered bad form to do it right in front of the first dealer. He or she is not going to like it, and the second dealer isn't going to like it either.

6. *Don't argue about grading.* The dealers build their reputation on grading. If they say a particular coin is an MS-63 or an MS-65, then they will feel compelled to stick with that grade *no matter what you say.* It quickly becomes a matter of pride. Trying to get a dealer to lower or raise a grade once he or she's committed to it is like getting the dealer to admit a mistake. Most simply won't do it and will get offended at you for insisting.

7. *Do argue about price.* You think the coin you're selling is MS-65, the dealer calls it MS-64. Okay. Agree that hypothetically the grade is MS-64, but this particular coin is such a fine MS-64 that it's worth an MS-65 price. See?

8. *Do bargain—don't play games.* It's not like a jar of mayonnaise in a grocery store, where the price is set no matter what. Rather, it's like a market in a Third World country. The seller asks too high a price, the buyer asks too low. Which one gets the better deal depends to a large degree on how good a bargainer each is.

Expect dealers to ask prices that they will come down on. When you sell, ask for more than you expect to get. It's what everyone does. It's the way to get a good deal. It can also be fun.

But remember that it's not a game. At the end, if the dealer meets your price or you meet the dealer's, *You're now committed to the sale.* Once the dickering is done and a price is struck, stick to it. If you make a deal only to try and weasel out of it a few moments later, your name will quickly be passed around as someone to avoid. Not only won't you get a chance at the good deals, but you probably won't get the ear of many more dealers.

9. *Don't bother dealers who are busy.* Remember, buying and selling is going on all around you on a bourse floor, and money is changing hands. You may think your transaction is more important, perhaps because it involves more money than one the dealer is currently handling. It may be more important to you, but it probably isn't to the other customer and may not be to the dealer, depending on what his inventory is. If you interrupt, you're sure to get the dealer angry.

In addition, some dealers simply won't have time to talk with you. These are the wholesale dealers who come to the show almost exclusively to buy and sell to other dealers. You can usually tell who they are by the large crowd of dealers standing around their booth.

Don't be upset with them, and don't waste your time on them. You can spend a whole afternoon just waiting to get in a few words. There are plenty of retail dealers. Go see one of them.

Can you deal wholesale? Not unless you become a dealer yourself.

10. *Don't let anyone know how much or how little money you have.* Lots of money attracts muggers. Too little money causes others to lose interest. You know what you can afford. Try to get it.

Chapter

9

BUYING COINS BY MAIL AND PHONE

Many highly successful investors have long used the public mails to purchase their coins. They've found that they can obtain excellent buys in this fashion. (Remember the mail auction bids discussed in the last chapter?) Here we'll discuss buying direct from dealers through the mail as well as point out some disturbing tendencies in a new area, telemarketing of rare coins.

MAIL-ORDER DEALERS

As we've noted, there are the very large rare coin dealers and there are the mom-and-pop shops. There is, however, often a third and seldom-mentioned breed, the mail-order dealer. This can be, of course, either a large or small operation, but very frequently it's somewhere in between. Typically, the mail-order person is a smaller dealer who's working his or her way up. Or the mail-order person may be located in a part of the country where there is little walk-by business—in other words, a dealer trying for a wider market.

Mail-order dealers regularly advertise in all the numismatic publications, including *COINage, Coin World, Numismatic News,* and so forth (for a complete listing of publications see Chapter 11). They usually state the type of coin they are offering for sale, its condition and its price. Infrequently, mail-order dealers may include photos, but photo reproduction in popular publications is usually not of sufficiently high quality to warrant this. In addition these dealers (or sometimes very large auction houses) will advertise that they want coins and will publish their "want" lists. (They may also ask for customers' "want" lists and try to fill them with suitable coins.)

HOW TO ORDER BY MAIL

Each dealer will have specific requirements, but in general, to order by mail you will need to do the following:

1. Contact the dealer (or read the ad if this material is covered) to determine how payment is to be made.

2. Write to the dealer specifying which coins you want and how much you are paying. Get a letter from the dealer specifying what is to be purchased, the amount to be paid, when to expect delivery, and what guarantees and return privileges are offered. *This should all be in writing.*

3. Send payment, frequently a cashier's check. Some dealers will accept MasterCharge, Visa, and other credit cards.

4. Expect the coins to be shipped promptly by return mail. They should be well packed and *insured for their full value.* (The law requires delivery of merchandise ordered through the mail within a maximum of thirty days.)

5. Examine the coins. If they are as described, keep them. If not, repackage them securely and send them back by return postage, *again fully insured.*

6. If you've returned the coins, get your money back by return mail.

Most mail-order dealers have been in business for many years, and they go out of their way scrupulously to protect their reputations. (That is, after all, their source of livelihood.) Almost all offer money-back guarantees in case the buyer is unsatisfied with the coins. Once you've established a rapport with them, some will even send you the coins on acceptance—pay for them if you like them, return them if you don't.

Literally hundreds of thousands of people regularly buy and sell coins through the mail with these dealers, with only a minimal amount of problems. For the investor who wants a broader scope, mail order offers a bold opportunity.

WHAT TO WATCH OUT
FOR WHEN YOU ORDER

Knowing that most people order successfully by mail, however, does not mean that your particular transaction will be a success. You could always get the one bad apple in the barrel.

To help protect yourself there are a number of things you can do:

1. Find out how long the dealer has been handling mail orders. Virtually any dealer will be happy to tell you, and many give the years in business in their ads. Be careful with dealers who are just starting out.

2. Find out what city the dealer is in, and call the local postmaster. Find out if there are or have been any mail-fraud complaints against the dealer. *This is a must.*

Don't be bothered if just one or two complaints have been lodged against the dealer over the course of a number of years. In any business there are always going to be a few disgruntled customers who will create as much trouble for the dealer as possible. If you're concerned, call the dealer and ask for an explanation.

But be *very* alarmed if the postmaster tells you that they have dozens or hundreds of complaints! This is a definite warning sign. Don't think that everything is all right because the post office hasn't closed the place down. The post office works in a very slow fashion when it comes to mail fraud, and it could be years before action is finally taken.

3. Ask if the dealer is a member of a professional organization (ANA, ANS, PNG [Professional Numismatic Guild], and so on). If you have any doubts, call these organizations for a confirmation.

4. Be sure you understand the dealer's terms. Many require payment in full before they ship coins. Some will only accept returns under specific conditions and under time limits. For example, you may have only five days for approval.

5. Some dealers have minimum orders, usually ten to twenty-five dollars.

6. Be aware that quoted prices in publications are *not* firm. The coin market is volatile and moves quickly. However, in order to get their ads in magazines and papers, dealers must often draw them up weeks in advance. Thus, by the time they appear the prices of particular coins may be substantially higher or lower. Prices quoted in ads are normally considered "suggested." When you get the coins, you may find you are paying more—or less.

7. Don't expect actually to be able to buy every coin that you send for. Remember, the ad you read is probably being read by tens of thousands of other people. Any one of them may have sent in an order prior to yours. Virtually all mail-order offers to purchase are subject to prior sale.

8. Expect to pay extra for postage and insurance, unless you know the dealer very well and it's a big order. This can run upwards of ten dollars, depending on what you buy.

9. Many dealers won't accept C.O.D. orders; however, some dealers do offer toll-free phone numbers by which you can call your order in.

10. *Order small at first.* If this is the first time you've ordered from a dealer, buy just a few coins for just a few bucks. See what the dealer sends. See how the material is graded. See if it's been done fairly.

The idea is to build a relationship of trust between you and the dealer. As you gain more confidence, you'll feel secure in sending larger sums of money out to make bigger purchases. But the best way to start is to start small and build gradually.

WHAT TO DO
IF YOU GET STUNG

If you didn't follow the above ten cautions or if you got involved in an unusual situation where there was a dispute with the dealer, what can you do about it?

That depends on what happened. If the dealer has closed down and skipped town, you may simply be out your money. Check with the DA, but don't set your hopes too high. (Fortunately, this rarely happens.)

What's far more likely is a difference of opinion. Perhaps the dealer feels that the twenty days you took to make up your mind on the coins was too long. More commonly, the dealer may say that the coins you returned were damaged—you put your fingerprint on them. Who's to say?

The best way to solve this problem is to avoid it. If you have a good rapport with the dealer at the outset, it should never arise. However, should the dealer refuse to refund money that you feel is due you or fail to deliver coins as agreed, you have a series of options:

1. Contact the ANA. Be aware, however, that the ANA normally acts only for the benefit of its members; consequently, the first thing you may want to do is to join. Contact and complain to any other professional organization to which the dealer belongs.

2. Contact the dealer's postmaster. The post office may move very slowly when it comes to shutting a business down, but they do have one big lever—they can refuse to deliver mail. If they feel that there is fraud involved they can embargo a dealer's mail.

Since this, of course, can cause a dealer a world of trouble, complaining to the postmaster can put some pressure on.

3. Complain to the district attorney in the city where the dealer is located. Normally the DA can't be expected to act on a single complaint. But if there are numerous complaints, you may get some action.

4. Arbitrate. Keep talking with the dealer and try to work out a compromise that both of you feel is fair. This is often the best, though not always the most satisfying, way to handle this.

5. Write to the publication that ran the ad. Magazines and newspapers are used to getting occasional complaint letters, and if yours is the only one, chances are nothing

will happen. But if they are suddenly inundated with complaints about an advertiser, they may think seriously about running future ads from that source.

DEALER GUARANTEES AND
WHAT THEY ARE WORTH

Mail order dealers almost always offer guarantees (or else they could never induce anyone to buy coins through the mail). These guarantees operate at different levels. At the first level are guarantees that are easy to perform. At the last level are guarantees that are difficult if not impossible to perform. We'll start at the beginning.

1. Money back if the buyer is unsatisfied with the merchandise. This is always subject to a time limit, frequently a very short one. This is a basic guarantee that every mail-order dealer should offer.

2. Protection against counterfeit. Virtually all dealers guarantee to buy back any coins they sell that turn out to be fakes.

3. Buy-back. Some dealers agree to buy back any coin that you buy at the then-current market price. But remember, dealers have both "bid" and "ask" prices. If you buy at "ask," you will only be able to sell back at "bid," which will be substantially lower. In addition, some dealers may change their bid-ask. Thus when you go to sell back, they might give you a lower bid price.

4. Guaranteed buy-back. Although this rarely happens, sometimes a dealer will guarantee to buy back a coin for what you paid (or more) as long as you hold it for a specific period of time, say two years.

What are these various guarantees really worth? They are all worth as much or as little as the dealer wants them to be. A strong, honest dealer will honor these statements. If you happen to get that one bad apple, you may lose your money regardless of what agreements you have.

A special word about guaranteed-price buy-back. My

personal feeling is that this is a phony guarantee. All that it's saying, to my way of thinking, is that *if* the market goes up, the dealer will certainly buy back at the original price you bought for (which is certain to be lower than market). On the other hand, if the market goes down, the dealer can say "Sorry," in which case you still have no guarantee.

GET IT IN WRITING?

I've seen many authors tell their readers to "get it in writing" in order to be protected. It certainly is good advice, since the written word always supersedes the spoken word in a courtroom.

However, don't think that just because you have something in writing that you're protected. You're not. Whether it's coins or anything else, if the seller skips with your money and can't be found and doesn't leave behind any assets, your written agreement may not be worth anything in cash. Thus, get it in writing, *but* also know with whom you're dealing. Many times the handshake of an honest man is worth more than reams of paper signed by a dishonest one.

TELEMARKETING
OF RARE COINS

Telemarketing does not mean calling up a coin dealer and buying a coin. Rather, it means being called by someone you don't know who then tries to sell you a rare coin. There's a big difference.

There's nothing basically wrong with this kind of solicitation. Lots of perfectly respectable items and services from magazines to rug cleaning are sold this way. There's no reason rare coins can't be sold this way as well, and there are highly reputable coin houses that do it.

The problem, of course, is one of abuse. Certain unscrupulous schemers have opened "boiler room" operations and have ripped off the unsuspecting public for thousands of dollars. It's this group that one has to be on the alert for.

I recently received a call from such an operation. He knew that I was in some way involved in coins, but apparently not that I wrote on the subject. The caller's name was Mat. He sounded friendly and talked quickly.

"Hello, Bob? This is Mat from XXX coins in Florida. I heard that you were interested in rare coins, and I know you'll agree that coin investing is a great idea. [No pause for me to answer.]

"Bob, I know you're a busy person and I don't want to take up a lot of your time, but I have an investment opportunity here that I don't think you'll want to pass up. You've heard about rare silver dollars and the record prices they've been setting lately, haven't you? [No pause.]

"Bob, I know you've also read that according to a major financial house's report, rare coins are the top investment field [the Salomon Brothers report discussed earlier]. Well, our company has been buying silver dollars for some time now, and we are a wholesaler. We don't spend money advertising or pay for a fancy location. Instead we sell direct to the public over the phone, and we're able to pass along our savings. That means special discount prices for you.

"Here's what I mean, Bob. You know that an 1881-S dollar in MS-65 grade sells for five-thirty, don't you? Well, I can prove it to you. You've heard of the *Gray Sheet,* haven't you? It lists coin prices. Well, I'm looking at the current issue of the *Gray Sheet,* and there's the 1881-S and in black and white it's listed at five-thirty.

"Well, Bob, what would you say if I could get you that coin for just four-fifty? Think of it; that's wholesale price. The minute you bought the coin you'd be making 80 bucks profit.

"Bob, what do you think of that? I can get you that coin and a lot more, all at the same discount. It's just a matter of how much money you want to make. Just send me a binder for, say, two thousand, and I'll send you six coins, all at wholesale. And to prove their value, I'll enclose a copy of the latest *Gray Sheet* which I guarantee will state that each MS-65 coin I send you is worth at least eighty more than I'm charging. Now, how can you go wrong?"

It's a very intriguing argument, and if I didn't know anything about coins, I might not see clearly how I *could go* wrong. I certainly wouldn't send $2,000. But I might indeed send $480 for just one coin. So I made that offer just to see what would happen.

I suggested we start off small with just the one coin, the 1880-O dollar. I suggested that I would submit bank references and that "Mat" could send me the coin on ten days' approval. If it indeed turned out to be an MS-65 and I could find another dealer who would pay $530 for it, I'd buy it. (Why not? I would put up no cash and instantly make $80 profit.)

Mat said he didn't do business that way. He didn't know me (although he had chosen to call me), and the coin was valuable. It would have to be cash and carry.

I suggested a credit card transaction. (My bank allows me to refuse payment on any credit card transaction over $50, interstate and conducted by phone.) Matt said he didn't take credit cards. All right. In that case I suggested we change the subject and discuss the matter of the grading of the coin. Mat had another urgent phone call and had to leave. He said he'd call back later. He didn't.

As I stated at the beginning, I am not condemning all telemarketers. Some I'm sure are indeed legitimate coin dealers offering good coins for good prices.

However, I have seen the waves of letters from innocent investors who have been hit hard by unscrupulous telemarketers, those who have charged $450 and delivered coins worth $25.

NOTHING ILLEGAL

Notice, there's usually nothing *illegal* about what's going on here. The telemarketer may indeed deliver a coin in a package that has MS-65 written all over it. *But that doesn't mean the coin has value.*

The telemarketer can always argue that in his or her estimation the coin was indeed an MS-65 grade and hence, according to the *Gray Sheet* or some other source, was indeed worth the money. All that it has to be off is one or two grades for virtually an entire investment to be ripped off.

In recent years boiler-room operations, so called because they are frequently set up in the basements of large buildings where the boilers are, have stung thousands of would-be investors. These rooms are outfitted with dozens of phones and salespeople simply sit by the phones all day trying to solicit orders.

PROTECTING YOURSELF

To begin with, follow the same guidelines for buying from someone through the mail as noted above. If the dealer doesn't have a legitimate and longtime place of business, be wary.

In addition, try to find out as much about the person selling you the coins as possible. Ask about the person's experience in the field, particularly previous employment. Most coin salespeople bounce around a lot from dealer to dealer. Chances are that anyone legitimate will be able to name another dealer who may be better known and who can give a recommendation.

Finally, never talk price with telemarketers—talk grading. If they are legitimate, they'll respond. If not, chances are they'll hang up on you. After all, the crooks in this area are trying to find suckers who don't know anything about rare coins, not individuals who know what the field is all about.

Ultimately, the best advice is that if you don't feel perfectly comfortable, hang up. Remember, the seller invaded the privacy of your home or office with an unsolicited call. You don't owe him or her anything.

Chapter

10

INVESTING STRAIGHT TALK

As we noted early on in this book, collecting rare coins has proved to be a highly profitable endeavor. Those who have collected for periods of five, ten, or twenty years have shown substantial profits.

However, that does not mean that coin prices simply go up and up and never come down. Quite the contrary. Coin prices are typically cyclical. As anyone who has been in the business for any length of time can testify, they are characterized by periods of boom and bust.

Too often new investors come into the market during a boom period. Prices of coins go up almost every day, and it seems to matter little what is bought. To a new investor it can seem like the promised land. Buy anything and it turns to gold, in some cases literally.

Such investors usually get hooked on the fantasy that rare coin investing is a money machine. Just buy some coins, resell for a profit, use all the money you make to buy more, and pyramid yourself into financial independence.

These investors often take the worst beatings when the market reverses itself and prices fall. Unfortunately, they are also the ones who get disillusioned and walk away from the field vowing never to return. It's unfortunate because the problem is not with the field but rather with their perception of it.

A HISTORY OF
BOOMS AND BUSTS

I began watching the rare coin field in 1969. At that time we were in the midst of a miniboom. Prices for nearly every denomination, date, and mint mark were going up and, coming upon it by chance, as I did, I assumed that things were just going to keep going like that forever.

I was amazed just a few years later when the entire field plummeted into the doldrums. It seemed to sink and sink, and I began to believe that the whole thing was just a flash in the pan, a once-in-a-million occurrence.

At that time an old friend and collector, Maury Gould, took me aside and said, "Don't worry about this field. Look to the long term and you'll be fine. In the short term it's always up and down."

He was, of course, perfectly correct. The problem was that there was no real barometer that could be used to keep track of how the field was doing or what its history had been.

Thus it was in 1975 that I undertook, with the aid of veteran collector Lee Martin, to create a chart that would track the coin field. That chart eventually became *COINage Magazine*'s "Coin Price Averages," or "CPAs."

CPA

As originally conceived, the CPA would track 20 "key" coins. (As collectors know, "key" coins are typically those coins that are price leaders in a particular issue.) The average price of these twenty key coins, as determined by calling a selection of dealers, would then be averaged and the average would become an index. That index has been published monthly in *COINage Magazine* ever since.

Of course, over time, the index has had to be updated. Today two indices are used to reflect the monthly activity of the coin market in two areas. The first is the MS-65 category, in which sixty-eight key coins are used. This is primarily an investor's market. The second is the VF (Very Fine) category, in which fifty-three different key coins are used. This tends to be a collector's market.

Reproduced in this book is the CPA, going back to its beginnings, along with the two new indices.

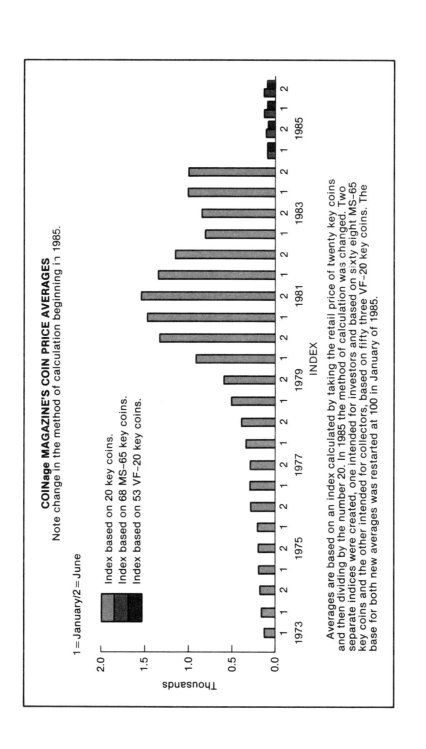

COINage MAGAZINE'S COIN PRICE AVERAGES
Note change in the method of calculation beginning in 1985.

1 = January/2 = June

Index based on 20 key coins.
Index based on 68 MS-65 key coins.
Index based on 53 VF-20 key coins.

Thousands

INDEX

Averages are based on an index calculated by taking the retail price of twenty key coins and then dividing by the number 20. In 1985 the method of calculation was changed. Two separate indices were created, one intended for investors and based on sixty eight MS-65 key coins and the other intended for collectors, based on fifty three VF-20 key coins. The base for both new averages was restarted at 100 in January of 1985.

HOW TO USE THE CPA

The CPA must not be taken as a final authority on the coin market. It *follows* rather than *leads* the market. Thus, whatever the indices state typically is where the market was a short time earlier, not where it currently is or is going to be in the future.

What is extremely useful about the CPA is that it suggests trends. It is also one of the longest-running (if not the longest-running) indices to follow the rare coin field.

Looking at the index, notice that the course of rare coins is not simply a steadily rising line. Rather, there have been very distinct ups and downs. Often the down periods have been as deep and sustained as the up periods.

For an investor with any acumen at all, this should suggest strong possibilities. With coins, historically speaking, it has been possible to buy cheap when the market is down, then sell expensive later on when the market is up. *And to do this over and over again.* In this sense, the coin market has been a regular money machine.

MARKET PECULIARITIES

It's important to understand a few oddities about the coin field. You might want to notch the corner of this page and return here for reminders later on:

1. When the market is going up, steeply up, then almost all coins are affected, from cents to gold. A strong market means everything goes up.

2. In a strong market, coin grading tends to get "advanced." By this I mean that when prices for MS-65 material zoom up, many of the investors for this grade of coin suddenly find that they are priced out of the market.

Hence, they begin looking for other grades to buy. Typically they buy the MS-63 coins. This causes a sudden demand for MS-63 material, and its prices start rising. Thus, the MS-63s advance to investor-grade material and investor prices.

In addition, coins that were formerly MS-63 are sometimes now graded as MS-64 under the pressure of the market, or, once in a great while, even MS-65. Thus the value increase can be enormous.

3. When the market cools off, the lower grades of coins drop off first and most steeply. Thus, as investor demand weakens, it will be felt first in the MS-63 coins, and they will tend to plunge in price long before the MS-65s begin to move down. Usually at about this time, those new investors who bought MS-63 begin to realize their error. They panic-sell, and this depresses the price for this grade even more.

Many a coin fortune has been made by buying up MS-63 coins at fire-sale prices when the coin market is weak, and then selling them at ridiculously high prices when the market booms. Of course, this takes a lot of confidence in one's perception of the future and a lot of money that can be put away and not touched.

4. When the market "busts," it does not usually do so across the board. Thus, for example, the price of cents, nickels, quarters, and halves could plummet. At the same time, because of their popularity, for example, the price of dimes, commemorative halves, and dollars could remain strong or even gain.

What's important to remember here is that the market does not move down across the board. The trick is to be positioned in those coins that will least feel the downward pull.

CAUTION

What should be apparent is that one of the keys to successful coin investing is timing. Knowing when the market is up or down and, even more important, when it's going to turn can be critical.

This desire to get a better grasp on timing has led some investors to rely too heavily on such devices as the CPA index. They take a look at what's happened in the past, then project that into the future.

This is called "technical analysis" and is highly suggestive. It seems to "prove" and "demonstrate" what is going to happen. But be aware that it contains an inherent flaw.

The flaw is that there is no guarantee that what has happened in the past will occur again in the future. Just because the market has repeatedly gone up and down does not *guarantee* that it will continue to do so. It could simply go down (or up) and stay there forever (although this is most unlikely).

Further, just because in the past a down (or an up) cycle lasted for twelve months or twenty-four months or whatever is no guarantee or even assurance that in the future a down cycle will last for a similar period of time. *It is extremely risky to try to predict the turns in the coin market just on the basis of any index.*

In other words, it is probably wise to temper guides such as the CPA with common sense and with a strong understanding of those factors that influence coin prices.

FACTORS THAT INFLUENCE COIN PRICES

Having looked at the technical side of things, let's now examine the fundamentals. We're going to cover five:

Inflation
Interest Rates
Economic Changes
Alternative Investments
Public Perception of Rare Coins

INFLATION

This is perhaps the single biggest factor influencing rare coin prices. Rare coins are seen as a form of "hard currency." They are typically viewed as holding their value during inflationary times. Thus, investors buy them as an inflation hedge.

This was amply demonstrated during the great inflation of 1978–1980. During that time the inflation rate in the United States soared to double digit rates for the first time in more than 50 years. Rare coin value soared as well. For every notch the inflation rate moved up, so did the rare coin field.

Similarly, as inflation was brought under control after 1981 and it fell, so did the overall value of the coin field (as evidenced by indices such as the CPA). Thus, rare coins, because of their hedging abilities, tend to follow what's happening in inflation.

Of course, what good would a rule be without an exception? In 1985 and 1986 inflation not only remained low but actually declined. Yet, during that period of time, many rare coin prices began rising. Instead of following the inflation curve, rare coins seemed to be diverging from it.

How can this apparent discrepancy be explained given the relationship between rare coins and inflation just suggested?

There are at least two possible explanations. First, many investors felt that inflation was artificially being kept low by a series of events, most particularly oil prices. The money supply was expanding, which should mean higher inflation in the future. Yet, oil prices were falling, reducing the cost of virtually everything, hence lower inflation.

Many investors felt that this was too good to be true and couldn't last. Eventually oil prices would rise and when they did, inflation would come back with a vengeance. Thus, these investors were possibly buying rare coins in anticipation of future inflation.

The second explanation is that there were other factors influencing the market that overrode low inflation. We'll look into these now.

INTEREST RATES

In general, low interest rates are good for rare coins; high interest rates are bad. In the period 1985–1986, when rare coins did well despite low inflation, we also had a period of low interest rates. Thus, it might have been that the beneficial effect of low interest rates during that time outweighed the detrimental effect of low inflation and this is why rare coin prices rose during this period.

The relationship between interest rates and rare coins is the same as for any hard investment. Namely, the substitution effect of invested money. It works like this:

Suppose you have $1,000 to spend. If interest rates are high, say 20 percent per year, and you put that money in the bank at those rates, you can expect to earn $200.

On the other hand, you could substitute that bank investment for a rare coin investment. But you have to ask yourself, Will my rare coins earn more than $200 for me within a year's time? (The coins have to earn more than $200 because they have certain drawbacks over a savings account, namely higher risk, liquidity problems, and insurance and storage costs.) If after all considerations the coins will earn sufficiently more than $200 to make the investment worthwhile, investors will then buy the coins. If not, then the money stays in the bank.

(This sort of substitution takes place in investors' minds all the time, and anyone who thinks it doesn't isn't really in touch with money.)

On the other hand, let's say interest rates are very low and the best an investor can hope for is 5 percent. The $1,000 will only earn $50 in a year. Now the same question gets asked. Only now the rare coin investment must compete with only a $50 alternative as opposed to a $200 alternative before. The chances are that rare coins will come off much better this time.

Thus high interest rates keep people away from rare coins while low interest rates favor coin investment.

ECONOMIC CHANGES

There are two schools of thought here. The first is that when the economy changes for the better, that is it grows, rare coin investments are favored. The reason is that during economic expansions, investors have money to spare and are looking for good investments. Typically, interest rates are low to medium, hence this is a time that favors rare coins.

The other school of thought says that rare coins are favored during moments of economic crisis. There's a war in the Middle East cutting off oil supplies. A major U.S. bank goes into default. There is a scandal on Wall Street. Whatever the scenario, suddenly we are faced with an upheaval that threatens to tear away the foundations of our economic order.

In times like this, rare coins tend to do very well. People panic. They realize that economic chaos is always just around the corner, and they look for a safety net. Rare coins, as a currency of last resort, along with gold bullion (and sometimes silver bullion), are often considered a safe haven.

There is one other sometimes-disturbing viewpoint that also needs mentioning. Since World War II we have become accustomed to times of either boom or recession. However, compared to the Great Depression, the recessions have been fairly mild.

There are those, however, who say that another great depression is just around the corner. These doomsayers point to the bloated federal deficit. They note the enormous loans given to Third World countries, with no real hope of repayment. They mention the uncertain prices of all commodities.

This viewpoint believes that a great depression is coming and—as during the last depression—all commodities, including rare coins, will not be highly valued. This "sky is falling" philosophy argues for investing in unfinanced property and for holding currency, but against stocks, leveraged real estate, and rare coins. It is an interesting concept, but one that few have thus far embraced. After all, if no new great depression should appear, the person who acted as noted above would be far behind the one who had invested in rare coins and similar "expanding economy" items.

ALTERNATIVE INVESTMENTS

A lot depends on what's for sale in the marketplace. If we walk into a grocery store's produce department and see that there are oranges and apples for sale, but right now strawberries are in season, chances are we'll opt for the strawberries. On the other hand, if we walk in and it's winter and there are just apples and oranges, we'll settle for one of those.

Investments work much the same way. Rare coins are always available. However, sometimes other investments are "in season." For example, during the late 1970s real estate was in vogue. People opted for it as a first choice. In the mid-1980s stocks have been popular.

As a consequence, rare coins have often felt the effect of being a stepchild to more popular investments. They have not been the "in" investment, hence they have not done so well.

Of course, there have been times—for example, during the high-interest, high-inflation 1980s—when rare coins did very well. *They* were the "in" investment, then.

A lot depends on investor whim and what's popular at the time.

PUBLIC PERCEPTION
OF RARE COINS

This has become an extremely important factor of late. It wasn't too many years ago when investors saw rare coins as strictly a hobby. It was fit for old men and young boys who had time on their hands. They collected Lincoln pennies (technically we currently do not have a penny—it's a "cent") and stored them in stuffy collections.

This perception held sway right up until about 1980, when the public in general and investors in particular were made aware by the media of the enormous surge in rare coin prices that was taking place. Since that time a new perception has appeared.

Today, due in no small part to the reports from financial

institutions of long-term profits in rare coins, many no longer view coins as a hobby but as a viable investment medium comparable at least to commodities or options if not to real estate and stocks. In fact, today many financial planners and advisors suggest that investors keep at least 5 to 10 percent of their portfolio in rare coins. (Prior to 1980 this would have been unthinkable.)

Thus, in the public's mind, rare coin investments have come of age. For now at least, this is a credible investment. And this credibility, in large measure, is what has led to the surge of investor interest in top-quality coins. A large part of the recent price rise of top-quality rare coins, in fact, can very possibly be linked to investors coming into the market and aiming for those coins *regardless of what other factors are at work.*

In other words, these investors don't know or don't care about the influence of inflation, interest rates, the economy, or alternative investments. All they know is that they should be in rare coins with at least part of their portfolio, and that's what they are up to. Thus, the perception of these people about the rare coin field may in large part be what's pushing the market up as of this writing.

In the future this could change. As of this writing, it is not possible, for example, to place rare coins in IRA or Keogh accounts. (It was at one time, but the rules were changed.) Should the law be eased allowing rare coin investments in these areas, we can almost be sure of a new surge of interest in the field.

THE BOTTOM LINE

Thus, from what has been said, I hope that you now see that investing in rare coins is something that can be immensely profitable, but which is by no means "guaranteed." It still takes perspicacity. You must be able to read both the fundamental factors and the technical charts. But if you do your homework and if your timing is right, your fortune could be just a few coins away.

Chapter

11

COIN
RESOURCES

I f you have read this book through, then you're probably asking yourself, Where do I go from here?

Obviously one way is to immediately begin investing and collecting coins. However, a well-known and well-cherished old adage in this field is, "buy the book before you buy the coin." The meaning, of course, is that knowledge is the true power.

Thus, as you expand your coin horizons, you will want to keep abreast of what's happening in the field as well as learn more about your special interests. To help you, this chapter is offered as a source for information. In it are listed all the major coin periodicals as well as a number of coin books that should prove helpful.

COIN PERIODICALS

COINage Magazine
2660 E. Main St.
Ventura, CA 93003

This is the largest-selling coin and precious-metals publication in the world. Published monthly in full color, it offers feature articles on both the hobby and investing. It presents the top authors in their field writing on their specialties. It is typically filled with advertising and is a good source of mail-order dealers.

Coin Dealer Newsletter (Gray Sheet)
PO Box 11099
Torrance, CA 90510

This is the weekly pricing guide that dealers and investors frequently use. It contains little to no editorial material. Instead it is usually about eight pages of bid-ask quotes on U.S. coins. There is some paid advertising.

Coin World
PO Box 150
Sidney, OH 45367

This is the largest-selling rare coin newspaper. Published weekly, it frequently runs to over 100 pages. Editorial content includes news stories on shows, recent finds, and items of interest to investors and collectors. It's also chock full of advertising and a good source for mail-order ads.

Krause Publications
700 E. State Street
Iola, WI 54990

This publisher offers three separate publications, *Numismatic News* (a weekly), *Coins Magazine,* and *Coin Prices.* The articles are frequently of strong interest to collectors. News items as well as prices *(Coin Prices)* are carried.

The Numismatist (The ANA Bulletin)
American Numismatic Association
PO Box 2366
Colorado Springs, CO 80901

This is the official bulletin of the ANA. It carries editorial material but usually features items of interest to members.

BOOKS

Hundreds of books have been written on various numismatic subjects. The few listed here are just a sampling:

Catalogue and Encyclopedia of *U.S. Coins*
by Don Taxay
Scott Publishing Co.
530 Fifth Avenue
New York, NY 10036

Coin Collectors Survival Manual
by Scott Travers
ARCO Publishing, Inc.
215 Park Avenue South
New York, NY 10003

A Guide Book of U.S. Coins (Red Book)
by R. S. Yeoman
(published annually)
Western Publishing Co.
Racine, WI 53404

Guide to the Grading of U.S. Coins (Brown Book)
by Martin R. Brown and John W. Dunn
General Distributors, Inc.
PO Box 234
Denison, TX 75020

Handbook of U.S. Coins (Blue Book)
by R. S. Yeoman
(published annually)
Western Publishing Co.
Racine, WI 53404

Modern World Coins
by R. S. Yeoman
(A series on world coins)
Western Publishing Co.
Racine, WI 53404

Morgan and Peace Dollars
by Wayne Miller
Adam Smith Publishing
4425 W. Napoleon Avenue
Metaire, LA 70001

Official ANA Grading Standards for U.S. Coins
American Numismatic Association
Western Publishing Co.
Racine, WI 53404

Penny Whimsy
by William H. Sheldon, M.D.
Harper & Row
49 E. 33rd Street
New York, NY 10016

Roman Coins
by David R. Sear
Seaby Publications, Ltd.
Audley House
11 Margaret Street
London W1N 8AT England

Standard Catalog of World Coins
by Chester L. Krause and Clifford Mishler
(updated annually)
Krause Publications
700 E. State Street
Iola, WI 54990

World of Coins and Coin Collecting
by David L. Ganz
Charles Scribner's Sons
115 Fifth Avenue
New York, NY 10003

Index

About the Author

Robert Irwin Wolenik is a
regular contributor to
COINage magazine, a leading
journal for coin collectors
and investors. Under the
pen name of Robert Irwin,
he has written more than
fifteen books on investment.
His most recent titles for
Franklin Watts have been
*Wealth Builders and
Profits from Penny Stocks.*

CONCEPTUAL STATISTICS FOR BEGINNERS

SECOND EDITION

Isadore Newman

Carole Newman

with PC wIZard by Wm. C. Croom, Ph. D.

UNIVERSITY
PRESS OF
AMERICA

Lanham • New York • London

University Press of America,® Inc.
4720 Boston Way
Lanham, Maryland 20706

3 Henrietta Street
London WC2E 8LU England

Library of Congress Cataloging-in-Publication Data
Newman, Isadore.
Conceptual statistics for beginners / Isadore Newman, Carole
Newman ; with PC wIZard by Wm. C. Croom. — 2nd ed.
p.   cm.
Includes index.
1. Statistics.   I. Newman, Carole.   II. Title.
QA276.12.N47   1993   001.4—dc20   93–39235 CIP

ISBN 0–8191–9420–4 (pbk. : alk. paper)

 The paper used in this publication meets the minimum requirements of
American National Standard for Information Sciences—Permanence
of Paper for Printed Library Materials, ANSI Z39.48–1984.

Table of Contents

Introduction

Most students, when faced with taking a statistics course, become immediately apprehensive. They are aware that they will be simultaneously confronted with unfamiliar terms, concepts, and computations, which they fear will be somewhat overwhelming. Even the most basic statistical textbooks tend to confuse the student.

The purpose of this book is to present the basic concepts and the terminology needed fo understand these concepts while keeping computation at a bare minimum. The emphasis has been almost entirely on developing an understanding of these concepts so that the student can interpret basic statistics and be better able to critically read the research being done in his or her area of interest.

In some instance, technicalities have been sacrificed for the purpose of conceptual clarity. This was done intentionally, since the authors believe the most appropriate way of learning statistics is first to build an understanding of the underlying principles. It is believed this procedure will provide the student with a firm foundation that will later facilitate the learning of computation and more sophisticated statistics.

Whenever possible, everyday language has been used instead of technical jargon. This is in keeping with research derived from Piaget's theory which indicates that the introduction of new material is most efficiently learned when that material is presented using a language most familiar to the student. Therefore, statistical and mathematical symbolism has been kept to a minimum.

All students who are statistically unsophisticated should benefit from reading this monograph. Chapters I, II and the beginning of Chapter III, which deals with the meaning of statistical significance, should be read and understood by all. The remainder of Chapter III, and Chapters IV and V introduce and define terms and concepts that are slightly more sophisticated. They will be most beneficial for the student who desires to learn more statistics; also, they will help all students conceptualize the relationship between certain statistical procedures and principles.

Chapter VI is a brief and conceptual introduction to research design and internal and external validity, based on a Campbell and Stanley tradition. It presents a conceptual model on which research designs can be placed on a continuum based on their internal validity. It is a crucial chapter for everyone who is interested in a basic understanding of research.

Chapter VII is a continuation of concepts presented in Chapter VI and extends them in the Campbell and Stanley tradition. It introduces quasi-experimental designs as well as time-series designs.

Chapter VIII is a paper entitled Type VI Error which was presented at the World Population Society. It deals with the conceptual problems in which many researchers find themselves entangled. Many sections of this paper are at a more sophisticated level than the rest of the text; however, the first seven pages can be read, understood, and useful to the beginning student.

The final chapter, Chapter IX, is a manual which explains the use of a PC program called Wizard, written by Dr. William Croom. This program is menu driven and contains the raw data mentioned in this text, so that one can easily run the problems and check answers. The program includes means, standard deviations, frequencies, Chi Square, t-test, and F-tests. It allows us to place the focus of this book on the conceptualization and interpretation, as intended, rather than on computation.

Objectives for Chapter I

After completing Chapter I, you should be able to:

1. define the terms descriptive and inferential statistics.

2. define the three measures of central tendency and state when it is most appropriate to use each one.

3. calculate a mean, median and mode.

4. identify the characteristics of a normal distribution.

5. define a skewed distribution.

6. identify the relative positions of the mean, median and mode on both a positively and negatively skewed distribution.

7. define variability.

8. define range, quartile deviation and standard deviation and state when it is most appropriate to use each one.

9. calculate standard deviation.

10. identify and state the characteristics of the normal curve.

11. define Z scores, T scores and stanines and explain how to interpret each one.

12. calculate a Z score.

13. define and interpret percentile, percentile rank, age equivalence and grade equivalence and state the advantages and disadvantages of each one.

Chapter I

Introduction to Statistics

This chapter is written for the primary purpose of introducing statistical terminology and concepts. An understanding of the material is basic to the efficient use of standardized test information, test construction, and the interpretation of many research articles.

Statistical procedures can be divided into two types: descriptive and inferential. When someone has test information on a large number of students, it becomes necessary to find an accurate manner to compile this data for the sake of efficiency and understanding. The statistical procedures developed for this purpose are called descriptive. Descriptive statistics are only used for describing the population on which one has data. They are not to infer to or describe groups or students on which information has not been collected. Almost all the statistical techniques presented in this chapter will be descriptive.

Inferential statistics, on the other hand, collects data on small samples from a group in which one is interested. The sample information, once collected and analyzed, is then used to infer to the entire population from which the sample came. In other words, one makes predictions about the entire population based on the information gathered about the sample. The statistical techniques that allow one to predict what a population will do on the basis of information gathered about a sample are called either sampling or inferential statistics.

Measures of Central Tendency: Average

To describe a population, statisticians usually consider the average score for the groups they are looking at (called the subjects). This "average" score is called the central tendency.

There are three basic measures of central tendency: the mean ($\overline{X}$), median (mdn) and mode. Each of these measures produces one score that describes or characterizes the performance of the whole group or population. By using the same measure of central tendency to report the average performance of two or more groups, one can more easily compare the average relative performance of these groups.

Mean ($\overline{X}$)

The most often used of the three measures of central tendency is the mean. Many people frequently use the terms mean and average interchangeably thinking that the mean is the only type of average one can calculate. While this is the most popular average used, it is not the only one.

The formula for calculating the mean is:

$$\overline{X} = \frac{\sum x}{N}$$

Where: $\overline{X}$ = mean

$\sum x$ = the sum of scores arrived at by adding all the scores together

N = the number of subjects or scores being added

For example, if one was interested in calculating the average mean performance of a group of five students on a particular test, one would proceed as follows:

Students	Scores
Sidney	95
David	80
Matthew	75
Carole	90
Isadore	<u>65</u>
Total	405

In this case, 405 is the sum of all of the scores ($\Sigma x = 405$). There were five scores added to arrive at the total (N = 5).

$$(\overline{X}) = \frac{\Sigma x}{N} = \frac{405}{5} = 81$$

Therefore, one now has a single score that represents the average performance of the group.

Median (mdn)

The median is simply defined as the middle point in a range of scores that have been put in order from lowest to highest or highest to lowest (rank ordered). This is used somewhat less than the mean. The median is calculated in such a way that it always lies at the center of a set of scores. This is not necessarily true for a mean.

For example, we can use the same scores in the previous illustration but we must first rank order them. The scores would then be listed as: 95, 90, 80, 75, 65. The score of 80 is the median since an equal number of the scores fall above and below it.

If a distribution has more than one person with the same score, it might be listed in the following manner: 60, 65, 70, 70, 71, 80, 80, 90. The score of 70.5 has four scores on either side of it; therefore, by definition it is the median. It is a score which no one actually received; however, 70.5 is the theoretical midpoint in the distribution. Therefore it is the median.

It becomes slightly more difficult to calculate the median when there are an even number of scores, as in the previous illustration, because the median will fall between the middle two scores. The following example also contains an even number of scores and a method for estimating the median.

Example: 60, 65, 70, 71, 75, 80, 81, 87

The two scores that fall at the middle of this distribution are 71 and 75. The median will fall between these scores; mdn = 73. The median score is 73 even though no one actually received this score. It was arrived at by locating the two middle scores (71, 75), adding them together (71 + 75 = 146) and then dividing by two (146/2 = 73). Seventy-three would then be a point in the distribution where 50% of the scores fall above it and 50% of the scores fall below it.

Mode

The least frequently used estimate of central tendency is the mode. It is the least stable which means it is likely to change very easily and drastically from sample to sample. It is also likely to be the poorest of the three measures of central tendency for representing the average group performance.

The mode is defined as the most frequently occurring score in a distribution of scores. For example, in the following distribution: 30, 60, 60, 60, 70, 70, 80, 80, 90, the mode is 60 because it is the most frequently occurring score in the distribution.

If we had a distribution in which two sets of scores occurred with equal frequency, each would be a mode. The distribution would be called bimodal.

Example: 30, 60, 60, 80, 90, 90

60 and 90 would both be modes of this distribution. If a distribution occurred in which three scores appeared with equal frequency, it would be a trimodal distribution, etc.

Appropriate Use of the Measures of Central Tendency

There are certain situations in which all three measures of central tendency will produce the same estimate, and there are other situations where the estimates will be drastically different. In these latter situations, it is necessary to determine which estimate is the most representative of the group performance. Most frequently, the shape of the distribution of scores determines the most appropriate measure to use.

Normal Distribution of Data

We assume data is normally distributed when the most frequently occurring scores are grouped in the middle of the distribution; and as scores move away from the middle in both directions (higher or lower than the average), they steadily decrease in frequency to an equal degree. Normally distributed data will always be in a bell-shaped distribution. Figure 1 is an example of a bell-shaped distribution.

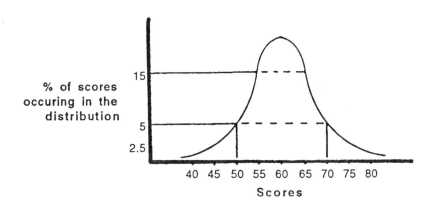

Figure 1

In this Figure, there were approximately an equal number of scores at 55 and 65 and, also, an equal but fewer number of scores at 50 and 70.

Very rarely does one's data or scores fall exactly in a normal or bell-shaped distribution. However, if the distribution of scores does not radically differ from this type of distribution, we tend to assume that the scores actually are normal. If the scores are normally distributed, then the mean, median, and mode will fall exactly at the same point. This is one of the characteristics of the normal curve, and it is illustrated in Figure 2.

As we can see by looking at Figure 2, the mode is the point in the distribution which occurs most frequently. The median is the point in the distribution where 50% of the scores fall above it and 50% fall below it. The mean is arrived at by adding all scores in a distribution and then dividing by the number of scores. In a normal distribution, the mean will be the score that is in the center of all scores. This is not true when the distribution is not normal.

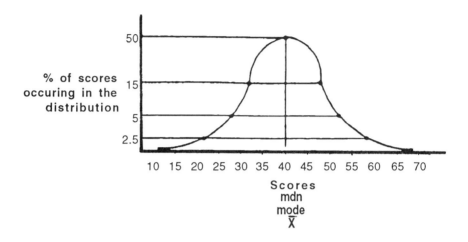

Figure 2

  To conceptually understand the function of the mean, one may think of a yardstick as being the base of our normal curve with each inch of the stick representing a score. Every time a score is received, we would place one poker chip at that point on the yardstick. For example, if three people received a score represented by the two-inch mark, then three poker chips would be placed on that mark on the yardstick. If this was done for every single score obtained and the scores were normally distributed across all 36 inches, then most of the chips would be piled on the 18-inch mark and numbers on both sides of the 18-inch mark would receive equal but increasingly less chips as we moved away from the score represented by the 18 inches.

  If we then took an ice pick and tried to balance the yardstick, the point at which the yardstick would be perfectly balanced would be the mean. This would be true for normally and not normally distributed data, but for a normal distribution this balance point will be exactly in the center of all of the scores in that distribution.

When the scores are exactly normally distributed (which is very rare if ever) the mean, median and mode will produce the same estimate of central tendency. However, the mean is the most stable estimate and will tend to fluctuate less. It is also a statistic which is the basis of the calculations of many other statistics. For these reasons, the mean is used more frequently than the other two measures of central tendency, and it is sometimes used inappropriately as will be discussed in the next section.

Skewed Distribution

Any distribution in which most of the scores are closer to one end than the other is called skewed. In other words, unlike a normal or symmetrical distribution, a skewed distribution will have most of its scores on one side and, therefore, would not be symmetrical.

Skewed distributions are referred to as being either positively or negatively skewed. In a positively skewed distribution, most of the scores will be on the lower end of the distribution (more low scores than high scores), and the long tail will be pointing toward the higher end of the distribution. An easy way to identify if a distribution is positive or negative is to put an arrowhead on the tail. If the arrow is pointing to the low end (left), the distribution is negatively skewed. See Figures 3 and 4 which also demonstrate the relationship between the mean, median, and mode on skewed distributions.

An examination of Figures 3 and 4 illustrates that the mean in a skewed distribution is always pulled toward the tail. In a positively skewed distribution, the mean will always be higher than the median or mode; and in a negatively skewed distribution, the mean will be lower than the median or mode. One can see that the mean is not at the center of the distribution, but it is affected by extreme scores while the median is not affected by extreme scores. It is the point in the distribution where 50% of the scores fall on either side of it no matter if the distribution is normal or skewed. The mode is the most frequently occurring score in the normal or skewed distribution.

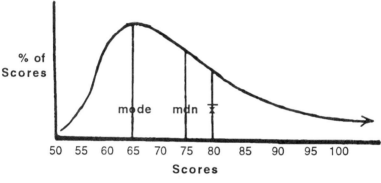

Positively Skewed Distribution

Figure 3

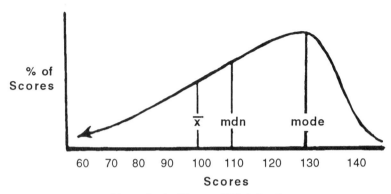

Negatively Skewed Distribution

Figure 4

When scores are skewed, the most stable and representative measure of central tendency would be the median.   For example, suppose ten students won the following sums of money:

$50.00
0.75
0.75
0.50
0.45   ← mdn 50% of the scores fall
0.35   on either side of this point

0.35
0.35
0.25
0.25
_____

$54.00

If we were interested in determining the average amount   of money that the students won, this number should be representative of most of the students. If we used the mean, we might be led to believe that most of the students won $5.40, which is obviously not representative

of actual winnings.   The mean is affected by extreme
scores and has been pulled toward the extreme end. The
median, on the other hand, is not affected by extreme
scores. It is the point in the distribution where 50% of the
scores fall above and 50% fall below. The median for the
above distribution is $.40, which is much more repre-
sentative of most students' winnings.

    If you were asked to calculate the average income in
the United States, and if a mean was used, you would
determine that the average income would be around
$60,000. This is because the distribution is positively
skewed and the mean is affected by and pulled toward the
extreme. See Figure 5 for an approximation of this distribution.

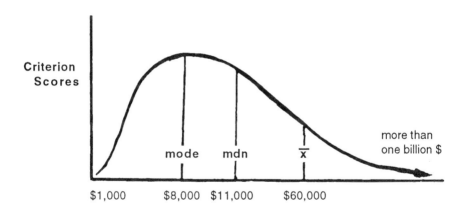

Figure 5

    The inappropriate use of statistics, as the mean is in
this case, has led some people to make the charge that
"statistics lie." This is an inaccurate statement since the
problem generally lies in employing an inappropriate
statistic. The mean should be used only if the data is
approximately normally distributed. Use under any other
conditions produces a distorted representation. The

median can be used for both normal and skewed distributions, but it is only preferable when the data is skewed. The mode is the least accurate and is generally not used. The only possible use it may have in the educational setting is for a quick and rough estimate.

Variability

Variability is defined as the degree the scores differ (vary) around the measure of central tendency. The more representative the measure of central tendency is for all scores, the less the variability. The less representative the central tendency measure, the more the variability.

There are three general estimates of variability: range, quartile deviation, and standard deviation. Of the three, standard deviation is by far the most important and will receive the greatest attention in our discussion.

Range

Range is the simplest and least accurate measure of variability. It is simply defined as the highest score in the distribution minus the lowest score. In some texts, it is defined as the highest score minus the lowest score plus one. (Hi-Lo, or Hi-Lo +1). If all the scores in the distribution are very similar, then subtracting the lowest score from the highest will produce a very small difference. This would indicate that there is little variability. At the very best, range is a quick and inaccurate estimate of the variability among scores in a distribution.

Quartile Deviation

The quartile deviation estimates variability by calculating the 25% (Q1) and the 75% (Q3) points in a distribution of scores. Then by subtracting Q1 from Q3 and dividing the difference by two, Q = (Q3-Q1)/2, the midpoint is determined. Q1 is the point in the distribution of scores where 75% of the scores fall above and 25% fall below. Q3 is the point in the distribution where 25% of the scores are above and 75% are below. The median can be called Q2 since it is the point in the distribution where 50% of the scores fall above it and 50% are below it.

Quartile deviation should be used whenever it is appropriate to use the median. Fifty percent of all scores in the distribution will fall between the median plus and minus one quartile (mdn ±1Q).

Standard Deviation

The most frequently used estimate of variability is the standard deviation. Conceptually, it is the average amount each individual score differs from the mean of its group. One way to calculate the standard deviation is to subtract the mean ($\overline{X}$) from each score and square the differences to eliminate negative numbers. The sum of the squares is then divided by the number of people and the square root is taken of this quotient.

$$S = \frac{\Sigma x^2}{N}$$

Where: $\chi2$ = score - mean quantity squared $(X - \bar{X})^2 =$ deviation score squared

N   = number of people in the group*

$\Sigma\chi2$ = sum of all deviation scores squared

If we compare the formula for standard deviation to the formula for the mean ($\bar{X} = \Sigma X/N$), we can see that conceptually the standard deviation is the square root of the mean of squared difference that each score differs from the distribution mean, on the average.   The following is a simple example given to demonstrate the computation.

X	$(X - \bar{X}) = \chi$	χ^2
6	(6-4) = 2	4
5	(5-4) = 1	1
4	(4-4) = 0	0
3	(3-4) = -1	1
2	(2-4) = -2	4

$\Sigma\chi = 20$ $\Sigma X = 0$ $\Sigma\chi2 = 10$

$$\bar{X}=\frac{\Sigma X}{N} = \frac{20}{5} = 4 \qquad S=\sqrt{\frac{\Sigma\chi2}{N}} = \sqrt{\frac{10}{5}} = \sqrt{2} = 1.41$$

In this example, the mean is 4, and on the average, each score differs from the mean 1.41.   The mean and standard deviation are most useful when the scores are distributed normally.   Some of the characteristics of the normal curve are:

———————————

*N-1 rather than N is used in the denominator when dealing with samples to correct for sampling error.

1. It is bell shaped
2. The maximum height is at the mean
3. It is asymptotic to the X-axis (theoretically, the tails of the curve approach but never touch the X-axis)
4. Approximately 68% of all the cases will fall between the mean ± one standard deviation ($\bar{X}$ ± 1 S = 68.26%)
5. $\bar{X}$ ± 2S = 95.44% (approximately 95%)
6. $\bar{X}$ ± 3S = 99.98% (approximately 99%)

The following I.Q. scores are assumed to be normally distributed with a $\bar{X}$ = 100 and S = 15. In a similar manner, approximately 95% of all scores will fall between 70 and 130; 99% of the scores will fall between 55 and 145.

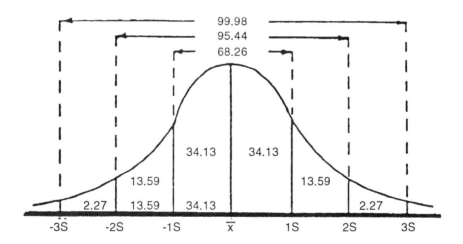

Figure 6

Using the mean and standard deviation, one can determine the percentage of people who will fall between a particular range of scores.

Standard Scores

Frequently, we want or find it necessary to compare scores that may have different means and/or different standard deviations. Comparison is facilitated by changing all scores involved to standard scores which will have a common mean and common standard deviation. The three most frequently used standard scores are Z scores, T scores, and stanines.

Z Scores

Z scores convert the raw scores into standard deviation units. For each distribution, Z always has a mean of "0" and a standard deviation of 1 ($\bar{X} = 0$, $S = 1$). The formula for Z scores is $Z = (X - \bar{X})/S = \chi/S$

where: X = any score in a set of scores
$\bar{X}$ = the mean of the set of scores
S = the standard deviation of the set of scores.

$$\chi = X - \bar{X}$$

The following example illustrates how raw scores can be converted to Z scores.

X	$(X - \bar{X}) = \chi$	Z
(1) 70	(70–56) = 14	1.55
(2) 60	(60–56) = 4	.44
(3) 50	(50–56) = −6	−.66
(4) 54	(54–56) = −2	−.22
(5) 46	(46–56) = −10	−1.11

Given that the $\bar{X}$ = 56 and the standard deviation S = 9.

$$Z = \frac{X-\bar{X}}{S}$$

$$Z_1 = \frac{70\text{-}56}{9} = 1.55$$

$$Z_2 = \frac{60\text{-}56}{9} = .44$$

$$Z_3 = \frac{50\text{-}56}{9} = -.66$$

$$Z_4 = \frac{54\text{-}56}{9} = -.22$$

$$Z_1 = \frac{46\text{-}56}{9} = -1.11$$

In the preceding example, the first person received a score of 70. This was converted to a Z = 1.55. This can be interpreted to mean that a score of 70 is 1.55 standard deviations above the group since Z scores are standard deviation units. Similarly, the fifth person's score of 46 was converted to a Z = -1.11. This individual was -1.11 standard deviation units below the mean for the group.

In the following example, the scores of two individuals on four different quizzes are presented. Frequently, the teacher averages all raw scores even though each quiz may have a different mean and standard deviation. These results can be very misleading. A more accurate and correct method of comparing would be to change all of the raw scores to Z scores and compare the Z scores since the Z scores more accurately show each person's relative position in the group; that is, where each score fits in relation to the mean of the group.

Table 1

Comparison of $\overline{X}$ and Z Scores

Test	$\overline{X}$	S	Matt XI	Carole X2	Matt Z	Carole Z
1	150	50	250	200	2.0	1.0
2	75	25	62.5	25	-.5	-2.0
3	50	1 0	80	50	3.0	0.0
4	300	100	300	500	0.0	2.0

$$\overline{X} = 173.1 \quad \overline{X} = 193.75 \quad \Sigma Z = 4.5 \quad \Sigma Z = 1.0$$
$$\overline{Z} = 1.125 \quad \overline{Z} = .25$$

By just calculating the mean of the scores, it would appear that Carole did better than Matt. However, this is incorrect since it does not take into consideration the different means and standard deviations. An inspection of Table 1 shows that, on most of the tests, Matt's scores are better than Carole's scores in relationship to the mean and standard deviation of each test. Matt's average Z score ($\overline{Z}$) on all four tests is 1.125, which means he is 1.125 standard deviation above the mean while Carole's $\overline{Z}$ = .25 which is .25 standard deviations above the average for all four tests. Changing raw scores to Z scores allows us to compare each person's score to the average performance of the group.

Looking at Table 1 again, we see that on Test 3, Carole has a Z = 0. This indicates that her score on that test was exactly at the mean of her group for that test. On Test 2, Matt's Z = -.5 indicates that he was 1/2 a standard deviation below the average of his group on Test 2.

We can also interpret Z scores in terms of the percentage of group members scoring above or below a particular Z score.

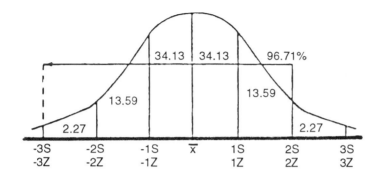

| -3S | -2S | -1S | x̄ | 1S | 2S | 3S |
| -3Z | -2Z | -1Z | | 1Z | 2Z | 3Z |

Figure 7

On Test 1, Matt's Z = 2. This means he scored two standard deviation units above the average on Test 1. By looking at Figure 7 one can determine the percentage of people in the group who scored lower than Matt on that particular test. In this case, approximately 97% of the people scored lower than Matt. We can determine this by adding up all the percentages under the curve that are less than 2 standard deviations or 2 Z scores.

There are many advantages for using Z scores over raw scores. In addition to the ones already discussed, they facilitate the weighting of tests. If we wanted to count one test twice as much as some other test, it is easy to change the raw scores to a Z score and multiply by two. By changing all raw scores to Z scores, it is generally more convenient for recording and scoring since they are always dealing with the same units which are generally within the range of +4 to -4.

One major limitation for using Z scores is that they are a function of the mean and standard deviation and are subject to the same restrictions. They are only appropriate when the data are normally distributed or approximately normally distributed.

T Scores

The T score is based on the same concept as the Z score. For any particular distribution of Z scores, the mean is 0 and the standard deviation is 1, ($Z = \overline{X} = 0$, $S = 1$) while for T scores, the mean is 50 with a standard deviation of 10, ($T = \overline{X} = 50$, $S = 10$).

The formula for T scores is $T = 50 + 10(Z)$. First, the Z score is found, multiplied by 10, and then 50 is added to it. This procedure eliminates the negative numbers in working with Z scores which decreases the likelihood of making clerical errors. This same idea is applied to the College Board Exams on which 500 is added to every score and Z is multiplied by 100.

T scores, like Zs, are subject to the same limitations. If the distribution of scores is not normal, it is difficult to interpret the Ts since they, like Zs, are based on the underlying assumption of normality. Standard scores such as Zs and T's will have the same distribution as the raw scores. If the raw scores are normally distributed, the standard scores will also be normally distributed.

Stanines

Stanines are fast becoming the most popular of all standard scores. The word stanine is actually a contraction standing for "standard nine point scale." Unlike the other standard scores, the conversion of raw scores to stanines does affect the shape of the distribution of scores. Stanines are assigned in such a way that the converted scores will always assume the shape of normal distribution.

When raw scores are converted to stanines, the raw scores are changed into one of nine values. The mean of a stanine distribution is always 5, and the standard deviation is 2 ($\overline{X} = 5$, $S = 2$). To make the conversion, the raw scores are rank ordered. These ordered scores are then divided into percentages, in which approximately the lowest 4% of the scores will all receive a stanine score of 1, the next lowest 7% receive a stanine score of 2; the next lowest 12% are stanine 3, the next 17% are stanine 4, the middle 20% are stanine 5. Stanines 6 - 9 consist of exactly the same percentages as stanines 1 - 4 and form the higher end of the normal curve. This same distribution can be approximated by first determining the median and calculating the same percentages working out from the middle. This may be preferable since it increases the probability of your distribution being symmetrical around the median.

In Table 2, the stanine groups are presented along with the theoretical percentages associated with each group and the approximate number of scores in each stanine for classes ranging in size from 25 - 35. These numbers are approximations. For example, if one took 17% of a group of 25 people to find the number of cases that should be in stanine 4, the number would have to be 4.25. We round off to get an even number of people and to maintain symmetry on both sides of a stanine score of five.

Table 2

Approximate Number of Scores in Each Stanine for Groups of Sizes 25 - 35

Approx. % of scores at each stanine Level	Lowest 4% Level	Lower 7% Level	Low 12% Level	Low Avg. 17% Level	Avg. 20% Level	High Avg. 17% Level	High 12% Level	Higher 7% Level	Highest 4% Level
STANINES	1	2	3	4	5	6	7	8	9
Size of group									
25	1	2	3	4	5	4	3	2	1
26	1	2	3	4	6	4	3	2	1
27	1	2	3	5	5	5	3	2	1
28	1	2	3	5	6	5	3	2	1
29	1	2	4	5	5	5	4	2	1
30	1	2	4	5	6	5	4	2	1
31	1	2	4	5	7	5	4	2	1
32	1	2	4	6	6	6	4	2	1
33	1	2	4	6	7	6	4	2	1
34	1	2	5	6	6	6	5	2	1
35	1	2	5	6	7	6	5	2	1

Stanine scores are also limited in their usefulness. The most appropriate use of stanines is when the trait being measured can be assumed to be normally distributed. If the trait is not normally distributed, the stanines will misrepresent the relative position of scores. Other limitations are that stanines tend to lose information since more than one raw score may have the same stanine. The more reliable the test, the more likely that this loss of information is meaningful. However, this is not a problem if one is interested in de-emphasizing small differences. Also, we must consider as a limitation the unfamiliarity of the general population with this form of score expression. This lack of understanding on the part of the public restricts the usefulness of stanines.

The major advantage of standard scores over raw scores is that they have specific means and standard deviations which are always whole numbers and are, therefore, easier to maniupulate. They facilitate our ability to differentially weigh any number of tests based on what we perceive to be their importance, and they make it much easier to compare tests in a meaningful and appropriate manner.

A major disadvantage is that they assume a normal distribution. If a normal distribution does not exist, it is very difficult to accurately interpret standard scores. There is also a general lack of familiarity on the part of the general public with the terms and use of standard scores. This limits their use since it becomes difficult to convey meaningful information. An additional disadvantage in the use of stanines is that while Z and T scores actually represent every score in the distribution, stanines group scores so that we lose information concerning differences among scores in the same stanine.

eighth grader would do in this content area. It does not say anything about how well her son would do on an eighth grade test in such subject areas as algebra or geometry.

Age Equivalence

Age equivalence is conceptually the same as grade equivalence. It is calculated in the same manner and has similar advantages and limitations. The major difference is that where grade equivalence is divided into ten intervals for each year, age equivalence is divided into twelve. A student with an age equivalent reading score of 9-11 is reading at the level of an average child who is nine years, eleven months old.

CHAPTER SUMMARY

In this chapter, we have presented the basic statistical concepts that are most commonly used. Understanding of these concepts is necessary for the intelligent use of tests and grading in the educational setting.

A differentiation was made between descriptive and inferential statistics. It is descriptive statistics that classroom teachers are generally required to deal with including measures of central tendency, measures of variability, standard scores, percentiles and grade equivalence.

The three measures of central tendency are the mean, median and mode. The mean is the most appropriate measure when the data at least approximates a normal distribution. For skewed distributions, the most representative measure of central tendency is the median. The mode is at best a quick but highly inaccurate and unstable estimate. In a perfectly normal distribution, these three measures all fall exactly at the same point.

The degree to which scores vary around the measure of central tendency is the variability. Three measures of variability are range, quartile deviation and standard deviation. Standard deviation is most often used and is appropriate whenever the mean is used. It, like the mean, forms the basis of many inferential statistical procedures.

Teachers frequently compare scores from different tests inappropriately. They generally do not consider differences in means and standard deviations. The best way to avoid this error is to convert raw scores to standard scores.

Standard scores have a common mean and a common standard deviation. One type of standard score is a Z score which has a mean of 0 and a standard deviation of 1. T scores have a mean of 50 and a standard deviation of 10. Standard scores allow for more accurate comparisons without changing the shape of the distribution.

Another type of standard score is the stanine, having a mean of 5 and a standard deviation of 2. Unlike the other standard scores mentioned, when changing raw scores to stanines, the shape of the distribution is changed to approximate a normal curve.

Percentiles and percentile ranks are very frequently used to report students' relative performances. Their frequent use is partially due to the apparent ease with which they can be understood. They describe a student's relative position compared to other students. However, a problem exists if the data is not evenly distributed. They tend to exaggerate differences in the middle of the distribution, and they minimize differences at the extremes.

One of the most misunderstood methods of reporting a child's performance is grade equivalence. The most appropriate use of grade equivalence is in the elementary school. They are less appropriate in the high school where there is less continuity of subject matter.

The major confusion in reporting grade equivalence is thinking that a fifth grader who has a grade equivalence of 8.0 is capable of doing eighth grade work. In actuality all it means is that the child is performing that particular task as well as an average eighth grader would perform on the same task.

Before a teacher can successfully communicate with a parent, he or she must have a clear understanding of the concepts presented here. The teacher must be able to clearly interpret test results and understand the limitations inherent in each method of reporting these results. Only then can the information be effectively used to help the student and to keep parents informed.

OBJECTIVES FOR CHAPTER II

After completing Chapter II, you should be able to:

1. define correlation.

2. define and interpret correlation coefficient (r).

3. identify the characteristics of r.

4. plot a scattergram for data presented.

5. estimate r for a set of given scattergrams.

6. define r^2

7. define rho.

8. tell when it would be appropriate to use r, rho or eta.

9. define reliability.

10. define three methods for estimating reliability.

11. list aspects that affect reliability.

12. define validity.

13. list and define six types of validity and state the strengths and weaknesses of each.

Chapter II

Correlation, Reliability and Validity

Correlation

Correlation is a measure of the degree of relationship between two or more variables. Variables in this case are defined as: anything one is interested in measuring, including such things as test grades, grade point averages, sex, height, etc. If we are interested in determining the relationship between sex and IQ scores, sex would be one variable and IQ scores the other. The correlation between these variables would indicate if a relationship exists and the magnitude of that relationship. With this information, we could, perhaps determine if males or females have higher IQ scores, on the average.

Correlation Coefficient (r)

The correlation coefficient is the most commonly used measure of correlation. Also referred to as the Pearson Product Moment Correlation Coefficient or the Pearson r, it is an index that measures the degree of **linear** (straight line) relationship between two variables. The size of r can range from +1 through 0 to a -1.

A correlation of r = 0 means that there is no relationship between the two variables we are interested in measuring. For example, it is likely that r would be zero between the variables of hair color and shoe size. Another way of saying this is that knowing a person's hair color, does not allow for guessing that person's shoe size any better than by chance alone. Therefore r = 0.

If the correlation between two variables is +1 or -1, a perfect relationship exists between these two variables. In reality there are very few, if any, perfect relationships. The only one that comes to mind is the correlation between birth and death. If a person is born, he or she will eventually die; therefore you can predict perfectly without error that anyone born will die. That is, the correlation between birth and death is perfect.

One can predict equally well if the correlation is a +1 or a -1. A +.8 correlation is also as predictive as a correlation of -.8. The positive or negative sign only indicates the direction of the relationship and not the magnitude. The magnitude of the relationship is indicated by the number, regardless of the direction. The closer the number is to 1, the greater the magnitude. Thus, a correlation between two variables of $r = -.9$ would indicate a greater ability to predict than would $r = +.8$.

A positive sign or no sign in the correlation indicates that the two variables are related in such a way that if one increases the other also increases and if one decreases the other decreases. A negative sign indicates a negative relationship which means that as one variable increases the other decreases.

An example of a positive relationship would be the relationship between the amount of gasoline consumed and the number of miles driven. Another example of a positive relationship would be between a student's IQ score and his grade point average. This is not a perfect correlation, but it is positive. Generally, the higher one's IQ, the higher the grade point average (GPA) (see Figure 9).

Table 3

IQ Scores and Grade Point Averages

Student	IQ Score	GPA
1	130	92
2	70	55
3	80	60
4	80	50
5	130	80
6	120	90
7	120	80
8	110	80
9	110	77
10	120	82

Student	IQ Score	GPA
11	110	75
12	100	80
13	100	78
14	100	72
15	100	70
16	100	60
17	100	60
18	90	60
19	90	55
20	100	70

The scores would then be plotted for each student (see Fig. 11).

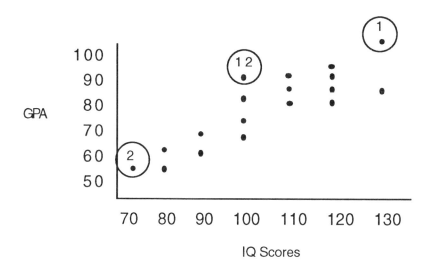

FIGURE 11

In Figure 11 three of the plotted points have been numbered for explanatory purposes. Student 1 had an IQ of 130 and a GPA of 92. Student 2 had an IQ of 70 and a GPA of 55. Student 12 had an IQ of 100 and a GPA of 80. All other students' IQ and GPA scores were plotted in the same manner. The result is a figure known as a scattergram.

Figure 11 indicates a positive relationship because the plotted points go from low in the left hand corner to a high in the right hand corner. If the plot went from a high in the left hand corner to a low in the right hand corner, this would indicate a negative relationship (see Figures 12 and 13).

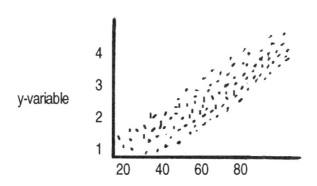

Figure 12.   Positive Relationship

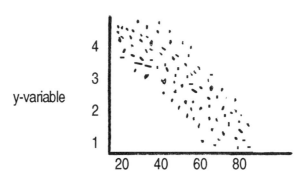

Figure 13.   Negative Relationship

When the correlation is perfect, all plotted points will form a straight line (-1 or +1; see Figure 14). For these perfect correlations one can predict exactly, without any error, by reading from the X axis to the line and then across to the Y axis.

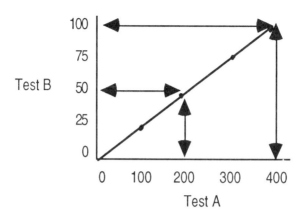

Figure 14.   Correlation Between Test A & Test B

For example, we can predict perfectly that if a person got 200 on test A he would get 50 on test B. We can predict just as well going from B to A as we can from A to B. So if we know a person received a score of 100 on test B, we can predict a score of 400 on test A.

A perfect correlation (r) means that every single point falls on a straight line; no point deviates from that line. As we stated earlier, very rarely if ever, does this occur.

Figure 15 illustrates a more common situation in which all points do not fall on the line. It is basically a scattergram with a straight line drawn to represent the average of the points. The straight line is calculated in such a way that each point will deviate from it to a minimum degree. The formula for calculating this line is the formula for the correlation coefficient.

Interpretation of r

Assume we have a situation as presented in Figure 17, and we know that the standard error of estimate (Sxy) is equal to 10. We can then say that in 68% of the cases the actual score the individual received will be within the limits of the predicted score ± 1Sxy. In the example on the next page, the predicted score for subject 1 is 55. The Sxy is 10. Therefore, we can assume that 68% of the time the actual score (in this case 58) will fall between 55 - 10 and 55 + 10 (45 to 65). We can also assume that 95% of the time the actual score will fall within the limits of the predicted score plus and minus 2Sxy. In the case of subject 1 we can assume 95% of the time his or her actual score will fall between the predicted score of 55 and ± 2Sxy, or between 35 and 75. This concept is the same as the concept discussed in Chapter I for the mean and standard deviation.

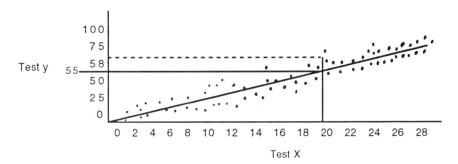

Figure 17

The smaller the standard deviation and the standard error of estimate, the more accurate are our predictions. In the case of r, the closer r is to 1, regardless of its sign, the smaller is the Sxy. Therefore, our prediction increases in accuracy as the correlation increases. (See Chapter 3, Table 7 for examples of how to use a table to determine if r is significant.)

r^2

The best way of interpreting r is in terms of the percentage of variance it accounts for. This can best be explained by an example. The correlation between the College Board Examination and success in college is r = .4. If we square r, that is, .4 x .4 = .16 (or 16%), this will tell us how much variance is being accounted for when we use the College Boards to predict success in college. In this case only 16% of the reasons someone does well or does poorly on the College Boards are the same as the reasons someone does well or does poorly in college. Therefore, 84% of the reasons (variability) for success in college are not being accounted for by the College Boards. Even if the correlation is highly significant, that is, it can predict better than chance (better than 50-50 chance), to interpret it we must know more than its level of significance. One must also know the amount of variance accounted for, which is calculated by squaring r.

Rho

Rho is really a special case of r, and it is generally an underestimate of r. Theoretically, it should be used in preference to r when one cannot make the assumption that the data is interval, but can assume it is ordinal (rank ordered). Rho is generally easier to calculate than r when the number of subject pairs is relatively small. If the N is larger than 20 or 25, it then becomes difficult to calculate by hand.

A caution when interpreting r or rho is that one must keep in mind that r and rho are measures of straight line relationships. If the relationship is curved, then r and rho would be an underestimate of the true relationship. For example, there is experimental evidence that a curved relationship exists between anxiety and performance. That is, people with low and high anxiety levels have poor performance while people with mild anxiety have higher performance (see Figure 18).

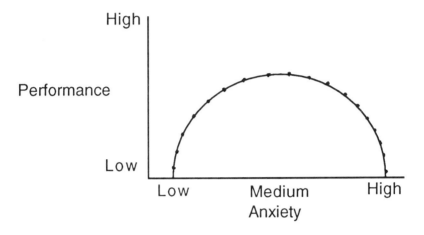

Figure 18. Curved Relationship

If one calculated an r or rho, the r and rho would be 0 indicating that there is no linear relationship. This does not mean that there is no relationship nor does it mean that we cannot predict perfectly. In the case presented in Figure 18, there is perfect prediction. Low and high anxiety scores for this individual produce low performance, and medium anxiety produces high performance. In this case and others where one expects a curved relationship, the correct correlational technique to estimate the relationship would be the correlation ratio, also called eta (η).*

———————————

*A more detailed explanation of eta (η) can be found in Nunnally, J. C. Psychometric Theory (2nd ed.). New York: McGraw-Hill Book Co., 1978, pp. 146-150; and Lomas, R. G., Statistical Concepts. New York: Longman, 1992, pp. 31-32.

Reliability

Correlation is very frequently used to estimate reliability. The reliability of a test is defined as the consistency of the measure. This means that the test, no matter what it is measuring, will produce the same value or one very close to it every time it is used.

Methods for Estimating Reliability

The consistency of a test is generally expressed in terms of r. If r is equal to 1, the test is considered to be perfectly reliable. If $r = 0$, the test is totally unreliable. If r is negative, the reliability of the test is difficult to determine because negative relationships should not occur when dealing with reliability. In general, the reliability coefficient should be .9 or higher before a test is considered reliable.

Test-Retest Reliability

One way of determining reliability is through the test-retest method. This necessitates giving the students the test and then retesting the same students with the same instrument at a later date. If they get the same or nearly the same score both testing times, then the test is considered to be reliable. However, if the scores differ widely the test is considered unreliable. The major shortcoming to this method of reliability measurement is that since the students are being retested on the same items, they may remember some of the items from the first testing. This recall may help them improve their performance during the retest which will decrease the test reliability. Another shortcoming is that the longer the time period between testing, the greater the likelihood that differential or new learning will occur. This learning would also affect test performance and therefore reduce reliability.

Equivalent Form Reliability

The equivalent forms method reduces the problem of recalling previous questions. This method is based on the assumption that one has two equivalent forms of a test that measure exactly the same thing. One popular method of constructing these equivalent forms is to construct twice as many items as are needed for one test and then randomly assign them to either form A or form B.

Each student receives both test A and B. One-half of the students are tested on test A first and then test B, and the other half are given test B first and then test A. The score on both forms for each subject are then correlated and produce an estimate of the reliability for the test.

Internal Consistency

Unlike the other two methods of estimating reliability, the internal consistency method does not require two testings. It also depends on correlation to estimate its reliability, but it correlates the test items within the same test. That is, if one gets a high estimate of reliability using internal consistency, this means that all of the items on the test are basically measuring the same underlying concept.

The two major methods of calculating reliability using internal consistency are the split-half method and the Kuder-Richardson formula 20 (KR 20). When using the split-half method, the items of the test are divided in half. Frequently, this is accomplished by splitting the odd and even numbered items, or almost any other split can be used, except splitting by grouping the items in the first half of the test against those in the second half of the test. The number of correct items are then calculated for each of the two groups of items, and these are correlated to arrive at a value of reliability for that test. The major problem with this technique is that it estimates reliability based on half of the number of items. Since reliability increases as the number of items increase, this method underestimates the reliability of the test. To correct this problem, the Spearman-Brown Correction Formula is generally applied.

KR 20 also provides an estimate of reliability based on a single administration of a test. Conceptually it averages the correlation between every item and the over-all test. The higher this average is, the more reliable the test. If the test is measuring more than one underlying concept, so that every few items are measuring unrelated concepts, then the KR 20 will tend to produce a low reliability coefficient even though the same test may produce a high reliability coefficient using test-retest, equivalent forms, or even possibly split-half. Even with this major limitation, primarily because of its convenience and statistical soundness, KR 20 is becoming the most widely used estimate of test reliability. It is being used to report the estimates of reliability of standardized tests.

Aspects that Affect Reliability

The reliability of a test can be altered by any one of the following factors:

1. Increasing the number of items on a test will increase the reliability.

2. Objective methods of scoring will increase test reliability.

3. Having a test measure one particular concept is likely to increase the reliability. However, the items should not be interdependent.

4. Constructing the items so that they are approximately equivalent in item difficulty will increase reliability.

5. Tests administered in a more standardized manner will have higher reliability.

One must remember that saying a test is reliable only means that it will consistently produce the same test results for a respondent. It does not mean that if we constructed an intelligence test with a high reliability coefficient that we would actually be measuring intelligence. For example, we could construct a test to measure intelligence and use height as the indicator of intelligence; that is, the taller the person the more intelligent. Our test would probably be highly reliable, especially for adults, since. their height is not likely to fluctuate between testings. Therefore, we could have a test that is highly reliable because we can consistently get the same values. In essence, reliability alone will not guarantee a good test, but without it the ability to interpret and use a test will be greatly limited because the inconsistent results will highly increase the error in prediction.

Validity

The most important characteristic of any test is its validity. The validity of a test is commonly defined as the degree to which a test measures what we want it to measure. For example, if we constructed a test to measure students' mathematical abilities, the validity of that test would be the extent to which that test was capable of measuring the students' actual mathematical abilities. One never really knows the true validity of a test; we only estimate. There are many methods for estimating validity. Often one method has more than one name. The five types of validity that will be discussed here are face, content, concurrent, predictive, and construct validity.

Face validity. The least accurate estimate of a test's validity is face validity. It is arrived at by the students' reaction to the test. If the test appears (to the students) to be measuring that which it purports to measure, it has face validity. One type of face validity may be **expert judge validity** which is a little more sophisticated. In this case, content experts instead of students judge the validity.

Content validity. Content validity has also been called definition validity and logical validity. Generally, the content validity of a test is estimated by demonstrating how representative the test items are of the content or subject matter the test purports to measure.

Concurrent validity. Concurrent validity is estimated by how well a test correlates with another test that has already had its validity estimated. For example, if we are interested in constructing an intelligence test we can estimate its validity by correlating it with well established intelligence tests such as the Stanford-Binet or the Wechsler Intelligence Scale for Children (WISC). If our test correlates highly with the other tests we may reasonably assume that it has concurrent validity.

Another way of estimating the concurrent validity of a test is by identifying people who have been assumed to be highly intelligent and people who have been assumed to be low in intelligence. We could then administer this test and see if the people who have been identified as highly intelligent score high, and those identified as low in intelligence score low. This kind of validity is called **known group validity**.

Predictive Validity. The major difference between concurrent and predictive validity is that in predictive validity one predicts into the future on the basis of the test results and then checks that prediction. If the prediction is correct, or if he can predict significantly better than by chance, the test has predictive validity. The higher the correlation between the test and the outcome, the better the predictive validity. Concurrent validity, on the other hand, may look at the same types of relationships but it is not predicting into the future; it is more present oriented. That is, the correlation between the test and its criterion occur at approximately the same time. Predictive validity and concurrent validity, when taken together, have been called **criterion validity**, **empirical validity**, and **statistical validity**. All three terms are basically describing the same characteristic.

Construct validity. Construct validity is a conglomeration of all other types of validity. It is most important when one is interested in interpreting a test score as a measure of some particular construct or attribute, such as intelligence, creativity, neurosis, etc.

When one is interested in construct validity, there is generally no one criterion that is acceptable as a measure of the construct. There is most likely a series of criteria that the test should relate to in differing degrees. How his test should relate to the various criteria is dictated by the theory of the construct. For example, someone may have a theory of intelligence that may include academic success, financial success, relatively good scores on the other intelligence tests, and popularity among co-workers. The theory may further predict that the relationship between the test and the above mentioned criteria may be the following:

1. The test should correlate highest with economic success and popularity.

2. There should be moderate correlation between the test and academic success.

3. The lowest correlation will be between the test and other intelligence tests.

The test could then be correlated with the above criteria. Construct validity exists to the degree that the results are in the predicted directions.

Obviously, the above methods of estimating validity vary in their degree of usefulness. Any estimate of validity is generally better than no estimate, but there are times when no estimate is better than poor estimates because you think you have validity when you do not. This may lead to a false feeling of security in your test, and you may make totally unjustifiable decisions based on your test.

When estimating the usefulness of a particular test, it is important to consider the type of estimate of validity reported. Many of the most widely used standardized reading tests generally report only content validity. Even tests that report under the heading of construct validity are frequently inappropriately titled. A close examination generally reveals that they have used no more than content or face validity. Since content and face validity are unrelated to the test's ability to predict, it would be inappropriate to consider a score achieved on these tests as an indicator of probable success. However, these tests are frequently used as indicators of success. This does not mean that the tests are unable to predict success, but since the validation procedures that were used did not estimate its predictive ability, one has no estimate of how accurately the tests can indeed predict.

Probably the most useful types of validity are predictive and concurrent. However, construct validity is the best of all but it is the most difficult to ascertain. If one has construct validity, one also has predictive, concurrent, and content validity.

It is important to keep in mind that we never really have a totally valid test. We can only estimate its validity; and because of this, there are always errors in prediction. If one can be sure that a test has a high estimate of validity, reliability estimates will be less important. One can have reliability without having validity; but if the test is valid, it is also reliable. It therefore follows that most of the time spent in test construction should be devoted to improving validity and not the reliability. This is contrary to most common practices.

Chapter Summary

To determine the degree of relationship between variables we use a technique called correlation. The most common correlational technique for linear correlations is the Pearson Product Moment Correlation (r). It ranges in magnitude from +1 to -1 with r = 0 indicating no relationship at all.

An easy method for determining the degree of relationship between variables is plotting a scattergram. The closer the points approximate a straight line, the greater the degree of correlation.

To interpret a correlation at least two things have to be considered: the standard error of estimate (Sxy) and the proportion of variance accounted for (r^2). The standard error of estimate is conceptually similar to and is interpreted in the same manner as a standard deviation (s). r^2 provides information on the proportion of the variance that can be accounted for by the correlation.

A major caution when using and interpreting r is that it is a linear technique. If the relationship is not linear, other techniques such as eta (η) should be used. Rho is appropriate to use when the N is small, the relationship is linear, and you cannot make the assumption that the data are at least interval. In other words, the data are ordinal (rank ordered) .

Correlation is very frequently used to measure a test's reliability. There are three methods for estimating reliability. These are test-retest, equivalent forms, and internal consistency. Each of these methods has its strengths and weaknesses. One method of measuring internal consistency that has become very popular is the Kuder-Richardson (KR 20).

It is important to keep in mind that reliability is necessary but not in itself sufficient for the meaningful interpretation of a test; we must also know the test's validity. Validity is the most important aspect of any test. It is the ability of a test to measure the trait or attribute for which it was designed. The procedures to estimate validity can generally be classified into five areas: face, content, concurrent, predictive, and construct validity.

Concurrent and predictive validity together have been called criterion validity. Generally, this is the most useful and practical estimate of validity. Construct validity is made up of all of the other types of validity. It is the best estimate of validity, but it is the most difficult to obtain.

In the construction or choosing of a test, one should determine the type of validity used. One then must determine if this is appropriate for the intended use of the test.

Objectives for Chapter III

After completing Chapter III, you should be able to:

1. define statistical significance.

2. distinguish among the .05, .01, and .001 levels of significance.

3. define the Null Hypothesis.

4. define and state the relationship between a Type I error and the Alpha (α) level.

5. define and state the relationship between a Type I and Type II error.

6. define statistical power.

7. define a one-tailed and two-tailed test and state when it is appropriate to use each.

8. identify tests of significance and tell when it is appropriate to use them.

9. define robust.

10. explain the meaning of the statistical statement, $p \leq \alpha$

11. look up a given t, χ^2, F and r in a table and determine if they are significant at the .05, .01, and .001 levels.

12. determine how large the t or r value has to be for a one or two-tailed test for $\alpha = .05$ and $.01$.

13. state the similarities and differences between t and F-tests.

Chapter III

The Meaning of Statistical Significance

Just about every day we can find someone anxious to tell us about an article or study that reported significant results. This often wrongly infers that a big difference exists. In reality the magnitude of the effect cannot be determined by just stating that it is statistically significant. One would also have to know the probability level (alpha, α), the size of the sample (N), the mean ($\bar{X}$) and standard deviations (S). Only then does one have the information to intelligently interpret the usefulness and meaning of the significant finding.

When something is statistically significant, it is unlikely to occur by chance. Chance is operationally defined by some alpha (α) level. In psychology and education, the alpha levels that are generally used are .05, .01, .001. The alpha level you pick is a **subjective** decision. It may be one of these three or any other.

If an alpha of .05 is decided upon; and if we then test some relationship and conclude that the relationship is significant at the .05 level, we are saying that the relationship we found is unlikely to·have occurred by chance alone. It does not tell us the magnitude; it merely states that there is a relationship other than zero relationship. The relationship is only likely to occur by chance 5 times out of 100. Therefore, we are conceptually willing to assume that the relationship really does exist and is not just a chance occurrence.

If an alpha level of .01 (α = .01) is decided upon and found significant, then the relationship of this magnitude is only likely to occur by chance 1 time in 100; and if a relationship is found significant at α = .001, then it will only occur 1 time in 1000 by chance alone.

If one converted these decimal values to fractions, it is more easily seen that (.05 = 5/100, .01 = 1/100, and .001 = 1/1000). If something is found to be significant at the alpha level .05, the conclusion that a difference exists in the population one hopes to infer to from the sample is likely to be wrong 5 cases out of 100 (5/100). At the .01 level one would be wrong 1 time in 100 (1/100), and at the .001 level one would be in error 1 time in 1000 (1/1000).

One should also be aware that by increasing the number of subjects one increases the probability of finding statistical significance, even though this does not necessarily change the magnitude of the relationship. For example, if five boys took an I.Q. test and had a mean score of 105 with a standard deviation of 15, and five girls had a mean score of 100 with a standard deviation of 15, these two groups would not be found to be statistically different at an alpha level of .05 or at any of the more stringent levels (.01, .001, etc.). However, given the same means and standard deviations (magnitude of effect), but increasing the subjects from 5 to 1000 for each group, would yield statistically significant results. The probability of this occurring by chance alone would be less than .05, and would therefore be statistically significant even though the magnitude of effect had not changed (In both cases, boys were 5 points higher than girls, on the average.). Therefore, increasing the N size inevitably increases the probability of finding statistical significance.

From what has been said, it is obvious that if someone says that something was found to be statistically significant, that information is not very meaningful unless we know the alpha level, the N size, and the effect size.

Type I Error

A Type I error is related to the likelihood (probability) of rejecting the statement that says there is no relationship or no significant difference between groups when that statement really is true. The statement of no difference is called the **Null Hypothesis**. In other words, a Type I error is the probability of rejecting the Null Hypothesis when the Null Hypothesis is true.

The probability of making a Type I error is determined by your alpha level. If you set your alpha level at .05, the probability of making a Type I error is 5 times in 100. Similarly, if an alpha of .01 is chosen, the probability of making a Type I error is 1 in 100.

Type II Error

A Type II error is not rejecting the Null Hypothesis when you should. In other words, there really is a relationship and/or a significant difference between groups, and you fail to reject the Null Hypothesis which says there is no difference.

The likelihood of making this error is inversely proportionate to the likelihood of making a Type I error (as the probability of making a Type I error increases, the probability of making a Type II error decreases; and as the probability of making a Type I error decreases, the probability of making a Type II error increases). If you hold your sample size constant and make your alpha level more stringent by going from $\alpha = .05$ to $\alpha = .01$, you decrease the probability of making a Type I error from 5 times in 100 to 1 time in 100; but you increase the probability of making a Type II error.

A Type II error is related to the power of your test. The **power** of a test is defined as the probability of detecting a difference when one exists. In a more powerful test, you are less likely to make a Type II error.[1]

One-Tailed and Two-Tailed Tests

Prior to computing a test of significance, one must decide whether to use a one-tailed or two-tailed test. A **two-tailed test** is actually a **non-directional** test. This means that the direction of the relationship(s) being tested is (are) not predicted prior to running the analysis.

For example, if we hypothesize that a significant difference exists between I.Q. scores of males and females, this hypothesis is non-directional because we did not state whose I.Q. scores would be higher; we just said they would be different.

However, when you have prior data indicating the direction of the relationship, it is more appropriate to use a one-tailed test. A **one-tailed test** is a **directional** test. An example of a one-tailed hypothesis would be . . . Male I.Q. scores will be significantly higher than female I.Q. scores. This is one-tailed because we are predicting who will be higher. If the prior data or theory indicated that female I.Q. scores should be significantly higher, and if our

---

[1]One can decrease the probability of making a Type I or II error by increasing the number of subjects used. This also increases the power of your test.

hypothesis stated that . . . Female I.Q. scores will be significantly higher than male I.Q. scores; this too would be directional because we are predicting who will do better on the I.Q. test.

A one-tailed test is more powerful than a two-tailed test. It is more likely to detect a difference or a relationship if one exists in the hypothesized direction. However, if a very strong difference occurs in the opposite direction, you must state your hypotheses have failed to be substantiated and that your results are **not** significant.

The same data **cannot** then be used to compute a two-tailed test of significance. The study should be replicated on a new sample and again you must decide whether to compute a two-tailed test or a one-tailed test in the same direction as before or in the opposite direction. If you are really not sure of the direction of the results, you are obligated to use a two-tailed test.

Tests of Significance

We have previously discussed levels of significance, and we have alluded to tests of significance. In this section, we hope to briefly introduce the most common tests of significance used and show some of the relationships between these tests.

As you may recall from an earlier presentation (pp. 19-24), Z scores were defined as the score, minus the mean, divided by the standard deviation ($Z=(X - \overline{X})/S$). If we found a person's I.Q. test score had a Z score of 3 ($Z = 3$), this means the I.Q. score was three standard deviation units above the mean of the group. The **probability** (p) that someone would score three standard deviation units above or below the mean by chance alone would be 1 time in 100 ($p = 1/100 = .01$). For something to be found statistically significant, the probability (p) has to be less than the subjectively decided upon alpha level. In the previous example, if we set our α level at .05, and we wanted to determine if this person's I.Q. score was significantly different from the average, we can say it was, because the probability of his score being that high or higher by chance alone was less than the stated α level. If the calculated probability (p) is less than or equal to the subjectively decided upon α, (p $\leq \alpha$) then the finding is said to be statistically significant. If the alpha level was set at .01 (p = .01), then the results would still be significant since the probability was equal to alpha. However, if we set our alpha level at α = .001 and p = .01, then this would not be significant since it is likely to occur by chance 1 time in 100 and we will not accept anything as significant that is likely to occur by chance more than 1 time in 1000. In this case, the probability is greater than the alpha level and is, therefore, not significant.

t-Tests

If one looks at the t-test formula, which is generally one sample mean ($\bar{X}_1$) minus another sample mean ($\bar{X}_2$) divided by the standard error of the difference between means, ($S_{D\bar{X}}$, which is conceptually a standard deviation) then t = ($\bar{X}_1$ - $\bar{X}_2$)/$S_{D\bar{X}}$ is very similar to the Z score, $Z = (X - \bar{X}_1)/S$.

There are tables of significance for t-tests. One looks up the t-value in the table to determine if it is significant. If the probability value associated with the calculated t-value is less than or equal to the alpha level (p $\leq \alpha$), then the t-test is considered significant at that α. Generally, t-tests are run to determine if <u>two groups</u> are significantly different. It cannot determine if more than two groups are significantly different. It also assumes that the data being analyzed is interval.

How to Use a t-table

The following is an example of how to use a t-table. Let's assume two treatments for teaching reading are being studied. There are 16 people in Treatment 1 and 16 people in Treatment 2 (N=32). The research hypothesis states that there will be a significant difference between the two groups, but it does not predict the direction; so we have a two-tailed test. The alpha level is .05 (α = .05) and the degrees of freedom (df) = N-2, which equals 32-2=30. If the calculated t of the t-test is as large or larger than the table value corresponding to the .05 level and 30 degrees of freedom, then the two groups are significantly different at the .05 level. According to Table 4, this value is 2.04. It is the value found at the place where df (30) and α = .05 for a two-tailed test intersect.

If we made a directional hypothesis using the same example and stated that Treatment 1 will do better than Treatment 2 (and we find that Treatment 1 did do better), we would check the table for the .05 level for a one-tailed test with the same df = 30. In this case, the t we calculated would have to be as large as or larger than the table value of 1.72 to be significant at the .05 level. If, on the other hand, Treatment 2 was larger, we then have to conclude that there is no significant difference. We must come to this conclusion no matter how great the difference is between the treatments, because the difference is in the opposite direction of that which was predicted.

TABLE 4

Level of Significance for a One-Tailed Test

df	.05		.01	.005	
	Level of Significance for a Two-Tailed Test				
	.10		.02	.01	.001
1	6.3	12.7	31.80	63.70	636.7
5	2.0	2.6	3.40	4.10	6.9
10	1.8	2.3	2.80	3.20	4.6
20	1.74	2.1	2.52	2.81	3.9
30	1.72	2.04	2.50	2.80	3.6
60	1.68	2.00	2.42	2.70	3.5
120	1.66	1.99	2.40	2.61	3.4
	1.64	1.97	2.30	2.6	3.3

Note: df = N-2 is used for a t-test when the two groups being tested are **not** correlated (independent) when N is the total number of subjects in one study. Also note the table values are approximations.

Chi Square

Chi square (χ^2) is defined as the sum of the expected scores (E) minus the observed scores (0), squared, divided by the expected score $\{\chi^2 = \Sigma[(E-O)^2/E]\}$. The expected score is conceptually similar to a mean.

Chi square (χ^2) is a test of significance usually used when one is interested in testing to see if the frequency of occurrence is significantly different between groups. It can be used when dealing with nominal data such as frequency counts.

Similar to t-tests, you look up the χ^2 in a table to see if the probability level associated with it is less than or equal to the selected alpha level ($p \leq \alpha$). If it is, the χ^2 is significant and one would be able to conclude that the differences in frequency of occurrences between groups is not likely to be due to chance at that specified alpha level.

How To Use A χ^2 Table

The following example demonstrates how to use a χ^2 (Chi^2) table. Let's suppose someone tossed a coin and came up with heads 40 out of 50 tosses. We want to determine if this is significantly different than what we would expect by chance when $\alpha = .05$. In this case, there is only one sample, one coin.

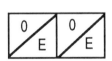

heads   tails

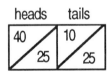

There are two cells, one heads and one tails. The top value is the observed toss of 40 heads and 10 tails. Below the diagonal is what we would expect by chance - 25 heads and 25 tails. In such a case, the degrees of freedom is equal to the number of cells minus one, which in this case is equal to 2-1=1. To determine if the calculated χ^2 is significant at the .05 level, one would go to Table 5 and look at the value at the point where .05 and 1 df intersect. If the calculated χ^2 is as large or larger than the table value of 3.9, then the χ^2 is found to be significant. This would mean that it is unlikely that a coin would come up 40 heads and 10 tails on 50 tosses. These results would occur no more than 5 times in 100 by chance alone, and one could assume the coin was probably biased.

This indicates that if a calculated χ^2 is greater or equal to the χ^2 value listed in the table, then the probability of obtaining a χ^2 this large would be less than or equal to the previously set alpha (not likely due to chance). Therefore, the χ^2 could be statistically significant, one could reject the null hypothesis (there is no significant difference), and accept the research hypothesis (there is a statistically significant difference). If the calculated χ^2 is less than the Table χ^2, then the opposite would be true.

χ^2 calculated $\geq \chi^2$ table value $p \leq \alpha$ statistically significant; reject Ho accept research hypothesis

χ^2 calculated $< \chi^2$ table value $p > \alpha$ not significant fail to reject H_O; reject research hypothesis

Table 5

χ^2 table

Level of Significance for a Two-Tailed Test

df	.05	.01	.001
1	3.9	6.7	10.9
2	6.0	9.2	13.9
4	9.5	13.3	18.5
10	18.4	23.2	29.6
20	31.4	37.6	45.4
30	43.8	50.9	59.7

Note: The df for a χ^2 in which there is only one sample is df = [(#C)-1] where #C is the number of cells.

The df for χ^2 in which there are more than one sample to compare: df = (C-1)(R-1) where C is the number of columns and R is the number of rows.

Also note that the table values are approximate and tend to be somewhat conservative.

In another case, let's assume we want to find if there is a significant relationship between political parties and income (the data are nominal). Since, in this case, we have more than one group to compare (political parties and income), the df = the number of columns minus one, times the number of rows minus one [df = (C-1)(R-1)]. We have three columns (C=3) and two rows (R=2) so df = (3-1)(2-1) = (2)(1) = 2.

Political Parties

		Democrat	Republican	Other
Income	High			
	Low			

We are interested in determining if there is a significant difference between political party affiliation and income at the .01 level. If the calculated χ^2 is as large or larger than the table value of 9.2 which is associated with 2 df and the .01 level, then there is a significant difference between political affiliation and income at the .01 level.

F-Tests

An F-test is the most frequently used test of significance. It is defined as the mean square between groups (MS_b) divided by the mean square within groups (MS_w) and is conceptually similar to differences in means between groups. The mean square within groups (MS_w) is conceptually the error in your data or how much variation you can expect by chance alone and is similar to the standard deviation. Therefore, $F = MS_b/MS_w$

The F-test can be used to determine if there is a significant difference between two or more groups or variables, simultaneously.

Like the others, an F is calculated and looked up in a table to determine if the probability associated with that F is less than or equal to the set α. Once again, if it falls within these bounds, then one can conclude that the groups are significantly different at that specified alpha level.

How To Use An F-Table

The following is an example of how to use the F-table. Since the F-test can test for differences between two or more groups simultaneously, the F-test requires two sets of degrees of freedom, one for the numerator and one for the denominator. The degrees of freedom-numerator (df_N) is equal to K-1, where K equals the number of groups. The degrees of freedom-denominator (df_D) is equal to N-K, where N equals the total number of subjects and K is the number of groups.

Let's assume you are interested in determining if there is a significant difference at the .05 level between ten methods for teaching reading (K=10). There are 11 subjects in each of the ten groups (N=110). The df_N = K-1 = 10-1 = 9, and df_D = N - K = 110-10 = 100. The table value associated with these two sets of df (9 and 100) is 1.90 (See Table 6). It is the value found at the place where df_N (9) and df_D (100) intersect. If the calculated F is as large or larger than 1.90, then there is a significant difference between the ten groups at α = .05. This doesn't tell you where the difference between the groups is, it just tells you that there is one somewhere. One may want to then run separate t-tests between the groups to locate the difference.

If the df listed in the table value does not exactly match what you have for your specific problem, you can interpolate (approximate).

Table 6

dfD	1	5	9	20	30	100	--
1	161	230	242	248	250	253	254
10	5.26	3.40	3.0	2.80	2.70	2.60	2.60
30	4.17	2.60	2.16	1.93	1.84	1.69	1.62
60	4.00	2.40	2.00	1.80	1.70	1.50	1.40
100	3.94	2.30	1.90	1.70	1.60	1.40	1.30
200	3.90	2.30	1.90	1.70	1.60	1.40	1.30
400	3.89	2.30	1.90	1.60	1.50	1.30	1.20
--	3.88	2.29	1.83	1.58	1.47	1.25	1.00

Note: The df for the numerator (dfN) is K-1 where K is the number of groups to be compared. The df for the denominator (dfD) is N-K where N is the total number of subjects in the study and K in the number of groups. Also note the table values are approximate for α = .05 only.

Similarities and Differences Between the F and t-test

1. Both tests give probability statements about statistical significance.

2. A t-test can only test the difference between two groups at one time.

3. Both tests require interval data as an underlying assumption.

4. t^2 is equal to F when you are testing the differences between two groups.

5. F-tests can test for interactions but t-tests cannot.

6. Both F-tests and t-tests are robust, which means that many of the underlying assumptions for both tests can be violated with very little effect on their accuracy.

All the tests of significance, Z, Chi square (χ^2), t, and F, are basically related.[3]

---

[3]Degrees of freedom (df) is a function of the number of independent replicates you have in your study which is similar to the number of subjects in the study.

For example:

$$\sqrt{F} = t \approx Z \approx \sqrt{2\chi^2} - \sqrt{2(df) - 1}$$

$$F = \frac{\chi_1^2/df_1}{\chi_2^2/df_2}$$

$t^2 = F$ (when testing the differences between only two groups)

As one can see from inspection of the formulae, Z is a function of χ^2, and F is a ratio of $2\chi^2$ with their respective df.

Basically, all these tests have the same or very similar underlying assumptions.[4]

One can also see by inspection of the formulae for calculating t and Z, they are very similar. However, t distributions vary with the df. When the df for the t-test is small, its distribution is skewed. As the df becomes larger

_____

[4]The t and F-tests are very robust. Edwards (1972) states that these tests are practically insensitive to violations of the assumptions of normality of distributions and heterogeneity of variance (unequal variance in your groups) as long as the number (n) of subjects in each group are equal (n1 = n2, etc.) and n $\geq$ 25.

than 30, the distribution approximates the normal distribution of the Z. When the t's df is over 400, the t-test and Z-test will produce, for all practical purposes, the same probability. Therefore, for a large df either Z or t can be used; but when the df is small, t should be used.

How To Use A Table To Determine If r Is Significant

Tables have also been developed to determine if r is significant for specific degrees of freedom. Table 7 is an example of this. The following is an example of how to use an r-table of significance.

Table 7

Level of Significance for r

One Tail
(predicting the direction of the relationship)

df	.05		.01	.005
	Two Tail (not predicting the directions of the relationship)			
	.10	.05	.02	.01
1	.98	.997	.99	.999
5	.67	.76	.84	.87
10	.50	.58	.66	.71
20	.36	.43	.50	.54
30	.30	.35	.41	.45
60	.22	.25	.30	.33
100	.17	.20	.23	.26

Note: The df for r is generally N-2 where N is equal to the number of pairs of subjects in the study. Also note the values in the table are approximate.

Let's assume 32 people took both an I.Q. test and a creativity test (N=32). We are interested in determining whether the correlation (either positive or negative) between the two tests was significant at the α = .01 level. Since it doesn't matter if the correlation is positive or negative, it is non-directional (two-tailed test). The df = N - 2 = 32 - 2 = 30. You would then enter the table at df = 30 and α = .01 for a two-tailed test to obtain a value of .45. If the calculated r is as large or larger than .45, it means there is a significant relationship between intelligence and creativity at the .01 level.

Now let's assume we use the same example but do a directional (one-tailed) test. We hypothesize that there is a positive relationship between I.Q. and creativity. This time, we enter the table at the same degrees of freedom, but at α = .01 for a one-tailed test, and obtain a value of .41. If the calculated r is as large or larger than the table value of .41, it means there is a significant positive relationship between the tests. If the relationship found is negative, we must state that it is not significant since it is not in the direction we hypothesized.

Chapter Summary

Chapter III has dealt with statistical significance. Merely stating that something is significant does not provide us with enough information to intelligently draw conclusions. We must also be given the probability level, sample size, mean, and standard deviation.

The probability level tells us the probability that the relationship is not likely to be due to chance. We also know that as the sample size increases, the likelihood of finding significance also increases even though the magnitude of the relationship (magnitude of the effect) has not changed. The magnitude of the effect or relationship is indicated by the mean and standard deviation.

Statistical significance is operationally defined by the alpha level one chooses. This is a subjective decision. However, in the fields of education and psychology one usually selects .05, .01, or .001. The alpha (α level) is the subjective probability statement of how often one is willing to accept something occurring by chance and still regard it as a non-chance occurrence.

The probability of making a Type I error is the same as the alpha level selected. It is the probability of saying a relationship exists when no relationship really exists. It is the probability of falsely rejecting the Null Hypothesis which states there is no relationship. A Type II error is failing to reject the Null Hypothesis when it should be rejected.

When testing for significance, one a priori decides on making a one- or two-tailed test. A one-tailed test is a directional test and should be used only when you have prior information indicating the direction of the results. It is a more powerful test when used appropriately. A two-tailed test is non-directional and should be used when no prior information exists.

The most commonly used tests of significance are the Z, t, χ^2, and F. They are all functionally related. The t and F-tests are very robust. Many of their underlying assumptions can be violated without affecting their results. The t-test is a special case of the more general F-test. Whatever you can do with a t can be done with an F-test, but the F-test is capable of doing more.

These tests of significance are used for calculating the probability of a relationship existing between variables. The values of these tests of significance are then generally looked up in tables to determine their probabilities. These probabilities are then compared to what one has previously decided to accept as a subjective alpha level. If the probabilities are equal to or less than ($p \leq \alpha$) the alpha decided upon, we state the relationship was found to be significant at that specified alpha level. In other words, the alpha level is our criterion for accepting something as being significant, and the probability (p) is calculated to see if it meets our criterion. If it does, we say it is significant; and if it does not, we say it is not significant.

Examples of how to read and use tables of significance were also presented. When using these tables, the calculated value must be as large or larger than the associated table value for a specified df and α level in order for the test to be significant.

Objectives for Chapter IV

After completing Chapter IV, you should be able to:

1. graph data presented in tabular form.

2. identify the area of interest on a graph.

3. define interaction.

4. define disordinal and ordinal interaction.

5. identify main effects and simple effects on a given set of data.

6. explain when it is appropriate to interpret main effects and simple effects.

7. explain when it is appropriate to graph data using a solid line and when to use a dotted line.

Chapter IV

Introduction to the Concept of Interaction

In reading through the literature one often encounters statements concerning interaction. Understanding this concept is frequently difficult, especially since it is usually introduced using a traditional statistical procedure as an explanation. The purpose of this chapter is to introduce the basic concept of interaction, conceptually and graphically, not mathematically. The explanation to be given should enable the reader to better interpret and understand the meaning of significant interaction.

Example of Plotting Interaction Data

Before one can have interaction, there must be at least four groups. The simplest example of this is a 2 x 2 table.

Table 8

		Treatment 1	Treatment 2
Sex of Teacher	M	30	20
	F	20	80

Assume the mean for Treatment 1, when there is a male teacher, is 30. The mean for Treatment 2, with a male teacher, is 20. The mean for a female teacher in Treatment 1 is 20, and for a female in Treatment 2 is 80. The means for each of the groups are reading achievement scores. For example, the mean on a reading achievement test for the students who were in Treatment 1, with a male teacher, was 30. The mean for students in Treatment 2, with a female teacher, was 80. These four means can be presented graphically as in Figure 19.

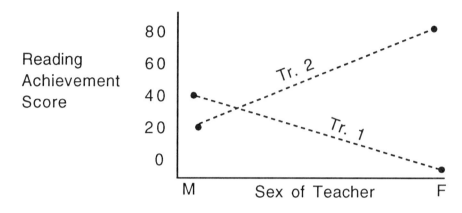

Figure 19

It is a good idea to plot them before attempting interpretation so you can see the relationship between the variables.

Definition of Interaction

The definition of interaction that we will deal with is: Interaction exists when there is a significant differential effect across the area of interest. In other words, the lines are significantly not parallel.

The area of interest when discussing interaction in graphic form is whatever is labeled on the X-axis (Y I___).
$$X$$

In the above example, the area of interest is the sex of the teacher.

What Can Be Interpreted When There Is Significant Interaction?

Let's assume a t-test was conducted between Treatments 1 and 2 (the two methods of conducting reading), and it was found to be significant at the .05 level. In the above example, the mean for Treatment 1 would be 25 or (30 + 20)/2, and the mean for Treatment 2 would be 50 or (20 + 80)/2. Since Treatment 2 has significantly higher reading achievement scores, some may want to suggest that Treatment 2 be used in preference to Treatment 1. This would be an inappropriate conclusion since looking at the graph clearly indicates that Treatment 2 is only better when there was a female teacher. However, Treatment 1 was better when the teacher was male.

In the above example, there are two major variables (factors) also called **main effects**. One is Treatment (1 and 2), and the other is Sex of Teacher (male and female). If there is significant interaction, one should not, and technically cannot interpret the main effects. This is the reason why it is inappropriate to interpret the main effects of the treatment in the previous example. One cannot logically or technically say that Treatment 1 is better than Treatment 2.

As indicated, interaction may be conceived of as lines being significantly different from parallel when they are graphically plotted. In the above example, the plotted lines crossed. However, lines can also be significantly non-parallel without crossing.

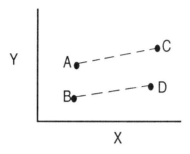

Figure 20A

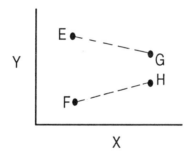

Figure 20B

We also stated previously that interaction is a differential effect across the area of interest and that the X-axis is the area of interest. In other words, on the two figures above, if there is a significant interaction, the difference between points A and B will be significantly different than the difference between C and D. Similarly, the difference between E and F will be significantly different than the difference between G and H. By definition, these lines are significantly non-parallel.

Two examples of parallel lines follow (Figures 21A and B).

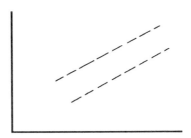

Figure 21A

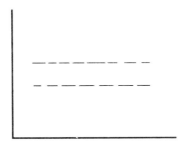

Figure 21B

In graphs that resemble these, it would be appropriate to interpret main effects since there is no interaction.

Ordinal and Disordinal Interaction

There are two types of interaction, ordinal and disordinal. When the lines plotted cross within the values on the graph, the interaction is **disordinal**.

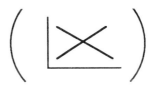

When the plotted lines do not cross within the values on the X-axis, this has been operationally defined as **ordinal interaction**.

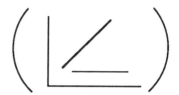

The first example presented in this chapter (Figure 19) was a case of disordinal interaction since the lines crossed, and Figures 20A and 20B were ordinal since the lines did not cross within the area of interest.

It was stated earlier that when there is interaction, one cannot interpret main effects. This is technically true. However, it may sometimes make logical sense to interpret main effects when there is ordinal interaction.

The more traditional statistical texts will state that only simple effects (looking at each group independently) must be interpreted when there is significant interaction. In our first example, there were four groups; therefore, to interpret the simple effects, one would look at each of these groups separately. The conclusions based on this interpretation would be that Treatment 2 is more effective when there are female teachers, and Treatment 1 may be more effective when there are male teachers (depending on whether or not the difference is significant).

Plotting Interaction for Three Treatments Across Sex

For another example, let's assume that there are three treatments and sex of the teacher.

Table 9

Treatment

		1	2	3
Sex of Teacher	M	65	75	90
	F	70	80	20

Let's also assume that the six groups have the means presented in the boxes on a reading achievement test. That is, the mean of Group 1, which is Treatment 1 with male teachers, is 65, and so forth for the other five groups. If one were to graph these means, they may appear similar to Figure 22.

Even though we have six groups in this case, we still only have two main effects, treatment and the sex of the teacher. As stated, if there is significant interaction, one cannot technically make statements about main effects but can only discuss simple effects (looking at each of the six groups separately).

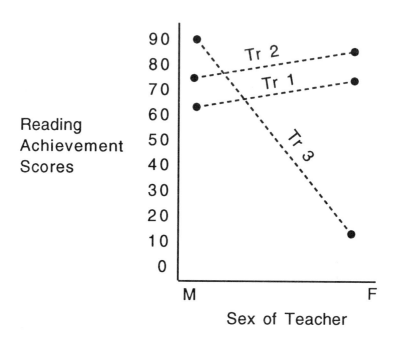

Figure 22

As one can see by looking at Figure 22, even though Treatments 1 and 2 appear to be parallel (therefore not interacting with each other) they both interact with Treatment 3, over the area of interest (the sex of teacher).

One possible interpretation of this data is that Treatment 3 may be the most desirable to use when the teacher is male, and it is potentially the worst treatment when there is a female teacher. Treatment 2, on the other hand, may be the most appropriate if both male and female teachers had to be used. These are examples of statements of simple effects since we cannot make a more general statement such as Treatment 1 is the best regardless of the teacher's sex, etc. In other words, in this example a decision as to which treatment is to be used must be based on the treatment and whether the teacher is male or female. These data are also an example of disordinal interaction since the lines cross within the area of interest.

Dotted and Solid Lines

Up to this point we have used dotted lines to connect points on the graphs. The accepted symbolic representation is to use a dotted line when connecting points over an area of interest that is made up of **dichotomous or categorical variables**. In other words, a dotted line is used when the area of interest has a variable that is not at least ordinal in value. A solid line is used to connect points when the area of interest consists of at least **ordinal** data (it can be ordinal, interval, or ratio). Examples of when a solid line should be used are when I.Q., time, income, age, years of experience, etc., are the variables on the X-axis area of interest).

If the data looked like the following, it should be graphically represented by using a solid line (see Table 10 and Figure 23).

Table 10

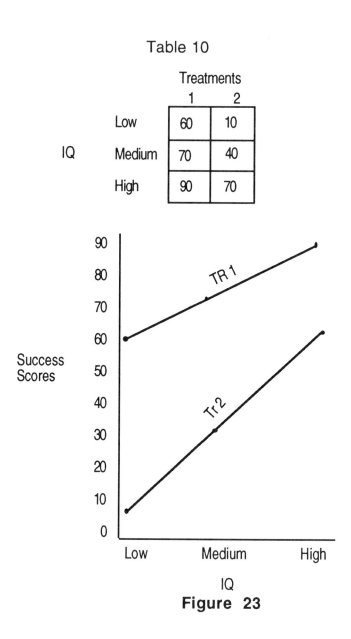

Figure 23

As one can see, the lines do not cross within the area of interest (IQ); therefore, if there is significant interaction, it would be ordinal interaction.

Chapter Summary

In this chapter, interaction was defined as the differential effect across the area of interest (whatever is on the X-axis). In other words, the magnitude of the differences will be significantly different for various values across the X-axis and is depicted graphically as significantly non-parallel lines.

Disordinal interaction occurs when the lines cross within the area of interest. When they cross outside of the area of interest, the interaction is ordinal.

The variables on the X and Y axes are called the main effects. These are not technically interpretable when there is significant interaction. This is always the case with disordinal interaction; but sometimes, when the interaction is ordinal, it may be logically interpretable.

When interaction exists, it is always appropriate to interpret the simple effects. This is accomplished by looking at each group independently and comparing it to every other group.

To graphically plot data, we may use a solid or dotted line. A dotted line is used when the data are not at least ordinal in nature, and a solid line should be used when the data are at least ordinal.

Objectives for Chapter V

After completing Chapter V, you should be able to:

1. list the purposes of research design.

2. interpret the meaning of a significant F when it is run on two or more groups.

3. given any two-factorial design (2 x 2, 3 x 3, etc.), draw the cells and identify the main effect and simple effects.

4. given an analysis of variance table and the total number of subjects, calculate the degree of freedom for the main effects, interaction, within, and total.

5. interpret the F-test for factorial design.

6. given a three-factorial design (2 x 2 x 2, 2 x 2 x 3, etc.), draw the cubes and identify the main and simple effects.

7. list the important considerations when using factorial design, as stated in this chapter.

8. define and discuss the problem of intact groups.

9. name the variable that is always statistically analyzed.

10. determine the Total df when given Between groups df and Within groups df.

11. determine the Between groups df when given the df for the main effects and interaction.

12. state the relationship between determining Total df and Total SS.

Chapter V

Introduction to Factorial Design and its Interpretation

Most published research tends to use analysis of variance (the F-test) to analyze factorial designs. This is used so frequently that people have confused the two. Analysis of variance is a statistical procedure, and factorial design is a design.

Purpose of Research Design

The purpose of design is to control for certain variables while testing others. After the research questions have been decided upon, the researcher then designs his study to control variables that he thinks may be of concern or eliminate variables that he thinks may contaminate the study.

The following is a list of how research design helps the researcher:

1. It controls variance.

2. It sets up the variables in such a way that the relationship between them can be adequately tested.

3. By analyzing the design, one can determine which statements can legitimately be made and the limitations.

Generally, design can be taught in two ways. One method is the Campbell and Stanley procedure. This stresses the conclusions that can be made from the analysis of the design, the limitations, and the population to whom the results can or cannot be generalized. This method also stresses the logical alternative explanations that may have caused the difference, other than the variables controlled for by the design. The Campbell and Stanley method does not stress the statistical procedures necessary to analyze the design since there are potentially many appropriate procedures.

The second method is factorial design. This method has its greatest stress on the statistical procedures for analyzing the design. This chapter will briefly discuss this second procedure to the extent that the reader will be able to interpret it when a factorial design is seen in the literature. We will not go into the statistical calculations.

One-Way Analysis of Variance Design

The simplest design is a one-way analysis of variance design. The simplest of these is testing to see if there is a difference between two groups; for example, Treatment 1 and Treatment 2. In this design, Treatment 1 is the only factor, and it is therefore not a factorial design because factorial designs must have at least two factors.

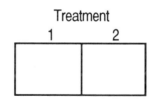

Figure 24

This is similar to a t-test between two groups. As was pointed out in Chapter 3, when you have only two groups, the F-test is actually equal to t^2; and you get the same results.

Another analysis of variance example in which the F-test is more appropriate than the t-test because there are more than two groups, is when there are five groups (see Figure 25).

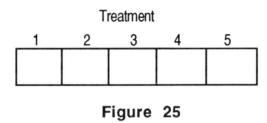

Figure 25

If we ran an F-test on the five groups and found it to be significantly different, we would not know what caused the difference only that some group or combination of groups was significantly different. Quite often, when a significant F is found, some researchers will go back with a t-test or F-test and test for the significant difference between specific groups to locate the difference. (There are more technically accurate procedures to do this, but they will not be discussed here.)

Example of a 2 x 2 Factorial Design

The simplest example of a factorial design is a 2 x 2 design which must have at least two factors, and each factor must have at least two levels. In other words, the simplest factorial design will produce at least four groups (2 x 2 = 4). As stated in Chapter 4, this is the minimum number of groups needed to test for interaction. (See Table 11 for an example of this design.)

Table 11

		Male	Female
Treatment	1	40	60
	2	80	55

Note: the scores in each of the cells are means for the dependent variable of reading achievement

In this example, we have two factors, Sex and Treatment. Sex has two levels, male and female, and Treatment has two levels, 1 and 2.

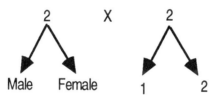

The factor sex is considered one main effect, and the factor treatment is the second main effect. These two main effects with their two levels create four groups which are:

Treatment 1 - male
Treatment 1 - female
Treatment 2 - male
Treatment 2 - female

When one looks at the separate groups, they are called the **simple effects**.

Quite often when one presents the analysis for a factorial design in table form, the effects are sometimes represented by letters. For example, sex may be represented by the letter A, treatment by the letter B, and the interaction by A x B (sex x treatment). The table that presents these results generally takes the form of Table 12.

Table 12

Source	df	S S	MS	F
A (sex)	1			1.5
B (treatment)	1			10.2
A x B	1			12.2
Within (error)	100			
Total	103			

To interpret Table 12, you really only need the **source**, **df**, and **F**. As stated in Chapter 3, to determine if an F is significant there must be two sets of degrees of freedom, the degrees of freedom numerator(df_N), and the degrees of freedom denominator (df_D). Since there are three F values in this particular table, two sets of degrees of freedom are needed for each F. In the general cases we are dealing with, the df_D will always be the df associated with the within (error), which is 100 on this table. The second df, the df_N is the degrees of freedom associated with each of the sources of variability listed in the column Source. In this table, there are three sources of variability that are controlled for; the sources of variability due to sex, the source of variability due to treatment, and the source of variability due to the interaction between sex and treatment.

Calculating Degrees of Freedom

The degrees of freedom are calculated in the following manner:

For the A main effect: df = a - 1
Where: a = number of levels of A (sex),
in this case a = 2
df for A = a - 1 = 2 - 1 = 1

For the B main effect: df = b-1
Where: b = number of levels of B (treatment),
in this case b = 2
df for B = b - 1 = 2 - 1 = 1

For the A x B interaction: df = (a-1) (b-1)
df for A x B = (2-1) (2-1) = (1) (1) = 1

For the within (error): df = N - K
Where: N = total number of subjects in this study (we
assumed N = 104)
K = number of groups
df for within = 104 - 4 = 100

Total df: can be obtained by adding up all the others or by N - 1.

If one was interested in testing to see if there is a significant effect due to sex, one would look up the F value in the table using the df associated with sex and within. In this case, if the alpha level was set at .05 ($\alpha = .05$), it would be found to be not significant. In other words, sex did not account for a significant amount of variance. In checking to see if there was a significant difference due to treatment, one would enter the F-table using the df associated with treatment and within. At an alpha of .05 this would be significant indicating that treatment accounted for a significant amount of variability. Following the same procedure for interaction, one would use the df values for the within and interaction. This would also be found significant at the $\alpha = .05$ level.

If you recall from Chapter 4, when significant interaction exists, it is technically not appropriate to interpret the main effects even if they are found to be significant, as treatment is in our example. If there is significant interaction, it should be graphed, as demonstrated in Chapter 4, to determine if the interaction is ordinal or disordinal. If we assume that the dependent variable being measured is a reading achievement score, which would be graphed on the Y-axis, sex may be considered the area of interest and would be graphed on the X-axis, as in Figure 26. If the scores obtained were like the ones in our example, then the interaction would be disordinal, and no interpretation of main effects can be made.

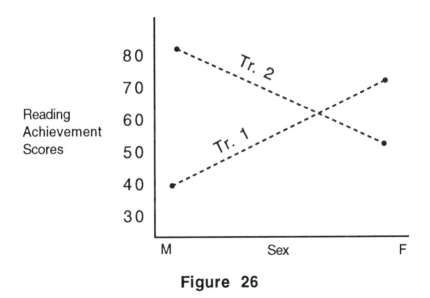

Figure 26

Example of a 2 x 3 Factorial Design

In a 2 x 3 design, we have two factors, one of which has two levels and the other has three levels. There are six groups (2 x 3 = 6). Let's assume the first factor is I.Q. and it has two levels, high and low. The second factor is treatment, which is three methods of teaching arithmetic. (See Figure 27 as an example of a 2 x 3 factorial design).

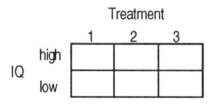

Figure 27

Note: There are six groups.
　　　Group 1 is people who have high I.Q. and were in Treatment 1;
　　　Group 2 is people who have high I.Q. and were in Treatment 2;
　　　Group 3 is people who have high I.Q. and were in Treatment 3;
　　　Group 4 is people who have low I.Q. and were in Treatment 1;
　　　Group 5 is people who have low I.Q. and were in Treatment 2;
　　　Group 6 is people who have low I.Q. and were in Treatment 3.

The traditional analysis of variance table will look like the following example, which assumes that the total number of subjects is 100.

Table 13

Source	df	SS	MS	F
A (IQ)	(a-1 = 2-1) = 1			4.1 (S)
B (treatment)	(b-1 = 3-1) = 2			6.3 (S)
AxB	(a-1)(b-1) = (1x2) = 2			.2 (NS)
Within (error)	(N - k = 100 - 6) = 94			
Total	(N - 1) = 99)			

Note: a = number of levels of the A main effect (factor I)
        b = number of levels of the B main effect (factor 2)
        N = total number of subjects in the sample, in this case we
            assumed 100 subjects
        K = total number of groups (2 x 3 = 6)
        S = significant, ns = nonsignificant

If the F-ratios were looked up in a table, one would find the interaction is not significant at the α = .05 level. (The df_N would equal 2 and df_D would equal 94.) Since the interaction is not significant and the main effects are, *it is legitimate to interpret main effects.

The A main effect (I.Q.) only has two groups; therefore, one can easily interpret this to mean that there is a significant difference between high and low I.Q. However, no directionality is given. To determine which group scored higher on the dependent variable (criterion), one must look at the means ($\overline{X}$) for the high and low I.Q. groups.

_____

*The df for determining the significance of the A main effect are 1 and 94 and for the B main effect, the df are 2 and 94.

The B main effect was also found to be significant; but since there are three groups, the interpretation of the significant F just means that there is a difference somewhere in the three groups (the same interpretation as if we were doing a one-way analysis of variance on three groups).

Example of a 2 x 2 x 2 Factorial Design

Here we have three factors, each with two levels. Let's assume Factor A = treatments, Factor B = sex, and Factor C = I.Q.   This would be depicted as a three-dimensional figure (a cube) (See Figure 28).

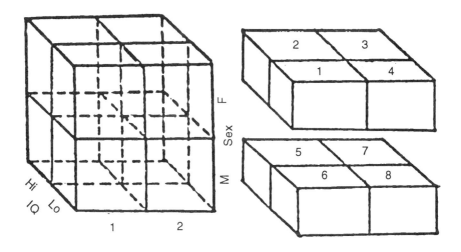

Figure 28

In a 2x2x2 factorial design, there are eight groups (2x2x2=8) and three factors (three main effects). The eight groups are:

Group 1 = females with low I.Q. in Treatment 1
Group 2 = females with high I.Q. in Treatment 1
Group 3 = females with high I.Q. in Treatment 2
Group 4 = females with low I.Q. in Treatment 2

Group 5 = males with high I.Q. in Treatment 1
Group 6 = males with low I.Q. in Treatment 1
Group 7 = males with low I.Q, in Treatment 2
Group 8 = males with high I.Q. in Treatment 2

These groups make up the simple effects.

The analysis of variance table for this is somewhat more complex since there are three main effects which allows for three two-way interactions and one three-way interaction. This is illustrated in Table 14.

Please see Appendix R for a brief discussion and an example of a correction for multiple comparisons.

Table 14

Source	df	SS	MS	F
A (treatment)	(a-1) = 2-1 = 1			7.2 (s)
B (sex)	(b-1) = 2-1 = 1			1.5 (ns)
C (IQ)	(c -1) = 2-1 = 1			4.5 (s)
A x B	(a-1)(b-1) = (2-1)(2-1) = 1			.7 (ns)
A x C	(a-1)(c-1) = (2-1)(2-1) = 1			1.2 (ns)
B x C	(b-1)(c-1) = (2-1)(2-1) = 1			.8 (ns)
A x B x C	(a-1)(b-1)(c-1) = (2-1)(2-1)(2-1) = 1			1.1 (ns)
With (error)	(N-K) = (200-8) = 192			
Total	N-1 = 199			

Note: a = levels of the A main effect (2)
        b = levels of the B main effect (2)
        c = levels of the C main effect (2)
        K = total number of groups (2x2x2=8); in this example there
            are 8 groups
        N = total number of subjects (assumed for this example to be
            200)
        s = significant, ns = non-significant

The significance for the main effects and interactions is looked up in the F table in exactly the same way as in the previous example. You need two sets of df for each. In this case, the df_D will always be 192, and the df_N for each one of these is one. If any of the two-way interactions was found to be significant, then the main effects could not technically be discussed. However, in this case, there is also a three-way interaction, which if found to be significant, would mean that the two-way interactions could not be discussed. In this event, each of the eight groups would have to be discussed and compared separately.

Important Considerations

1. In the beginning of this chapter, we stated that the purpose of research design is to control variance. The more variables (**factors**) we have in a design, the more variance we can control.

2. The more factors and levels of factors one has, the more groups one has and the more subjects one needs.

3. One rule of thumb when working with factorial design is never to have less than five subjects in a group, even though the analysis can be run with two subjects. It is desirable to have at least twenty subjects per group.

4. There are many assumptions that underlie analysis of variance which we will not deal with. However, it is important to mention that the F-test is very robust, and one does not have to worry about most of the assumptions especially if two conditions exist. These are that there are at least twenty subjects in each group (the more the better) and that all groups have the same number of subjects.

5. One assumption that must be met is that of independence of measurement. This means that each subject's response on the **dependent variable** (**criterion**) is independent of any other subject's response. For example, suppose we had two groups (ten people each) of individuals in group therapy. Group 1 received Rogerian Therapy and Group 2 received Gestalt. N, in this case, would not be twenty. It would be two since each subject's success in therapy is not independent of the other members in the group. The only things that are independent are the groups. This has been referred to as the problem

of **intact groups**. It occurs very frequently in the field of educational research. For another example, when one is testing to determine which treatment is most effective, four different classes of thirty students in a class may be used. The N would be 4 instead of 120. This could make a dramatic difference in determining whether or not there is statistical significance.

6. Only the dependent variable (criterion) gets statistically analyzed. It is the score that is used to compare each of the groups (simple effects and main effects).

7. The Between Subjects and the Within Subjects = Total Subjects. Similarly, the Between df plus the Within df = Total df. In a factorial design (for example 2x2), the Between df is equal to the df of the A main effect plus the df of the B main effect plus the df of the A x B interaction. Therefore, Total df = Between df plus Within df (Between df = Adf + Bdf + A x Bdf) and (Total df = Between df + Within df).

8. In a three-dimensional factorial design (for example 2x2x2), the Between df = df for A main effects plus the df for B main effects plus the df for C main effects plus the df for A x B plus the df for A x C plus the df for B x C plus the df for A x B x C. Total df = Between df plus Within df. This same principle applies to the subjects.

Chapter Summary

Chapter 5 has dealt with the basic interpretation of factorial design. The purpose of research design is to control for variability (variance). This allows for adequately testing relationships and enables us to determine appropriate conclusions and the limitations.

The simplest design is a one-way analysis of variance design in which there is only one factor that may have any number of levels. The simplest factorial design is two-factorial design (2 x 2) having two factors (main effects) of two levels each, creating four groups (simple effects). A three-factorial design has three factors (three main effects). The number of simple effects is determined by the levels of each factor (2 x 2 x 2 = 8; 2 x 3 x 2 = 12; 6 x 3 x 4 = 72). In the 6 x 3 x 4, the A main effect has six levels, the B main effect has three levels, and the C main effect has four levels.

To determine if an F is significant, two sets of degrees of freedom are needed. The degrees of freedom-numerator (df_N) is always the df associated with that particular main effect. The degrees of freedom-denominator (df_D) is always the df associated with the Within. The Between df plus the Within df equals the Total df.

If there is a significant interaction, one can only interpret the simple effects in a two-factorial design. When dealing with a three-factorial design, one cannot interpret the main effects if any of the two-way interactions is significant. Similarly, one cannot interpret any of the two-way interactions if there is a significant three-way interaction. A significant three-way interaction means there is a significant interaction between at least two, two-way interactions.

To avoid worrying about the underlying assumptions, one should have as large an N as possible and keep equal numbers of subjects in each group. As a rule of thumb, the N should not be less than five subjects per group.

A problem frequently encountered in educational research is one of intact groups. The N is always the number of independent replications. It is not necessarily the number of people involved. One should also keep in mind that only the dependent variable (criterion) gets statistically analyzed.

Objectives for Chapter VI

After Completing Chapter VI, you should be able to:

1. identify and define:
   A. pre-experimental design
   B. three types of ex post facto research
   C. quasi-experimental design
   D. true-experimental designs

2. discuss internal and external validity as they relate to each of the designs in Objective 1, a-d.

3. identify and define internal validity.

4. identify and define external validity.

5. identify, define, and give examples of independent variables (active variables) that can be manipulated.

6. identify, define, and give examples of assigned or attribute variables that cannot be manipulated.

Chapter VI

Introduction To Research Designs:*

Internal and External Validity

Ideally, the purpose of research design is to control for all possible alternative explanations other than the one being investigated. To the extent that the research design can do this, the design is **internally valid;** and to that extent, one can infer causal relationships. Designs with total internal validity are referred to as "true experimental designs."

True experimental designs require so much control that they can be generally only conducted in a laboratory setting. Therefore, when you are doing research in an applied setting, the controls you need for true experimental designs are generally lacking so other designs must be used. These alternatives are generally classified as pre experimental, quasi experimental, and ex post facto designs.

Pre-experimental designs have virtually no internal validity, even though they have an independent variable that is capable of being manipulated. An example of this type of design might be pretest-treatment-posttest (0-X-0).

_____

*The following presentation has been heavily based upon the work of Campbell & Stanley's Classical monograph Experimental and Quasi-Experimental Designs for Research, 1966.

This common design is generally used to infer that the treatment caused the change in scores from the pretest to the posttest. However, many other explanations are possible, such as the pretest may have sensitized the subject which improved posttest scores, or that time lag between the pre- and posttest may have caused the difference. Another example of a common pre-experimental design is one in which a treatment is given to one of two groups and the groups are tested for differences. This is symbolized by $\underline{X\ O}$. However, there is no way of knowing
$$\overline{O}$$
if the treatment caused the difference or if the two groups were different to begin with since they were not initially tested for equivalence. As one can see, pre-experimental designs do not have very much control even though they have an independent variable which can be manipulated by the researcher (an active variable).

Quasi experimental designs have a little more control and have independent variables that are under the control of the experimenter. However, they do not have enough control to be considered true experimental. Generally, in quasi-experimental designs, one does not have enough control over the situation to randomly assign subjects to treatments or to have control over the scheduling of the testing or treatment. However, some of these quasi-experimental designs may range from very little to a great deal of internal validity depending upon the specific situation.

Ex post facto research is generally a term that describes research which is initiated after the independent variable (the variable of interest) has already occurred or the independent variable is a type that cannot be manipulated such as age, race, sex, economic status, etc. Ex post facto research has been subject to more criticism by research methodologists than any other research. Some of this criticism is justifiable, and some is not. This is the type of research that has been predominately done in the field of education. Since it is very important to understand some of the strengths and weaknesses of ex post facto research, a later section will be devoted to it.

The following table represents the theoretical relationships between pre-experimental, quasi-experimental, ex post facto and true experimental designs in terms of internal validity (see Table 15).

Pre experimental and ex post facto designs with no hypotheses are generally considered to be the weakest in terms of internal validity, that is, no causal inferences should be made. Ex post facto research with hypotheses has potentially much more scientific value. However, ex post facto research with hypotheses and tests for alternative hypotheses is considerably more powerful in terms of internal validity than the preceding designs, and it even may be better than some types of quasi experimental designs, depending on the strength of the controls. Obviously, true experimental design is the most powerful in terms of internal validity.

External validity is defined as the ability to generalize results from the testing situation to the general population which was not tested. In research, one finds that as the experimental controls are increased, one's ability to generalize beyond the controlled testing situation is decreased. Therefore, the most controlled designs with the greatest internal validity tend to have the least external validity. So, if one looked at the experimental, quasi experimental, and ex post facto research, true experimental research would have the least amount of external validity while ex post facto research would have the most. Following is a more detailed discussion of ex post facto research.

Table 15

The Continuum of Internal Validity
as Related to the Various Possible Research Designs

CRITERIA WITH WHICH TO JUDGE INTERNAL VALIDITY	1. Lowest Pre-Experimental Designs	2. Ex Post Facto with No Hypotheses	3. Ex Post Factor With Hypotheses	4. Ex Post Facto With Hypothesis & Tests of Alternative Hypotheses	5. Quasi-Experimental Designs	6. Highest True Experimental Designs
1. Random Assignment Occurs Within Design:	NO	NO	NO	NO	NOT GENERALLY	YES
2. Definite Controls for Scheduling:	NO	NO	NO	NO	QUESTIONABLE YES/NO	YES
3. Independent Variable is Active and Can be Manipulated by the Experimenter:	YES	NO	NO	NO	YES	YES
4. Independent Variable is Assigned/Attribute and Cannot Be Manipulated by the Experimenter	NO	YES	YES	YES	NO	NO

Klein's Modification of Newman's 1976 Continuum of Research Design.

Ex Post Facto Research

Throughout the literature one can find ex post facto research almost delegated to an inferior position among the types of research designs and methodology. The terms "ex post facto research" and "correlational research" are sometimes used interchangeably. When one does correlational (ex post facto) research, causation cannot be inferred. Therefore, many methodologists have issued numerous warnings emphasizing the dangers and possible misinterpretations of research in which the experimenter does not have control over the independent variables.

In ex post facto research, causation is sometimes improperly inferred because some people have a propensity for assuming that one variable is likely to be the cause of another because it precedes it in occurrence, or because one variable tends to be highly correlated with another (for example: Smoking--the independent variable, assumed to cause cancer--the dependent variable). This obviously does not necessarily mean because two variables are correlated and one precedes the other that they are not causally related. However, while a correlated and preceding relationship is necessary, it is not sufficient for inferring a causal relationship.

To assume a causal relationship, one must have internal validity (all other explanations for the effect on the criterion [dependent variable] are controlled for and the only possible explanation for changes in the dependent variable must be due to the independent variable under investigation). Only with a true experimental design does one have the experimental control to achieve internal validity. Ex post facto research lacks this control for a variety of reasons. Some of these reasons are that there is an inability to randomly assign and manipulate the independent variable since in this research it has already occurred and is not under the control of the researcher.

A common weakness of ex post facto research is that the design is not capable of controlling the confounding effects of self selection. For example, suppose research was conducted to see what effect early childhood training had on motivation; also suppose a significant relationship between early independence training and later adult motivation was found. Therefore, one might incorrectly conclude that the independence training "caused" this adult motivation. Another explanation might be that volunteer subjects who had independence training were more likely to demonstrate a greater degree of adult motivation but what causes this motivation might be more related to what causes them to volunteer than it is to the independence training.

A better example may be data which indicates elementary school males score significantly lower on reading achievement than females; therefore, one may tend to assume that males are less competent in decoding this visual stimulus. One of many other reasons for their lower scores may be that in our culture, reading at the lower levels is considered to be more of a feminine activity and, therefore, males may receive less reinforcement for engaging in this activity and may even receive aversive comments from their peers, which could affect reading performance.

Obviously, one can go on with examples of ex post facto research which cannot appropriately assume causal relationships. Because of this well acknowledged weakness, many tend to regard ex post facto as inferior research that should not be conducted.

This is not necessarily true since it is the research question which determines whether or not its use is appropriate. If the research question is dealing with causation, ex post facto procedures are inappropriate. However, if the question deals with relationships, it is very appropriate.

Sometimes a research question of interest has independent variables that cannot be manipulated. Therefore, the researcher can either decide to do ex post facto research or no research at all.

The authors feel that, before deciding to conduct research, one should ask the question, "So What?" "So what if significance or non-significance is found?" Is this useful information?   When the "So What?" question is answered positively, the researcher may find that the variables are the type that require ex post facto research. The research that tends to be related to some of the most significant social problems, by its very nature, has to be ex post facto. (Kerlinger, 1972).

One of the most effective ways of using ex post facto research is to help identify a small set of variables from a large set of variables that is related to the dependent variable, for future experimental manipulation.

One can identify three major types of ex post facto research: **without hypotheses**, **with hypotheses**, and **with hypotheses and tests of alternative hypotheses**. Ex post facto research without hypotheses is one of the poorest types of research found in the literature in terms of internal validity.   It is sometimes called exploratory. Without replication, this research is potentially highly misleading, and one should be very cautious in using or interpreting the results.

Ex post facto with hypotheses tests previously stated hypothetical relationships. This type of research is much better; but there is still a danger of misinterpretation, and one must be cautious once again in interpreting the results of the investigation.

The third type tests stated hypotheses and alternative hypotheses. These are hypotheses that propose other explanations for the effect, other than the stated ones. These explanations are competing or rival hypotheses to the ones the researcher is interested in verifying. The more of these rival hypotheses that can be eliminated, the greater the internal validity of the design. However, one must still keep in mind that by its very nature ex post facto research can never have total internal validity. Therefore, causation can never be inferred.

Chapter Summary

In this chapter, the purpose of research design is defined as controlling for all possible alternative explanations. A design is internally valid and causal relationships can be inferred to the extent that the design controls for these alternatives. A design is externally valid to the extent the results can be generalized beyond the testing situation. Therefore, the most controlled designs tend to have the least external validity.

There are generally four classifications of research designs. These are:

1. **Pre experimental** - very little control, virtually no internal validity; therefore, no causal inference should be made.

2. **Quasi-experimental** - a little more control, but not enough to randomly assign subjects to treatments or

to control scheduling of treatments. Internal validity ranges from very little to a great deal, depending on the situation.

3. **Ex post facto** - the independent variable has already occurred or cannot be manipulated. The design may be very weak in internal validity or relatively strong depending on whether there are hypotheses and tests for alternative hypotheses. They tend to have the most external validity.

4. **True experimental** - regarded as totally internally valid. One can infer causation, but these designs require so much control that a laboratory setting is necessary. Therefore, they are not practical for most situations one wishes to investigate. They tend to have the most internal validity.

It was also stressed that causation can only be assumed when all other explanations for the effect are controlled for and the only possible explanation for change must be due to the independent variable under investigation. If the research question is concerned with finding a causal relationship, then ex post facto procedures are not appropriate.

Finally, researchers should be concerned with the "So What?" question. They should be concerned with whether the information produced will be useful, and they should be able to state why their research question is worth investigating before they invest their time, money, and labor.

Objectives for Chapter VII

After completing Chapter VII, you should be able to:

1. identify some of the common symbols used in diagramming research design.

2. define:
   a. one shot case study
   b. a pretest/posttest case study
   c. a simulated before-after design
   d. a two group-posttest only, nonequivalent design
   e. a pretest/posttest nonequivalent design (a quasi-experimental design)
   f. a longitudinal time series design
   g. a posttest only experimental and control groups randomized design
   h. an experimental and control group matched subjects design
   i. before and after true experimental design with a control group
   j. a Solomon 4-group design

3. For each of the above designs, be able to discuss the internal validity.

Chapter VII

Further Discussions on Research Designs

It is convenient to represent research designs with a diagram. The diagrams that are used to represent designs are called paradigms. Studying a paradigm makes it easy to plan, interpret, and analyze research.

In this chapter, ten designs will be presented. These ten represent the more common designs that are used in educational and behavioral science research. There are many more designs that could be presented; however, many of these additional designs are modifications of the basic ten presented in this chapter. Thus, the reader who understands these fundamental designs will have the basic tools for interpreting most research.

In representing research designs with paradigms, symbols are used that must be explained to the reader. The following is a list of symbols used in this chapter and a brief description of the meaning of each:

X   This refers to the experimenter's treatment for a group.

-X   no treatment or an absence of treatment.

In an experiment, one group might receive a treatment and a second group not. The second group is commonly called the control group.

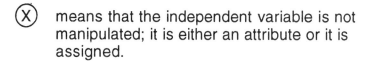   means that the independent variable is not manipulated; it is either an attribute or it is assigned.

O   a measurement or an observation. In educational research, O will frequently be some type of test score. For example, pretest and post-test. It can have any number of subscripts.

R   means the random assignment of subjects to groups.

M   means the assignment of subjects to groups using a matching procedure.

M_r means the assignment of subjects to groups by first matching subjects and then randomly assigning each matched subject

The first group of designs presented (1-6) are quite common but are somewhat inadequate in terms of internal validity. As each design is presented, its strengths and weaknesses will be discussed.

Design #1 - The One Shot Case Study (A Pre-Experimental Design)

1. X O

In this design, there is some form of treatment to a group followed by an observation of that group after the treatment to ascertain its impact.

Strengths: Scientifically, this design does not have any strengths because it lacks any form of comparison. Therefore, one can never be sure what the results mean. An example might be a teacher trying a new method of instruction in his class and asking the students to indicate how they liked it. Valuable information can be gained, but from a research standpoint, this is not a valid way to assess instruction.

Weaknesses: This design is extremely weak in that one really doesn't know what is obtained afterwards since no meaningful comparison has been made. This design is not very often found in the research.

Suggested Statistical Analysis: There is no meaningful way that this design can be statistically analyzed.

Design #2 - The Pretest, Posttest Case Study (A Pre-Experimental Design)

2. O_1 X O_2

This design differs from number one in that an observation is made before the treatment occurs. This allows the researcher to compare the group before and after the treatment to judge the impact of it.

Strengths: This design is relatively weak. It is stronger than number one, but only because of the one comparison. This design is frequently used in evaluating the effectiveness of instruction. It can be extremely useful if applied appropriately but highly misleading if not. An example might be, pretest before instruction (O_1), present instruction (X), and posttest after instruction (O_2).

Weaknesses: The major weakness is that one can't be sure that the treatment caused the difference between the pre and post measures. On the surface it might appear that the treatment caused a change in the group, but further analysis shows that a number of other factors could be influencing the results.

The following are alternative explanations of the possible causes of the change in our group: The terms are borrowed from Campbell and Stanley's classical work, Experimental and Quasi-Experimental Designs for Research.

History could account for the change in a group. History means any extraneous event other than the treatment that intervened between the pre- and post-measures. For example, if a school district was investigating the effect of a new set of arithmetic textbooks on achievement by measuring achievement at the beginning and end of the year, Design #2 might be chosen. But what if during the year all the students moved into a new building? This would be an example of a history factor that might effect the results of the study. In other words, the researcher wouldn't know if it were the new books or the new school that caused the results of the study.

Another example might be a researcher investigating the effects of integration on student attitudes toward people of different races. In our example, the history factor is the death of Martin Luther King one week before questionnaires were distributed to students. Obviously, such an event would drastically affect student responses and confound the results in an unknown way.

Maturation is another factor that could account for a change in a group. Maturation means any growth or development that normally takes place independent of an experimental treatment. An example might be the analysis of the impact of a school lunch program on student's growth. Part of the change that occurs in students during such a program would normally occur as part of their maturation. Often, history and maturation are confused because they both are related to something occurring in the time between the pre- and post-tests. The distinguishing point to keep in mind is that **historical effects** are happening **external to the subject** while **maturation**

effects are related to **changes internal to the subject**. Examples of these internal changes may be psychological such as boredom or physiologial such as fatigue.

Testing refers to factors associated with measuring devices that actually cause change to occur. This may happen when a pretest sensitizes people to an experimental treatment and actually causes them to behave differently during the treatment. An example of this would be a teacher's evaluation of the impact of a Values Clarification Program on the moral development of students. If the teacher gave a pretest that asked questions about morality, the pretest might possibly get the students concerned about the topic and thus influence them to be unusually receptive to the Values Clarification Program. This same phenomenon can also take place with other factors such as achievement.

For example, a teacher might be interested in investigating the effects of an instructional procedure that could improve his students' performance in arithmetic. He decides to test the students before and after instruction. Although he does not have to use the same test on both occasions, he, at least, has to use a pretest and a posttest that are equivalent in terms of the content area they represent, their difficulty, etc. But the fact that the students had taken a pretest that was equivalent to the posttest might have provided them with an opportunity to "practice." Therefore, any improvement in their posttest scores could be due to the fact that they were pretested rather than due to the treatment. This type of pretesting effects is usually referred to as "practice effects."

In summary, it can be said testing effects are the results that the first test has on the performance on the second test.

Instrumentation refers to effects due to unreliable measurement instruments. If one had an unreliable pretest measurement, any change in the posttest measurement might be due to the instability of the measurement device, rather than the treatment.

Also, when one is using mechanical, electronic, and other sorts of instruments that are in need of calibration or that might get affected by prolonged usage, it is necessary to make sure that any differences between the pre- and posttest are not due to changes in the instruments. In addition, certain research questions might require the use of observers rather than tests or instruments. If there is no consistency among the observers or if the same observe is not consistent over a period of time, any difference between pre- and posttest could not be legitimately considered as due to treatment. Therefore, it is necessary to use more than one observer and to make sure that each observer's judgments are highly related with those of other observers (interrater reliability).

Statistical Regression is defined as the effects of extreme pretest scores tending to regress toward the mean on posttesting. For example, if subjects were selected for a study simply because they scored extremely low, and for no other reason, then when they are posttested, they will tend to score higher, regardless of treatment. Both are examples of extreme cases regressing towards the mean of the population. Therefore, one can get significant differences between pre- and posttest scores just because extremes were selected initially. Regression is a statistical phenomena that will occur whenever groups are selected on the basis of extreme scores and for no other reason.

Experimental Mortality is the loss of subjects between testing. For example, we can start with 100 subjects on a pretest with an average IQ of 95 for the sample. If, for some reason, 50 people dropped out before posttesting, the average IQ of the remaining 50 might be 150. Therefore, the difference between pre- and posttest scores would, in all likelihood, not be due to the treatment, but due to the differential loss from pretest to posttest (mortality).

Selection Bias occurs when subjects are assigned to two or more comparison groups and not all groups are given the treatment. If these groups are initially different before treatment, then any difference between posttest scores may be due to the initial differences rather than treatment. An example of this might be assigning a treatment of individualizing instruction to highly motivated children and traditional instruction to children with little motivation. If the groups were tested for gains at the end of a unit, any difference found might, in fact, be due to initial motivational differences, rather than treatment differences.

The purpose of the "Better" research designs is to eliminate as many of the above type of factors that contaminate research as possible.

These contaminating factors, such as maturation, testing, history, etc., which are threats to internal validity, must be considered when evaluating research. They are useful mind sets to aid an individual in asking the types of questions which will help in identifying good or poor research, and appropriate or inappropriate research conclusions. They are also useful questions to ask before designing or conducting one's own research.

Suggested Statistical Procedures for Design #2 (O_1 X O_2)

Gain scores are most frequently used to analyze Design #2. To do this, the pretest scores are simply subtracted from the posttest scores to determine gains. A t-test or some other statistical test is then used to determine if the gains are significant. However, if one is looking at frequency or nominal data, a Chi square, or Sign Test should be used. The most powerful statistical technique to use on this design may be residual gain analysis. This procedure conceptually holds constant gains expected to occur in the posttest, based upon the pretest scores (slope of the pretest). The procedure then tests to see if the gains are significantly greater than one would expect from the pretest regression line.

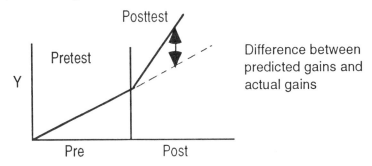

This procedure is statistically more sophisticated and complex, but it also helps to control for the regression effect.

Design #3 - The Simulated Before-After Design (A Pre-Experimental Design)

3.   X O_1

          O_1

This design uses two groups to enable a comparison of before and after treatment change, but only one group actually gets the treatment. One group is tested before and the second group is tested after receiving the treatment. Interpretation of results is based upon a comparison between the experimental and control groups. The assumption is that the groups are equivalent. One must be careful in interpreting the results of studies using Design #3.

Strengths: This design does afford some comparisons for the researcher, but the basis for the comparison may be very limited because of uncertainty about equivalence of the groups. Also, this design controls the possibility of a pretest-treatment interaction since the group pretested doesn't get the treatment. Pretest-treatment interaction is an example of testing as a factor affecting the internal validity of a design. In this design, there would be no pretest to affect the experimental group nor in any way sensitize its members to the treatment.

Weaknesses: The major weakness of this design is that one is not sure of the degree to which the two groups are similar (selection bias). This can be a very serious limitation. Other limitations that one should be concerned with are such things are history, maturation, and maybe instrumentation, depending upon the extent to which the instrument may be effected by time.

Design #3 might be used by a teacher who has tried a new approach to instruction and given a posttest. As a control group, the teacher might use another class that happened to get the same test as a pretest. This design would be normally used when, for some reason, a pretest was not given to the experimental class. Generally, this design is not a very good one and is not used very often.

Suggested statistical procedures for this design are the same as those suggested for Design #2 (see Design #2).

Design #4 - Two Groups - Non-Equivalence (A Pre-Experimental Design)

4. $X \quad O_1$ or $X \quad O_1$

-----------   ------------

$-X \quad O_2$ O_2

This design involves the use of an experimental and a control group which differ in that one group receives the treatment and one doesn't. It allows a comparison to be made and is employed quite often in educational research. An example might be a teacher using a new method on one class and not using the method on the other class. A comparison is made between the two groups after the treatment is completed.

Strengths: The major strength of this design is that it does allow a comparison between an experimental and a control group. Also, it represents the typical practical situation that exists for many educational researchers--a comparison between two existing classes. Furthermore, the internal validity of this design is not jeopardized by the confounding effects of history, maturation, testing, regression, and mortality.

Weaknesses: The major weakness is that one can't be sure that the groups are equivalent since there is no attempt to control the composition of the groups. Although this weakness is very severe, it can be lessened by obtaining information that describes the groups on important variables, thus, helping to document their equivalence. This is an example of selection bias which was discussed earlier. Another problem one should consider in this type of design is that of **intact groups**. In an intact group, the subjects are not independent of each other. Therefore, one must use the number of groups and not the number of individual subjects in calculating the N size. This is a concern that should be considered for every design, but especially for designs occurring in natural settings.

Suggested Statistical Procedures: If the data are nominal or frequencies, nonparametric statistical techniques such as a Chi square or Sign Test, would be most appropriate.

If the data are ordinal, interval or ratio, the appropriate statistical techniques would be a t-test or a F-test. (It is the personal bias of this author that parametric procedures are more powerful and are preferable to non-parametric techniques when the data are at least ordinal. This is not consistent with presentations in many traditional texts, but it is based on more than ten years of Monte Carlo studies which generally support this position. These comments pertain to the other designs also.

Design #5 - Experimental-Control, Pre- and Post-test Design (A Quasi-Experimental Design)

5. O_1 X O_2 O_1 X O_2

   ------------------ OR ----------------

O_3 -X O_4 O_3 O_4

Design #5 is a little better than Design #4 because of the inclusion of a pretest for both groups. However, one still has the problem of nonequivalent groups because the experimenter has not actively designed the groups to be equivalent through randomization or some other means. The pretest does provide information about group equivalence which enables a more refined analysis to be undertaken.

This design might be used by an educational researcher interested in two different teaching approaches. The researcher arranges for pretests to be given to all classes. Thus, one group, possibly one-half of the classes, receives one method of instruction and the other group, the remaining classes, receives the other method of instruction. At the conclusion of the experiment, a posttest is given to both groups and the results are compared. Also, the researcher can compare the average gains (posttest minus pretest) for each group or even use the more powerful statistical techniques that quantitatively remove pretest differences.

Strengths: Although the researcher is not manipulating assignment of subjects to groups, the pretest gives an indication of how similar the groups are. This design is quite practical in that students may remain in intact classes. This design does eliminate many of the history factors that might influence results as well as maturation. On the whole, the practicality of this design makes its usage widespread despite some remaining questions about internal validity.

Weaknesses: Design #5 is efficient to the degree that the groups are equivalent. To the degree the groups are not equivalent, one cannot assume that the treatment (the independent variable) is causing the difference. For example, if the groups are different, the control group may gain more than the treatment group. In this case, it is possible that the treatment was not effective for the experimental group; but since the groups were initially different, the same treatment may have caused even greater gains in the control group if they had received it. This is referred to by Campbell and Stanley as **interaction**. Therefore, one cannot conclude that the treatment is significantly better or worse, since it may depend on which group received it.

Another possible weakness may be the **regression effect**, if the groups were picked for extreme scores on the pretest. **Mortality** is also a threat to any pre-, posttest design. One should always check to see if there was any differential loss in subjects between pre- and posttests and whether this loss may account for the difference in gains. The effects of mortality can be assessed by analyzing the number and/or types of subjects that started in both groups and ended in both groups.

Suggested Statistical Procedures: Posttest minus pretest scores (gain analysis) is generally used. However, analysis of covariance in which the pretest scores are covaried is the most powerful technique for analyzing this type of data. Details of this procedure can be found in any standard statistical text, such as Popham's Educational Statistics: Use and Interpretation; McNemar's Psychological Statistics; Edward's Experimental Design in Psychological Research; or Ferguson's Statistical Analysis In Psychology and Education.

Design #6 - The Longitudinal Time Design (A Quasi-Experimental Design)

6. O_1 O_2 X O_3 O_4

This design is very popular in developmental psychology where researchers are interested in studying growth and maturation, although it can also be used to study learning over a period of time. The distinguishing factor in Design #6 is the number of measurements before and after treatment (there can be more than two). In educational research, this type of design might be employed to investigate the effects of a preschool program. Successive measures throughout elementary school are designed to measure the permanence of such a program. This design can be expanded to included a control group for additional comparisons and increased validity, for example:

$$O_1\, O_2\, O_3 \quad X \quad O_7\, O_8\, O_9$$
--- OR
$$O_4\, O_5\, O_6 \; \text{-X} \quad O_{10}\, O_{11}\, O_{12}$$

$$O_1\, O_2\, O_3 \quad X \quad O_7\, O_8\, O_9$$

$$O_4\, O_5\, O_6 \qquad O_{10}\, O_{11}\, O_{12}$$

Strengths: The additional pretest(s) allow the researcher to control for the reactivity of the measurements (also called pretest sensitization). The additional posttests afford the opportunity of assessing the permanence of gains. Another very important strength is that the multiple observations serve to illustrate the effects of maturation both with and without the experimental treatment. As previously mentioned, the addition of a control group increases the strength of this design considerably.

Weaknesses: A weakness of this design is that the **frequent testing**, especially over a span of years is cumbersome and often subjects are lost for any number of reasons. Another potential threat to the internal validity is **mortality**. In general, this design is mediocre in internal validity, but it is important in longitudinal research. The addition of a control group makes it a good design with a fair amount of internal validity.

Suggested Statistical Procedures: One method used frequently with this type of design is simply graphing on the X-axis the observations (independent variable) and on the Y-axis the criteria measures (the dependent variable).

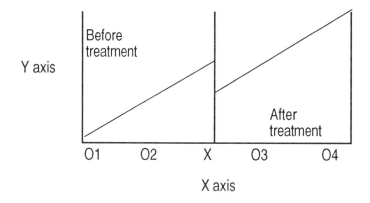

One should avoid the tendency to average all the pretest scores and test them against the posttest scores. This can be very misleading.

The most appropriate way to analyze this design requires a fair amount of statistical sophistication. The researcher looks at the intercept and slope of the line before treatment (X) and compares it to the intercept and slope of the line after treatment (X). This type of analysis is specifically appropriate for behavior modification designs. (See Kelly, Newman, and McNeil, 1973)

Since there are underlying statistical difficulties in analyzing such data, it is a good idea to consult a statistician before the analysis.

Design #7 - Experimental and Control Groups, Randomized Subjects (A True Experimental Design)

7.   X O_1 R X O_1
   R   OR
        -X O_2 R O_2

This design represents the classically designed experiment. The groups are equated by randomization and one group is randomly (R) designated as experimental and the other as control. The experimental group receives a treatment, the control group doesn't and the two groups are compared after the treatment to assess its impact. An example would be a school investigating a non-graded program on an experimental basis. One-half of the first graders are assigned by random means to experimental classes. The remaining students are assigned to control classes. At the end of the school year, comparisons are made between the two types of instruction. In this example, the researcher would probably measure more than one variable on the posttest. Achievement, attitude toward school and other important variables could be compared.

Strengths: Design #7 is considered to be an outstanding design from a scientific point of view. Its main strength lies in the fact that the control group enables a legitimate comparison to be made between groups. This is the first design observed so far that incorporates the equivalent control group into the design. Related to the idea of the **equivalent control group** is the technique of randomization. **Randomization** is the procedure that makes this design effective. When subjects are randomly assigned to treatments, one is allowed to assume that the groups are equivalent on all possible variables and differences between groups can be assumed to be the result of chance alone. This design provides adequate controls for all threats to internal validity.

Weaknesses: The major weakness of Design #7 is in the area of external validity. The problem is that most classes in schools are not constituted randomly. Therefore, the application of research results based upon Design #7 is only as valid as the process used in obtaining groups that allows one to use randomization procedures. When students are grouped homogeneously into tracts, to some the degree they are different from students that are grouped with no bias whatsoever. This problem can be solved by making classrooms the unit of observation instead of individual students. This solution necessitates an extremely large study since sample size would be determined by the number of classes in the study.

Another weakness of this design is that it is usually quite difficult to randomly assign subjects in many applied settings such as schools. The weakness is usually a matter of practicality in the normal routine of school operations.

Extensions: This design can be extended to include studies with more than two groups in which randomization is used. As more groups are added to a study, one finds that the notion of a control group (no treatment) may become inapplicable. It may become convenient to think of these groups as comparison groups, each getting different treatments, instead of the classical experimental-control group design. The logic of the investigation is still the same: groups are treated exactly the same on all except one variable whose effect is observed on some criterion. This design is the simplest form of the posttest only control group design.   Further examples would be:

$$R \ X_1 \ O_1 \qquad\qquad X_1 \ O_1 \qquad\qquad X_1 \ O_1 \qquad R \ X_1 \ O_1$$

$$\underline{OR} \ \ R \ X_2 \ O_2 \quad \underline{OR} \ \ R \ X_2 O_2 \quad \underline{OR} \ \ R \ X_2 \ O_2 \ \text{etc.}$$

$$R \ X_2 \ O_2 \qquad\qquad X_3 \ O_3 \qquad\qquad X_3 O_3 \qquad R \ X_3 \ O_3$$

$$X_4 \ O_4$$

Suggested   Statistical   Procedure: If the criterion variable is a frequency (nominal data), then a Chi square, Sign Test, or some similar procedure is suggested for statistical analysis.   If the data is ordinal or interval in nature and there are only two groups, then a t-test is appropriate.   If there are more than two groups, then an F-test would be most appropriate.   However, depending upon the number of groups and the research question, analysis of covariance or blocking procedures may be used to increase the power of the statistical analysis.

Design #8 - Experimental and Control Groups, Matched Subjects (A True Experimental Design)

$$
\begin{array}{llll}
8. & \quad X \quad O_1 & \qquad M_r \ X \ O_1 \\
M_r & & \qquad\qquad\quad OR \\
& -X \quad O_2 & \qquad M_r \quad\ \ O_2
\end{array}
$$

Design #8 is quite similar to #7 except in the method used to assign subjects to groups.   In Design #8, subjects are assigned to groups by matching them first on some attribute or attributes.   In addition, it is important to note that, as each pair of matched subjects is selected, the assignment of members of the pair to groups is done randomly.   If a researcher wanted to study the effects of lectures vs. independent study on achievement in biology, for example, subjects would probably be matched on IQ or previous biology achievement. If subjects were matched on IQ, for example, the researcher would then randomly assign the members of each matched pair in the sample.

However, one of the major problems with matching is the difficulty in obtaining subjects. Therefore, one may lose some power because many unmatched subjects may have to be eliminated from the subject pool.

Randomization is generally regarded as the best technique for equating groups because of its greater precision and relative ease in implementing.

Suggested Statistical Procedures: The statistical procedures are the same as those suggested for Design #7. However, if analysis of covariance is used, one can covary (hold statistically constant) the variable that was used for matching, allowing more subjects to be used. Therefore, more power is obtained without having to match.

Design #9 - Before and After, With Control Group (A True Experimental Design)

$$
\begin{array}{cccccccc}
 & O_1 & X & O_2 & & R & O_1 & X & O_2 \\
R & & & & OR & & & & \\
 & O_3 & \text{-}X & O_4 & & R & O_3 & & O_4
\end{array}
$$

Design #9 includes the use of a pretest with groups that have been equated by means of randomization. The pretest results will demonstrate to the researcher the effectiveness of randomization as a means of equating groups. In addition, the pre- and post-measures allow the researcher to assess the impact of treatment using gain scores. Of course, the use of equated groups in this design allows comparisons to be made between experimental and control groups.

An example of Design #9 would be research on the effectiveness of a new mode of instruction, for example, programmed instruction vs. traditional, on end of year achievement in arithmetic. Students are randomly assigned to two groups and given a pretest at the beginning of the school year. The experimental group of classes uses programmed instruction in arithmetic and the control group does not--other conditions are hopefully the same for each group. At the end of the school year, all students are tested in achievement again. Usually, the same test or a parallel form of it is used. The researcher then compares the average gains during the year to see which group has gained the most.

Strengths: This design is very strong in internal validity. The use of both randomization and the pretest provides sound evidence of the history and maturation. Also, the ability to analyze gain scores is welcomed in some research situations, especially when assessing achievement over the period of a school year.

Weaknesses: The major weakness is the practical difficulty of using randomization in many applied settings. Sometimes, it is just not practical in a school situation. Also, the use of a pretest may cause some disruption of normal activities and might predispose subjects to react unusually to the treatment. For example, a pretest of racial attitudes might affect the subjects' sensitivity to an experiment investigating the impact of encounter groups on racial attitudes (threat to external validity). Likewise, an achievement test at the beginning of a school year might affect students' and teachers' motivation toward an arithmetic course. This phenomenon is called pretest sensitization. In comparison to the other designs, however, the weaknesses of Design #9 in terms of internal validity are minor.

Suggested Statistical Procedure: The procedures suggested for this design are the same as those suggested for Design #5.

Design #10 - The Solomon (A True Experimental Design)

10.   (Group I)   R O_1 X O_2

       (Group II)   R O_3 O_4

       (Group III)   R   X O_5

       (Group IV)   R O_6

Design #10 is the most elegant of the designs in this chapter in terms of the internal validity that is insured by its use. In essence, it is really a combination of Designs #7 and #9. The Solomon, named after its originator, allows the researcher to make a number of comparisons. Again, using randomization insures that the comparisons rest on sound ground. History, maturation, and pretest sensitization are all controlled in this design.

An example of its use would be a study of the effect of watching a movie on drug abuse upon attitudes toward drugs. Groups I and II are administered a pre-treatment questionnaire which assesses attitudes toward drugs.

Groups III and IV are not given the pretest so that any possible pretest sensitization will be evident in comparison between Groups I and II and Groups III and IV. At the end of the movie on drug abuse or the control group's movie on recreation, the drug questionnaire is administered again but this time to all the groups. Differences between Groups I and III compared with Groups II and IV show the impact of the film on drug abuse attitudes. Remember that all four groups were equated before the experiment by randomization.

Strengths: This is by far the strongest design for the control of internal validity. Group equivalence through randomization and the four different groups allow comparisons to be made which answer all the internal validity questions.

Weaknesses: The major weakness with Design #10 is its practicality. The Solomon Design is difficult to set up in many situations. Randomization, four different groups, and some pretesting, are factors which make Design #10 diffi-cult to implement. The difficulty of implementation detracts from the usefulness of this design. An additional weakness is that, because this design has four groups, it requires twice as many subjects as Designs #7 or #9, which only have two groups. Since this design requires procedures that are unlike the routine of the average school, generali-zation to the average school is limited.

Suggested Statistical Procedures: One method of statistical analysis is to put this into a 2 X 2 analysis of variance design. For example:

(Treatment)

		yes	no
(Pretest)	yes	Group I	Group II
	no	Group III	Group IV

This design gives information about the effects of the treatments and the effects of pretesting as well as the effects of the treatment interacting with the pretest (i.e. A - main effects, B - main effects, AB - interaction).

Chapter VIII

Type VI Error: Inconsistency Between the Statistical Procedure and the Research Question*

Isadore Newman, Robert Deitchman, Joel Burkholder,
Raymond Sanders, The University of Akron ;
Leroy Ervin, Jr., Oberlin College

While a great deal of money and energy is currently being directed toward research, there also seems to be a general lack of acceptance of the relevance of research findings. This skepticism is somewhat justifiable, and we will attempt to discuss what we feel are the major causes of this state of affairs. These issues may explain to some extent why less and less monies are being made available for certain types of research.

One reason people ignore research findings is that the statistical models used have frequently been unrelated or tangentially related to the research question of interest. There are a variety of reasons for this, some of which will be discussed in this paper.

---

*Paper presented to the World Population Society, Western Regional Meeting; January 24, 1976, aboard the Queen Mary, Long Beach, California.

We would like to gratefully acknowledge the assistance of Dr. Ralph Blackwood, Dr. Keith McNeil, and Dr. Charles Dye for their editorial comments.

1. The courses that teach research methods generally emphasize data analysis rather than practicing appropriate methods and procedures for asking and developing research questions. These courses do not adequately develop the skills of evaluating the research question and the statistical models that are most capable of reflecting the research question.

Quite often students coming out of these courses tends to select a familiar, "canned" standard statistical design, or package (cookbook approach) such as a 2 x 3, or 2 x 2 x 3, because they have not been taught to develop their own models to reflect the research question. Therefore, they use these standard models which dictate the question being investigated. Sometimes a researcher is aware that these models do not completely represent the true research question. When this happens, he or she may then make inferential jumps from the data. These influences may well be inappropriate. In some cases, the researcher is unaware that the models are not really reflective of the research questions; sometimes the unsophisticated researcher allows the statistical model to totally dictate the research question. Under these conditions, we find research that is technically correct but is not relevant because it is not related in a pragmatic way to a specific problem.

2. People often misinterpret or misapply research findings because they confuse statistical analysis with experimental design. Traditional analysis of variance, in which the design and statistical procedures are totally related, has fostered this confusion.

One sometimes finds even the most respected of colleagues making statements such as:

a. We can only infer causation when the research is analyzed through traditional analysis of variance.

b. If we use regression or correlation, we cannot infer causation.

Remember, causal relationship can only be inferred through experimental design. No statistical technique allows us to infer or assume causal relationships.

In an issue of the Harvard Review, Luecke & McGinn (1975) wrote a paper entitled, "Regression Analyses And Educational Production Functions: Can They Be Trusted?" Their conclusion was that we cannot appropriately infer causation from regression techniques. This is an obvious statement since causation cannot be inferred from any statistical technique, whether it be regression, analysis of variance, t-test, etc. However, their conclusion has been inappropriately generalized beyond this. In some quarters it has been accepted to the extent that some believe causation cannot be inferred anytime regression is used regardless of the research design. This stems from the earlier problem of confusing statistics with design.

Regression is a statistical procedure and should be used in relationship with some design in the Campbell & Stanley tradition (1969). A researcher should begin by asking a research question that reflects an area of interest. The study should then be designed so that it can answer that research question. The research design should include how data will be collected, how subjects will be selected, how treatments will be administered, etc. (See Fig. 1) . To the extent that this design has internal validity, one can infer causal relationships between the independent variables. If this design is internally valid, no matter what statistical technique is used to test it, such as regression, correlation, etc., one can legitimately assume causal relationships.

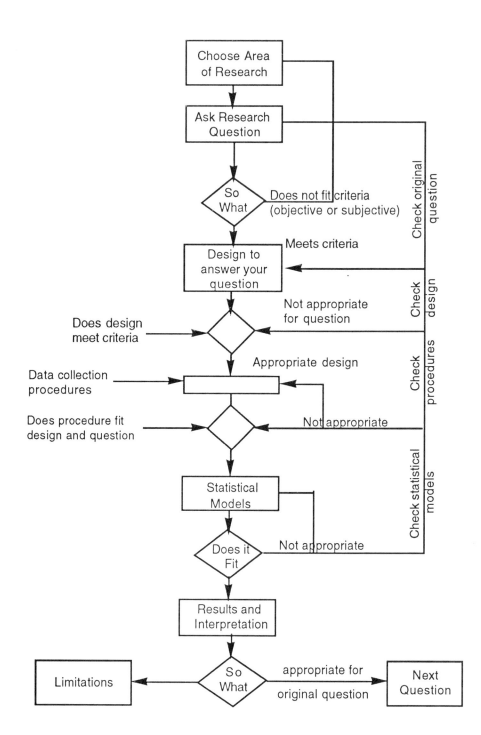

Figure 1

If the research design is ex post facto, i.e. where the independent variable is not under the control of the researchers, no matter what technique is used, one could not infer causation. All the studies on desegregation and busing such as the Coleman Report (1966), Jensen, Jencks, et al. (1972), and Gerald & Miller (in press) are of this nature. It is not technically legitimate to infer causation when the design is ex post facto. Even though a variety of statistical techniques such as path analysis as developed by Blalock (1962, 1964, 1970, & 1972) and component analysis developed by Mood (1971) have attempted to get at causal relationships of ex post facto data through the manipulation of regression techniques, one still cannot technically infer causation (Newman & Newman, 1975). Causation cannot be inferred from an ex post facto design even if you analyze data with ANOVA. These techniques tend to eliminate some rival hypotheses, making the study somewhat stronger. However, they cannot eliminate all of the rival hypotheses so the study cannot be totally internally valid and causation cannot be inferred. This is not to say that these studies are not very valuable. This simply says one cannot infer causation between the independent and dependent variable.

A necessary but not sufficient prerequisite for an experimental design is that at least one independent variable is active (under the control of the researcher). If there are no active variables in a research study, the study by definition would be ex post facto, even if the analyses is ANOVA. For instance, assume one study with a 2 x 2 factorial design looked at Black students in integrated

	Male	Female
Integrated		
Non-integrated		

schools versus Blacks who were not, and sex. If the subjects were not in the researcher's control, this study would then be an ex post facto design not a true experimental design since random assignment could not be employed. In effect, this is a straight correlational study even though one is getting A-main effects, B-main effects, and AB-interaction. It is not a true experimental design, and causation cannot be inferred. The statistical question being asked in such a design is whether there is a significant relationship between these independent variables and the criterion. Any inference about causal relationships would be inappropriate.

3. When the research question of interest is one of trends or functional relationships, one often finds the use of inappropriate statistical models which cannot accurately reflect the research questions (Newman, 1974).

When researching developmental questions, one is often more interested in functional relationships than mean differences. There is generally a continuous variable that is of interest, such as time, age, population sizes, I.Q., sex. When traditional analysis of variance is employed, continuous variables are forced into categorizations. This causes the researcher to lose degrees of freedom, and there is a potential loss of information. This loss is contingent upon how representative the categories are of the inflections in the naturally occuring continuous variable.

Since continuous variables are frequently artificially categorized, the analysis produced by such a procedure may not really reflect the researcher's question or interest. The most efficient method for writing statistical models that reflect trend or curve fitting questions is the general case of the least squares solution, linear model (Multiple Linear Regression Procedures, Newman (1974), McNeil, Kelly,

McNeil (1975), Draper & Smith (1966), Kelly, Newman, and McNeil (1973). This procedure allows one to write linear models which specifically reflect the research question.

Linear Regression is an excellent statistical tool for looking at a population trend or comparing multiple trends over time (Newman 1974, Ervin, 1975). The following examples are taken from a study comparing performance trends of underprepared students receiving special treatment with the performance of regularly admitted students requiring special assistance over four years (Ervin, 1975). Although the example provided is concerned with an educational issue at a single institution, regression is not limited to such situations. In fact, it has more flexibility than any other single statistical tool and can be used with large populations incorporating a sizable number of independent variables in a single model.

In Figure 2, a graph is presented that reflects the researcher's interest in learning if there are significant differences in trends (in this case slope differences) between Black subjects who received the Developmental Program (X_2) and Black students who did not receive the program (X_1), as it relates to their cumulative GPA.

This research question was then related as a specific hypothesis.

Hypothesis I : Are there significant differences in slopes for X_1 vs. X_2 in predicting cumulative G.P.A. for Black students at Oberlin?

The models needed to test this hypothesis are as follows:

Model 1: $X_{14} = a_0u + a_1X_1 + a_2X_2 + a_3X_3 + a_4X_4 + E_1$
Model 2: $X_{14} = a_0u + a_1X_1 + a_2X_2 + a_5X_5 + E_2$

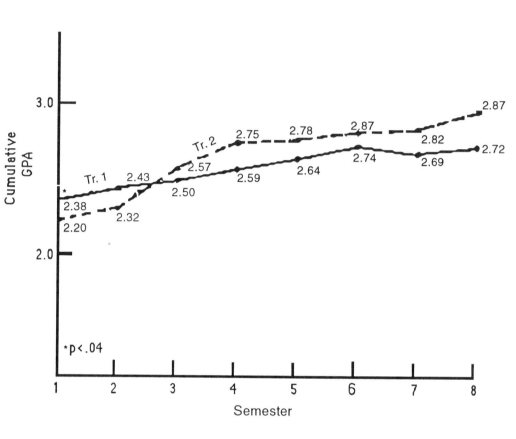

Figure 2

Table 1

CONCEPTUAL PRESENTATION OF THE THREE METHODS
FOR ADJUSTING UNEQUAL N'S

SOLUTION I	Total proportion of variance accounted for by the effect of major interest. Example: (n^2 for A = main effect)	Proportion of variance accounted for by the effect of the second most important variables holding constant the first most important variable. Example: (n^2 for B holding A constant)	Proportion of variance accounted for by the last important variable holding the first and second most important variables constant. Example: (n^2 for ns holding A and B constant)
SOLUTION II	Proportion of variance for one main effect holding the other(s) main effect(s) constant. Example: (n^2 for A-main effect holding a main effect constant)	Proportion of variance accounted for by the second main effect holding the other(s) main effect(s). Example: (n^2 for B-main effect holding constant A-main effect(s)	Proportion of variance accounted for by the interaction while holding constant all the main effects. Example: (n^2 for AB holding constant A & B main effects)
SOLUTION III	Unique variance accounted for by the first main effect holding constant the other main effect(s) and interaction(s). Example: (n^2 for A-holding constant B & AB)	Unique variance accounted for by the second main effect while holding constant the other main effects and interaction(s). Example: (n^2 for B-effect holding constant constant A & AB)	Unique variance accounted for by the interaction holding constant all the main effects. Example: (n^2 AB holding constant A & B main effects)

Where: X_{14} = cumulative GPA

X_1 = 1 if student had program, 0 otherwise

X_2 = 1 if student did not have program, 0 otherwise

X_3 = number of the semester for the subjects who had the program, 0 otherwise

X_4 = number of semesters for the subjects who did not have the program, 0 otherwise

X_5 = $X_3 + X_4$ = number of semesters for all subjects

U = unit vector, 1 if subject is in the sample, 0 otherwise

$a_0 - a_5$ = partial regression weight

$E =$ error $Y - Y$

If Model 1 is found to be significantly different from Model 2, this would indicate that there is a significantly different functional relationship (at some specific α level) between Black students who took the program and Black students who did not take the program in terms of their cumulative G.P.A.

There are an infinite number of other questions that could be asked, such as: Are there significantly different 2nd degree or 3rd functional relationships (curvilinear relationships) and are the means of the groups significantly different over all semesters or over specific semesters? etc. Then, regression models could be written that specifically reflect the questions of interest.

4. The problem of unequal Ns is really an intriguing one. It is of importance because it is a common problem for applied researchers; and, depending upon the models employed, it can produce widely different answers.

There are a variety of solutions to the unequal N's problem which can be divided into two major categories--

approximate and exact. Examples of approximate solutions are: randomly eliminating data and running the analysis on just group means, therefore, decreasing the number and power. A researcher using any of these solutions is generally aware of the limitations and problems.

What may be more misleading are the exact solutions which are all technically correct but which, like the mean, median, and mode, are answering different questions. The three exact solutions are the hierarchial model, the unadjusted main effects method, and the fitting constants method.

1. Solution I (Cohen, 1968; Williams, 1974). This requires a priori knowledge of which variables in a solution are more important or of greatest interest. With this approach, each effect is only adjusted for the effects that are of greatest interest.

2. Solution II (Williams, 1974). This solution requires that the main effects may not be adjusted while the interaction effects would be adjusted for the variance accounted for by the main effects.

3. Solution III. This method as a solution for disproportionality has been suggested and described most frequently (Winter, 1971; Schagger, 1959; and others). In this procedure, each main effect is adjusted for each other main effect, and the interactions are adjusted for all main effects. This procedure is similar to the analysis of covariance procedure suggested by Overall and Spiegel (1969).

By examining Table 1, one can see that the hierarchial method is most sensitive to detecting questions of major interest. It accounts for the total variance of the variance of the main effect, even though it overlaps with the variance of each main effect minus the variance of the other main effects. The third method of fitting constants may be most conservative of the three. It determines the unique variance accounted for by each main effect and the interaction. As one can see from Table 1, these three methods, which are all statistically accurate, are answering three different questions.

It is important to determine which of these methods are reflecting the question that we are interested in answering. One can only do this by being sensitive to one's research question and by being aware of the different statistical techniques which are more appropriate than others.

4. Still another area of concern for applied researchers is the relationship between statistical significance and N size. When the Ns are very large, any difference is likely to be statistically significant at extremely conservative alpha levels. It is the authors' position that it is to the advantage of the researchers and the implementers of research to always look at the R^2 (proportion of variance accounted for). This is a very important index to estimate the pragmatic importance of the study. This becomes especially important when the Ns are large and one finds significance at $p < .0001$. It is possible that the R^2 is accounting for 1% of the variability and 99% is unaccounted. It is important that the researcher be aware of the magnitude of effect as well as the statistical significance. Without this awareness, one increases the likelihood of inappropriately estimating the usefulness of the results.

5. Another error that sometimes occurs due to inappropriate statistical procedures is the loss of power (increase in Type II error, failure to reject a false null hypothesis). This may be due to not using a directional hypothesis when one should, especially when the N is small.

A relatively frequent error found in the literature is the statement that, "Significance was found, but in the wrong direction." This is incorrect because if it was in the wrong direction, one would have to fail to reject the null hypothesis; and therefore, conclude the findings were nonsignificant.

A possibly more dangerous error, because of its subtlety, is when a researcher makes a nondirectional test to "play it safe" and because most statistical text books suggest this procedure. He or she then might find statistical significance in the opposite direction from which the question was initially generated. (In other words, the researcher should have used a directional text, but did not.) Some researchers would then state that they have found statistical significance, but it is a conceptual error. In this case, statistical significance is likely to mean that there was something wrong with the initial logic or theory from which the hypothesis was derived, and a rethinking of the initial logic and procedure is called for. Therefore, this aspect must be carefully looked at before one can determine appropriate estimates of the findings' applicability. (See McNeil, et al., (1975), for an excellent discussion on the importance of directionality in hypotheses testing.)

Suggested Approach For Conducting Research

It has been suggested that the sequential steps for conducting research, which are presented in Figure 1, be adopted as a guide (Deitchman, Newman, Burkholder, and Sander (1975)).

At best, one should always generalize with caution. The magnitude of the relationship that one finds in a sample is quite often an overestimate of the magnitude of the effect in the population. Therefore, one should try to replicate whenever possible.

If one does not wish to or cannot replicate, the next best procedure of estimating the effect size in the population from a sample is by using shrinkage estimates. Shrinkage formulas are most appropriate as unbiased estimates of R^2 when the predictor variables are not solely selected on the basis of their initial correlation with the dependent variable (Newman, 1973).

One of the best estimates of shrinkage is a cross validation procedure. This procedure is described in detail in McNeil, et al. (1975). Three easily computed mathematical estimates of shrinkage (Wherry, McNemar, and Lord) are discussed and evaluated by Newman (1973) and Klein & Newman (1974).

In addition, anyone who is conducting or reading research should keep in mind the important difference between statistical methods and research design. As depicted in Figure 1, the first important step is to ask a relevant research question and then to decide on procedures and methods (design) which will lead to an answer for that question. This design should then be evaluated for limitations in terms of its internal and external validity. Once one establishes the basic research question and a design that is acceptable, specific hypotheses can be derived which can be statistically tested (keeping in mind that every test of significance is a test of specific hypothesis.) Linear models (regression models) can then be developed to reflect each specific hypothesis and to test each for significance. In this manner, when one gets statistical significance from a test, one knows specifically the hypothesis being tested. He or she also knows how accurately the results can be interpreted in terms of causation and its general ability, based upon the internal and external validity of the research design.

In Retrospect

We have attempted to convince trainers of researchers and the researchers themselves to beware of the Type VI Error. We believe that the examples will help the researcher to become sensitive to these types of problems. Bad research not only drives out good money but creates a large credibility gap where there should be none. From the authors' perspective, applied and theoretical research really only differ in terms of face validity which implies an attempt to answer the "So What" question of the research. It is to some extent an artificial dichotomy that applied researchers are dealing with the "So What" and the theoretical researchers are not. In reality, this is not true. Asking the "So What" question may be one of the discriminating features between good and bad research, regardless of orientation.

The authors of this paper feel that good research can benefit everyone, but poor research may harm everyone. We also believe that the suggestions presented in this paper, if followed, are likely to facilitate good research.

Chapter Summary

A Type VI Error was defined as the inconsistency between the researcher's question of interest and the statistical procedures employed to analyze the data. The reasons for these commonplace errors vary. They may be the result of courses which fail to emphasize logical analysis as a prerequisite to the statistical analysis, confusion caused by teaching traditional analysis of variance without differentiating between the statistic and the design, the misconception that causation can only be inferred from traditional analysis of variance, and forgetting that causation is a design question, not a statistical one.

A major problem discussed was disproportionality (unequal Ns). The three exact solutions, hierarchial models, unadjusted main effects, and fitting constants, were discussed in terms of conceptual questions and answers. Stress was placed on understanding that each solution is answering different questions. Therefore, one should not be concerned with which model is more statistically accurate, but with which one is more reflective of the researcher's question.

In dealing with a research question, one must consider practical as well as statistical significance. This means that N size, and effect size as well as probability level and power, must be considered.

Finally, a procedure is suggested for conducting research along with a flowchart. We feel that following the procedures outlined in the flow chart will help researchers avoid some of the pitfalls that lead to Type VI errors.

CHAPTER IX

wIZard!

Software Companion to

Conceptual Statistics for Beginners

To obtain the disk for the wIZard program, contact the author at:

7261 Engle Road
Suite 202
Cleveland, OH 44130
216-826-0444
FAX: 216-826-3606

The Software Companion to
Conceptual Statistics for Beginners

What is wIZard!

wIZard! is a personal computer program written especially for this textbook, Conceptual Statistics for Beginners. It will run on IBM or IBM-compatible personal computers only. The examples in the book were generated from the data files on this disk, so you can duplicate the examples on your own machine as you study. wIZard! allows you to focus on what you want to do with the data and to avoid the computational mechanics--this is in keeping with the "Conceptual" part of the title of the book. You can use your own data and perform a number of statistical analyses, based on the research question you ask, view the results on the monitor or print a copy to study later. wIZard! is not designed to be a complete data analysis system, so you won't find some features which are standard on larger statistical packages.

This Chapter

The aim of this chapter is to present some information which you need to know before you begin using wIZard!. In addition, it will serve as a handbook to which you can refer as you run the program. This chapter assumes you already know:

1. How to turn on the computer and "boot" it with the Disk Operating System (DOS).

2. How many disk drives you have, where they are, and what ll they are named.

3. How to format a floppy disk and how to make a copy of a disk (make a "backup").

If you are not sure about any of these, you will probably want to review the DOS manual or talk with a knowledge-able friend before you proceed.

Back Up your wlZard! Program Disk

The very first thing you should do is make a copy (backup) of the wlZard! program disk and put the original away in a safe place. Use the copy for your day-to-day work. If anything happens to the copy, you always have the original available to make another copy. You are free to make as many copies of wlZard! for your own use as you wish. In order to use wlZard!'s on-line help, you must have DOS on the same disk as wlZard!--follow these steps:

1. Format a floppy with the /s option. For example, if the DOS disk is in drive A:, put the blank disk in B: and type FORMAT B: /S. The "/s" option installs a copy of your DOS on the formatted disk. Because of the size of the new MS-DOS version 5, this will not work with a 360Kb floppy--there is not enough room for both DOS and wlZard! on the same disk. Use an older version of DOS, a bigger disk, or format without the "/s" option.

2. Put the wlZard disk in drive A: and type COPY A:*.* B: <ENTER> . This copies all the program files from the wlZard! disk to the disk in drive B:.

3. The newly-formatted disk will boot your computer and also run wIZard!.

If you have a hard drive (usually drive C:), copy the wIZard! disk to your hard drive. You might want to make a special directory for wIZard! to keep all the parts of the program together. Assuming wIZard! is in drive A:

C: <ENTER>	change to drive C:
MD \WIZDIR <ENTER>	make a directory called wizdir
COPY A:*.* C:\WIZDIR	copy everything from a: to c:\wizdir

Data Disks

It is a good idea to keep your data on a separate disk from the wIZard! disk, since wIZard! and DOS take up a fair amount of disk space all by themselves. If you do, respond with the appropriate drive and path when wIZard! asks for a file name. For example, if wIZard! is in Drive A: and your data disk is in B:, then the filename might be B:MYFILE.DAT. Read more about DRIVES and PATHS in your DOS users manual.

Changing Disks

Once wIZard! is loaded and running, you may remove the program disk and replace it with a data disk. The program disk must be in the drive only when it changes program segments, such as running on-line help or Options 5 and 6 (T-Tests and ANOVAS), or when returning to the Main Menu after having run those options. In each case, wIZard! checks to see if the proper disk is in the drive and warns you if it cannot locate the rest of itself. If you see the messages or,

Can't find WIZARD.EXE!

Can't find TANOVA.EXE!

you should check to be certain the wIZard! disk is back in the drive you started it from.

Entering Data into wIZard!

    If you are using this disk purely as a study aid to Conceptual Statistics, the data supplied on the disk is all you need to begin. If you want to analyze your own data, you will have to enter it yourself. For each option (except the two versions of Chi-Square), wIZard! will ask you how the data are to be entered--via the (K)eyboard, or read from a disk (F)ile. For small data sets, you may find it more convenient to enter the numbers directly on the keyboard. For larger sets, it is almost always easier to use a text editor or word processor to set up a data file beforehand because there is no way to edit direct keyboard entries once they are made.

    It is important to remember that data files must be in DOS "text" (also called ASCII) format. ASCII files do not have the special, unprintable characters in them that word processing programs use (for example) to determine where to hyphenate a word or to begin and end a run of underlining. If you can list the file to the screen with the DOS TYPE command and all the characters are readable, the file is in ASCII. If you get gibberish, Greek characters or smiley-faces mixed with a few readable characters, it is not.

Most word processors can write a DOS "text" file rather than saving the file in the usual way, so consult your particular word processing program's manual. Look for keywords such as "Text file" or "ASCII file". Read more about data files under "Option 8: Convert text to wIZard! files," below.

Missing Data

Not all data sets are complete in every respect. Subjects may drop out of your study; information may be uncollected or (more aggravating) misplaced. If you enter data by way of the keyboard, you must make sure beforehand that you only enter cases for which you have complete data. You cannot enter a "missing data" marker from the keyboard. If you use a word processor to set up a data file, missing data MUST be coded by entering "-99" (a minus sign and the numerals 99, without any spaces separating them).

The wIZard! Program Options

The remainder of this chapter presents each of the program options in outline form. You will learn what the program expects from you as input and what results you will get, as well as any cautions, tricks, or special terms that might not be immediately obvious. From now on, <ENTER> means, "Press the Enter key." The program itself will prompt you for the ENTER key by displaying a left-pointing arrow that looks like the one on the keyboard.

General Information

The various options are designed to be similar in their execution, so if you can run one, you can run them all. A few points are worth mentioning, though.

1. The program will present results one "screenful" at a time. You must press < ENTER> when prompted to see more. If you print the results, the printer will run until all results have been printed.

2. When wIZard! asks you for a filename, you can simply <ENTER> to automatically select the appropriate example from the book--any other name must be typed out in full, with path, if necessary.

3. Data can be represented both NUMERICALLY, like 1, 5, .09, or with ALPHA characters like M, T1, or FEMALE. You will gain in clarity if (for the T-test and ANOVA options) you enter ALPHA characters to identify groups, such as M for MALE or T3 for TREATMENT 3, since these will be printed out on the printout, making identification of contrasted groups easier.

   If you code data NUMERIC (for example, 0 if FEMALE and 1 if MALE), then you can get a frequency count of 1's and 0's, or even correlate them with some other variable. If you code "F" and "M" respectively, it is impossible to do arithmetic with the data beyond simple counting. What you gain in clarity you may lose in flexibility. In addition, if the data is actually coded "M" in the file and you reply "m" to a data prompt, wIZard! will never see any uppercase "M" data as being a part of the group you really wanted to select. A little thought before you code your data will help you ask the most appropriate questions of it.

4. If, for whatever reason, you need to stop wIZard! in the middle of the program, hit the Ctrl and ESC keys at the same time (you may also have to tap the ENTER key). You will immediately return to DOS.

5. wIZard! will detect a math coprocessor chip if one is present in the machine.

Starting wIZard! from a Floppy Disk

Put the wIZard! program disk in drive A: and boot your machine. At the A: prompt, type wIZard and <ENTER>. It will take a few seconds before you get the greeting screen. Remember to return the program disk to drive A: should you remove it for any reason. Remember--in order to use wIZard!'s on-line help, you must have DOS on the same disk as wIZard! See "Backing up your wIZard! program disk above.

Starting wIZard! from a Hard Disk

Change to the wIZard! directory and type wIZard! <ENTER>.

The Greeting Screen

The greeting screen is simply that; it lets you know you are running wIZard! and waits for you to press a key to begin the working part of the program.

Option 1: Means. Standard Deviations. Correlations

1. Select (M) to compute means or (C) to compute correlations. If you select (M)eans, the program produces a correlation matrix anyway, but if you select (C)orrelations, that's all you will get. Note that at this point, you may "a" to quit and return to the main menu.

2. Choose whether data will be entered on the (K)eyboard or read from a (F)ile. Keyboard entry restricts you to 20 variables--you may name them, or wIZard! defaults to "VAR1," "VAR2," and so on.

3. For Keyboard data entry: follow screen prompts.

4. For datafile input: wIZard! reads the file and presents means. Respond "Y" or "N" to see the correlation matrix. This can take some time with large data files.

5. For all: respond "Y" or "N" at the prompt to print the results. Make sure the printer is on and connected to the PC. Respond "Y" or "N" to do another run.

Option 2: Frequencies

1. For Keyboard data entry: follow screen prompts.

2. For datafile input: Specify file. Step through the variable names using "N" until variable you want to tally is presented. Select with "Y," or quit the whole thing with "Q".

3. Again, you may print the frequency distribution and do another run without returning to the main menu.

Option 3: IxJ Chi-Square

1. This option assumes you already know the frequencies of each cell in the chi-square design and want to compute the probability of non-independence. You supply the number of rows and columns, then type in the observed frequencies as you are prompted. wIZard! calculates the expected frequencies and generates the necessary statistics. You may print the results.

Option 4: Chi-Square Goodness-of-Fit

1. Again, you must know the frequencies occurring in each cell. After you have entered the frequencies, however, wIZard! asks you whether you want the program to calculate the expected frequencies (C), or for you to supply them (S). If you choose (C), let the program calculate, the expected frequency for each cell is the number of observations divided by the number of cells. If you supply the expected values, you may, of course, make them anything you wish.

Option 5: T-Tests -- Independent

wIZard! first loads the T-Test/ANOVA part of the program.

1. For Keyboard data entry: follow screen prompts.

2. For datafile input: wIZard! first asks for the variable that distinguishes between the two groups. Cycle through the variable as they are presented and select the group

variable, then type in the values which will define the selection scheme. For example, if the group variable is EXTRAVERSION and the selection values are 3 and 8, then all those subjects having an extraversion score of exactly 3 will be group 1; all those with an extraversion score of exactly 8 will be group 2. If the selection values are "T1" and "T3," only those subjects in groups T1 and T3 will participate in the analysis.

3. Select the variable to test (the dependent variable). wIZard! calculates the T-statistic and displays the results.

Option 5: T-Tests -- Dependent

wIZard! first loads the T-Test/ANOVA part of the program.

1. For Keyboard data entry: follow screen prompts.

2. For datafile input: wIZard! already knows that each two sets of scores come from the same person, so all you have to supply is which variables you want to test. Whether it makes logical sense to test any two particular means is up to you.

Option 6: Analysis of Variance -- One-Way

wIZard! first loads the T-Test/ANOVA part of the program.

1. For Keyboard data entry: follow screen prompts.

2. For datafile input: proceed as you would with the Independent T-Test, but note that ANOVA can test more than two group means. Cycle through the variables, and select the variable that identifies the groups.

3. Enter the codes that distinguish the groups. Remember that any ALPHA labels must be exact.

4. Cycle through the variables again and identify the dependent variable.

5. wIZard! calculates results and presents some tables.

6. After the ANOVA results table, press <ENTER> to see the means and SDs of the groups. Make a note of these, because you will have to know the group means to make sense out of the rest of the results.

7. <ENTER>, and wIZard! gives you the option of running multiple comparisons (Schieffe test) to identify which means are significantly different. Answer "N," and you are asked if you want to print the results. Answer "Y," and...

8. Supply the alpha level you want to hold constant. <ENTER> defaults to .05.

9. The Probability Matrix can be read something like a correlation table (it is not, though). The probability that the mean of group N is NOT significantly different from the mean of group M is found by looking at the number at the intersection of row N, column M. The alert reader will note that the probabilities on the main diagonal are all 1.0 -- no mean is different from itself.

10. <ENTER>, to see the Significant Differences Among means at the alpha you chose. Groups of means on the

same line are not significantly different from one another, given the choice of alpha. Means on different lines are different enough from one another to reject the null.

Option 6: Analysis of Variance -- Two-Way

wIZard! first loads the T-Test/ANOVA part of the program.

1. For Keyboard data entry: follow screen prompts.

2. For datafile input: this is similar to the One-Way design, except in this case you must supply selection variables for two dimensions, the ROW variable, and the COLUMN variable. One-way analysis of variance allows you to test (say) for differences among three different treatments. Two-way analysis of variance allows consideration of another grouping variable, for example, gender.

3. Cycle through the variables and select the ROW variable. Enter the codes which differentiate the groups.

4. Do the same for the COLUMN variable. Note that ROWS and COLUMNS are sometimes called the A Main Effect and the B Main Effect respectively.

5. Cycle through the variables and select the dependent variable. wIZard! calculates the rest.

Option 7: Multiple Linear Regression

1. For Keyboard data entry: follow screen prompts.

2. For datafile input: First, cycle through the variables and select all of the variables you need for this particular run. Exit this VARIABLE SELECTION section by choosing option "S," for STOP selecting. Later on you will select subsets of those you have chosen for actual analysis, but you cannot add any variables without starting over, so make sure to select all of the variables you want.

3. The program reads the variables and does some internal computations. If you have a large datafile, this can take a while. Note that ALPHA variables will not give meaningful results. Don't use them here.

4. Cycle through the variables you have selected for the run and pick the dependent variable.

5. Cycle through the remaining variables and pick as many predictors as you want. You must pick at least one. When you have selected all the predictor for that run, choose "S" to STOP selecting variables and to proceed with the analysis.

6. wIZard! calculates R, the R Square, and probability. <ENTER>.

7. wIZard! displays the name of the predictor, the unstandardized regression coefficients, and the standardized regression coefficients (beta weights). Print them if you wish.

8. (Optional) You may write the results to a MODEL FILE on the disk to use with the "Model Comparisons" part of regression. How to set up MLR models is beyond the scope of this chapter. Suffice to say that wIZard! allows you to test models against one another or against the special case of the RESTRICTED model being set to an R-square of 0 (MODEL99).

9. If you choose to run Model Comparisons, note that wIZard! does not check for inconsistencies in the data. For example, you may compare models from two different datasets without wIZard! generating an error message. It is up to you to make sure your data is consistent.

Option 8: ASCII to wIZard! File Conversion

1. This option reads DOS Text files and converts them to wIZard! format. wIZard! cannot read any file until it has been converted. If you want to type your data directly in wIZard! format, use a text editor to see exactly what a wIZard! file looks like, but it is much easier to let wIZard! do the conversion for you.

2. Enter your data so that each row is a subject, each column, a variable. You must separate each variable by a comma. For example, here is a five subject, three variable file consisting of Test 1 raw score, Test 2 raw score, and gender coded NUMERIC (0 if female, 1 otherwise):

23,45,0
35, 78, 1
21, 56, 0
12, -99, 0   (Note the "-99", indicating missing Test 2 data)
20, 49, 1

Here is the same file with gender information coded ALPHA:

23, 45, F
35, 78, M
21, 56, F
12, -99, F
20, 49, M

3. For datafile input: <ENTER> the name of the ASCII file to be converted.

4. <ENTER> the name of the wIZard! file you want to hold the converted data.

5. <ENTER> the number of subjects, or N size.

6. <ENTER> the number of variables.

7. wIZard! will sequentially name the variables VAR1, VAR2, VAR3, and so on. You may enter your own names for them at this point. <ENTER> for the automatic naming default, or press "N" to name them yourself.

Option 9: Help Menu

1. Select on-line help by pressing the appropriate key. Note that Conceptual Statistics page references are included in the on-line help whenever possible. You may also browse through this manual while in the help mode.

REFERENCES

Ahamann, J. S., & Glock, M. D. (1971). Evaluating pupil growth: Principles of tests and measurements (4th ed.). Boston: Allyn.

Asher, H. B. (1983). Causal modeling (2nd ed.). Sage University Paper Series on Quantitative Applications in the Social Science, 07-003. Beverly Hills, CA: Sage.

Bentler, P. M. (1989). EQS structural equations program manual. Los Angeles: BMDP Statistical Software.

Bray, J. H., & Maxwell, S. E. (1985). Multivariate analysis of variance. Sage University Paper Series on Quantitative Applications in the Social Science, 07-054. Beverly Hills, CA: Sage.

Cronbach, L. J. (1960). Essentials of psychological testing (2nd ed.). New York: Harper & Row Publishers.

Downie, N. M., & Heath, R. W. (1959). Basic statistical methods. New York: Harper & Brother Publishers.

Dunteman, G. E. (1989). Principal components analysis. Sage University Paper Series on Quantitative Applications in the Social Science, 07-069. Beverly Hills, CA: Sage.

Ebel, R. L. (1965). Measuring educational achievement. New Jersey: Prentice Hall, Inc.

Educational Testing Service. (1965). Short-cut statistics for teacher-made tests. Princeton, NJ: Author.

Edwards, A. L. (1960). Statistical methods for behavioral sciences. New York: Rinehart & Co., Inc.

Edwards, A. L. (1972). Experimental design in psychological research (4th ed.). New York: Holt, Rinehart & Winston, Inc.

Ferguson, G. A. (1966). Statistical analysis in psychology and education (2nd ed.). New York: McGraw-Hill.

Flury, B. (1988). Common principal components and related multivariate models. New York: Wiley.

Harris, R. J. (1985). A primer of multivariate statistics (2nd ed.). Orlando, FL: Academic Press.

Joreskog, K. G., & Sorbom, D. (1988). LISREL 7: A guide to the program and applications. Chicago: SPSS.

Kaufman, L., & Rousseeuw, P. J. (1990). Finding groups in data: An introduction to cluster analysis. New York: Wiley.

Kerlinger, F. N. (1973). Foundations of behavioral research (2nd ed.). New York: Holt, Rinehart & Winston, Inc.

Klecka, W. R. (1980). Discriminant analysis. Sage University Paper Series on Quantitative Applications in the Social Science, 07-019. Beverly Hills, CA: Sage.

Lomax, R. G. (1992). Statistical concepts. New York: Longman.

McNemar, Q. (1963). Psychological statistics (3rd ed.). New York: John Wiley & Sons, Inc.

Newman, I., Frye, B. J., & Newman, C. (1973). An introduction to the basic concepts of measurement and evaluation. Akron, OH: The University of Akron.

Popham, J. W. (1967). Educational statistics: Use and interpretation. New York: Harper & Row, Publishers.

Swaminathan, H. (1989). Interpreting the results of multivariate analysis of variance. In B. Thompson (Ed.), Advances in social science methodology (Vol. 1, pp. 205-232). Greenwich, CT: JAI Press.

Tatsuoka, M. M. (1988). Multivariate analysis (2nd ed.). New York: Macmillan.

Thompson, B. (1984). Canonical correlation analysis: Uses and interpretation. Sage University Paper Series on Quantitative Applications in the Social Science, 07-047. Beverly Hills, CA: Sage.

APPENDIX A

TESTS OF SIGNIFICANCE FOR VARIOUS

TYPES OF DATA AND SAMPLES

A TABLE OF SUGGESTED TESTS OF SIGNIFCANT FOR VARIOUS TYPES OF DATA AND SAMPLES

*Kind of data	Single Group	Two Samples (Independent)	Two Samples Correlated (Dependent)	More Than Two Groups Independent	More Than Two Groups Dependent
Nominal (Category or Frequency data)	X^2 (Chi sq.) (for a single sample) Fisher Exact test	X^2 (Chi sq.) (Multi-sample)	McNemar tests	X^2 (Chi sq.) (Multi-sample)	Cochran Q Test
Ordinal (Rank data)	X^2 (Chi sq.) (for a single sample) Kilmogorov-Smirnov	X^2 (Chi sq.) (Multi-sample) Mann-Witney U test	Matched pair signed ranks	Kruskal-Wallis X^2 (Chi sq.)	Friedman analysis of variance
Interval or Ratio data	Single sample t-test	Independent sample t-test	Dependent t-test (correlated t-test)	One-way F-test	Repeated measures F-test

*The non-parametric tests are descripted in great detail in Siegel (1956). However, it is the author's opinion (supported by much empirical data) that quite often the use of non-parametric statistic is unnecessary and generally less powerful.

APPENDIX B

COMPUTATION OF A CORRELATION COEFFICIENT

AN EXAMPLE OF HOW TO COMPUTE CORRELATION COEFFICIENT

USING A CONCEPTUAL FORMULA

This appendix contains a computational example of:

A.   How to calculate r using Z scores along with

computations of the mean and standard deviations

need to compute a Z score.

B.   The raw score formula for computing r.

$$r = \frac{\Sigma(Z_x)\ (Z_y)}{N - 1}$$

where: r   is the correlation coefficient

Σ is summation

Z_x is each score of x changed to Z scores

Z_y is each score of y changed to Z scores

( ) ( )   is multiplication symbols

N   is the number of pairs scores (X or Y)

Subject	X	Y
# 1	10	8
# 2	6	5
# 3	4	5
# 4	8	9
# 5	7	11

First have to calculate Z_x score for x and then Z_y score for y.

for X

$$Z_X = \frac{X - \overline{X}}{S}$$

$$\overline{X} = \frac{\Sigma X}{N}$$

$$S = \sqrt{\frac{\Sigma \chi^2}{N - 1}} \qquad \chi = X - \overline{X}$$

$N = 5$

$$\overline{X} = \frac{35}{5} = 7$$

Subject	Score X	χ_1 $(X - \overline{X})$	χ^2	Zy $\quad \frac{(Z = X - \overline{X})}{S}$
1	1 0	3	9	$(10-7)/2.24 \;=\; 1.34$
2	6	- 1	1	$(6-7)/2.24 \;=\; -.45$
3	4	- 3	9	$(4-7)/2.24 \;=\; -1.34$
4	8	1	1	$(8-7)/2.24 \;=\; .45$
5	7	0	0	$(7-7)/2.24 \;=\; 0.0$

$\Sigma X = 35 \qquad \Sigma \chi = 0 \qquad \Sigma \chi^2 = 20$

$\overline{X} = 7 \qquad\qquad S = 2.24$

$$S = \sqrt{\frac{\Sigma \chi^2}{N - 1}} \;=\; \sqrt{\frac{2 0}{5 - 1}} \;=\; \sqrt{5} \;=\; 2.24$$

$$\text{for } Y$$

$$Z_y = \frac{Y - \overline{Y}}{S}$$

$$\overline{Y} = \frac{\Sigma Y}{N}$$

$$S = \sqrt{\frac{\Sigma y^2}{N-1}} = \sqrt{\frac{27.2}{4}} = 2.6$$

$$y = Y - \overline{Y}$$

$$N = 5$$

$$\overline{Y} = \frac{38}{5} = 7.6$$

Subject	Score Y	y $(Y - \overline{Y})$	y^2	Zy
1	8	.4	.16	(8-7.6)/2.6 = .15
2	5	-.26	6.76	(5-7.6)/2.6 = -1.00
3	5	-2.6	6.76	(5-7.6)/2.6 = -1.00
4	9	1.4	1.96	(9-7.6)/2.6 = .54
5	10	3.4	11.56	(11-7.6)/2.6 = 1.31

$$\Sigma Y = 38 \quad \Sigma y = 0 \quad \Sigma y^2 = 27.2$$

$$\overline{Y} = 7.6$$

$$Z_y = \frac{Y - \bar{Y}}{S_y} \qquad S_y = \sqrt{\frac{\Sigma y^2}{N-1}} \quad = \quad \sqrt{\frac{27.2}{5-1}}$$

$$= \sqrt{6.8} \quad = \quad 2.6$$

$$r = \frac{\Sigma(Z_x)\ (Z_y)}{N-1} \quad = \quad \frac{2.23}{4} \quad = \quad .56$$

Subject	Z_x	Z_y	$\Sigma(Z_x)\ (Z_y)$
1	1.34	.15	.20
2	-.45	-1.00	.45
3	-1.34	-1.00	1.34
4	.45	.54	.24
5	0	1.31	0.00
			2.23 = $\Sigma(Z_x)\ (Z_y)$

Note: If you already have the means and standard deviations and there are not too many scores, this procedures is relatively efficient.

An example of how to compute a correlation using a computational formula:

$$r = \frac{N \, \Sigma(X)\,(Y) \; - \; (\Sigma X)\,(\Sigma Y)}{\sqrt{[N\Sigma X^2 - (\Sigma X)]^2 \; [N\Sigma Y^2 - (\Sigma Y)^2]}}$$

Subjects	Score X	Score Y	(X)(Y)	X^2	Y^2
1	10	8	80	100	64
2	6	5	30	36	25
3	4	5	20	16	25
4	8	9	72	64	81
5	7	11	77	49	121

N=5 ΣX=35 ΣY=38 $\Sigma(X)(Y)$=279 ΣX^2=265 ΣY^2=316

$(\Sigma X)\,(\Sigma Y) = (35)\,(38) = 1330$

$(\Sigma X)^2 = (35)^2 = 1225$ $(\Sigma Y)^2 = (38)^2 = 1444$

$$\frac{5\,(279) - (35)\,(38)}{\sqrt{[5(265)-(35)^2][5\,(316)-(38)^2}} = \frac{1395 - 1330}{\sqrt{(1325-1225)\,(1580)-1444)}}$$

$= 65/ \sqrt{(100)\,(136)} \;\; = \;\; 65/ \sqrt{13600} \;\; = \;\; 65/116.62 \;\; = \;\; .56$

$$r = .56$$

APPENDIX C

COMPUTATION OF A CHI^2

AN EXAMPLE OF HOW TO COMPUTE A Chi^2

Example 1 $\chi2 = \sum \dfrac{(0\text{-}E)^2}{E}$

χ^2 = Chi Square
$\sum$ = summation sign
0 = observed scored
E = expected score (expected by chance)
df = (# of groups - 1)
      = 2-1 = 1

Let's assume that we have 90 students with 70 students enrolled in class 1; 20 in Class 2. We are interested in knowing if there is significant difference in enrollment (at α = .05).

$0_1 = 70$ $E_1 = 45$

What we could expect
by chance alone

$0_2 = 20$ $E_2 = 45$

df = 1

$\chi2 = \sum \dfrac{(0\text{-}E)^2}{E} = \dfrac{(70 - 45)^2}{45} + \dfrac{(20 - 45)^2}{45}$

$= \dfrac{625}{45} + \dfrac{625}{45} = 13.9 + 13.9 = 27.8$

$\chi^2 = 27.8$ df = 1   Significant

There are significantly more students enrolled in Class 1 than in Class 2.

<u>Example 2</u> 0_1 = 40 observed score

0_2 = 28 observed score

0_3 = 50 observed score

0_4 = 18 observed score

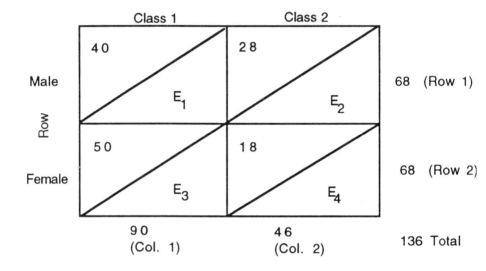

E_1 = (Row 1) * (Col 1)/total

  = (68 * 90)/136 = 45

E_2 = (Row 1) * (Col 2)/total

  = (68 * 46)/136 = 23

E_3 = (Row 2) * (Col 1)/total

  = (68 * 90)/136 = 45

E_4 = (Row 2) * (Col 2)/total

  = (68 * 46) 136 = 23

df = (# or Row - 1) (# of Col - 1)

  = (2-1) (2-1) = 1

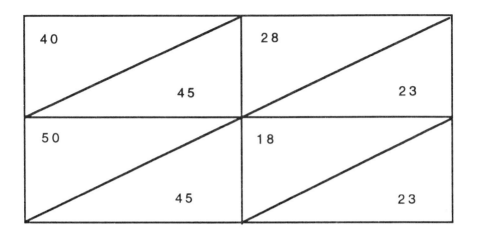

$$\chi^2 = \sum \frac{(0-E)^2}{E} = \frac{(40-45)^2}{45} + \frac{(28-23)^2}{23} + \frac{(50-45)^2}{45} + \frac{(18-23)^2}{23}$$

$$\chi^2 = \frac{25}{45} + \frac{25}{23} + \frac{25}{45} + \frac{25}{23} = 3.285$$

$df = 1 \quad \chi^2 = 3.285 \quad$ non significant ($\alpha = .05$)

APPENDIX D

COMPUTATION OF AN INDEPENDENT T-TEST

AN EXAMPLE OF HOW TO COMPUTE A t-TEST

The appendix contains computational examples of:

A. t-test for independent samples
B. t-test for dependent (correlational) samples

t-test for independent samples

Given the following data:

Control Subjects	Group Scores	Experimental Subjects	Group Scores	
# 1	5	# 6	0	df = (# subjects) - 2
# 2	7	# 7	2	
# 3	9	# 8	33	= 10 - 2 = 8
# 4	9	# 9	4	
# 5	10	# 10	6	df = 8

$N_1 = 5$ $X_C = 8$ (mean) $N_2 = 5$ $X_E = 3$ (mean)

$S_C = 2$ (standard deviation) $S_E = 2.24$ (standard deviation)
          for control   for experimental

$$t = \frac{\overline{X}_C - \overline{X}_E}{SD_{\overline{X}}} = \frac{(\text{mean of Control}) - (\text{mean of Exp})}{(\text{standard error of difference between mean})}$$

$$S^2_C = S^2_C = \frac{\text{standard deviation squared}}{\text{\# of subjects in group 1 (control)}}$$
$$\overline{N_E}$$

$$SD_{\overline{X}} = \sqrt{S^2_C + S^2_E} \longrightarrow S^2_E = S^2_E = \frac{\text{standard deviation squared}}{\text{\# of subjects in group 2}}$$
$$\overline{N_E} \quad \text{(experimental)}$$

$$SD_{\overline{X}} = .8 + 1.8 = 1.6$$

$$S^2{}_C = \frac{S^2{}_C}{N_C} = \frac{(2)^2}{5} = \frac{4}{5} = .8$$

$$S^2{}_E = \frac{S^2{}_C}{N_E} = \frac{(3)^2}{5} = \frac{9}{5} = 1.8$$

$$t = \frac{\overline{X}_C - \overline{X}_E}{S_{DX}} = \frac{8-3}{1.6} = \frac{5}{1.6} = 3.3 \text{ significant at } \alpha = .05$$

APPENDIX E

COMPUTATON OF A DEPENDENT T-TEST

Example of t-test for dependent sample

$$t = \sqrt{\dfrac{N-1}{\left[\dfrac{N \Sigma d^2}{(\Sigma d)^2}\right] - 1}}$$

N = # of pairs (# of subjects taking both tests, etc.)

d = difference between means

Subjects	Test #1	Test #2	d	d²
# 1	25	16	9	81
# 2	25	11	14	196
# 3	23	13	10	100
# 4	20	14	6	36
# 5	20	7	13	169
# 6	17	30	-13	169
# 7	16	8	8	64
# 8	14	15	-1	1
# 9	13	5	8	64
#10	11	6	5	25
			d=59	d²=905

df = (# of pairs)

df = 10 - 1 = 9

df = 9

$$t = \sqrt{\dfrac{10-1}{\dfrac{[10 \ (905)]}{59^2} - 1}} = \sqrt{\dfrac{9}{\left[\dfrac{9050}{59^2}\right] - 1}} = \sqrt{\dfrac{9}{\left[\dfrac{9050}{3481}\right] - 1}} = \sqrt{\dfrac{9}{(2.6) - 1}}$$

$$= \sqrt{\dfrac{9}{1.6}} = \sqrt{5.637} = 2.38$$

df = 9   significant at α = .05

APPENDIX F

COMPUTATION OF A ONE-WAY ANALYSIS

OF VARIANCE

AN EXAMPLE OF HOW TO COMPUTE A ONE-WAY ANALYSIS OF VARIANCE

Treatment #1   Treatment #2   Treatment #3

Total SS = Between SS + Within SS

$$\text{Total SS} = \Sigma\chi^2 = \Sigma x^2 - \frac{(\Sigma x_{tot})^2}{N}$$

$$\text{Between SS} = \left[\sum \frac{(\Sigma X)^2}{n}\right] - \frac{(\Sigma X_{Tot})^2}{N}$$

Within SS for
each group
$$= \Sigma\chi^2 = \Sigma x^2 - \frac{(\Sigma X)^2}{n}$$

N = total number of subjects in all groups

n_i = number of subjects in group i

Subj.	Treatment #1		Treatment #2		Treatment #3	
	X_1	X^2_1	X_2	X^2_2	X_3	X^2_3
1	9	81	6	36	4	16
2	12	144	8	64	4	16
3	12	144	9	81	5	25
4	13	169	11	121	9	81
5	14	196	11	121	8	64
	$\Sigma X_1=60$	$\Sigma X^2_1=734$	$\Sigma X_2=45$	$\Sigma X^2_2=423$	$\Sigma X_3=30$	$\Sigma X^2_3=202$

$$\underline{Total\ SS} = \Sigma X^2 - \frac{(\Sigma X_{Tot})^2}{N}$$

$$\Sigma X^2 = \Sigma X^2_1 + \Sigma X^2_2 + \Sigma X^2_3 = 734 + 423 + 202 = 1359$$

$$\frac{(\Sigma X_{Tot})^2}{N} = \frac{(\Sigma X_1 + \Sigma X_2 + \Sigma X_3)^2}{n_1 + n_2 + n_3} = \frac{(60+34+20)^2}{15} =$$

$$\frac{(135)^2}{15} = \frac{18225}{15} = 1215$$

$$1359 - 1215 = 144 = Total\ SS$$

$$\underline{Between\ SS} = \left[\Sigma\frac{(\Sigma X)^2}{n}\right] - \frac{(\Sigma X_{Tot})^2}{N}$$

$$\Sigma\frac{(\Sigma X)^2}{n} = \frac{(\Sigma X_1)^2}{n_1} + \frac{(\Sigma X_2)^2}{n_2} + \frac{(\Sigma X_3)^2}{n_3}$$

$$= \frac{(60)^2}{5} + \frac{(45)^2}{5} + \frac{(30)^2}{5} = \frac{3600}{5} + \frac{2025}{5} + \frac{900}{5}$$

$$= 720 + 405 + 180 = 1305$$

$$\frac{(\Sigma X_{Tot})^2}{N} = 1215$$

$$1305 - 1215 = 90 = Between\ SS$$

Total SS = Between SS + Within SS

Within SS = Total SS - Between SS

$$144 - 90 = Within\ SS$$

$$= 54\ Within\ SS$$

Source	SS	df	ms	F	Sign.
Between (Treatments)	90	(# of gr.)-1 3 - 1 = 2	BSS/dfB = 90/2 = 45	mS_b/mS_w =45/4.5=10	S
Within	54	# of subjects - # of groups 15 - 3 = 12	WSS/dfw = 54/12 = 4.5		
Total	144	N_{Tot} - 1 = 14			

$$\text{df Between} = (\text{The number of groups}) - 1 = 3\text{-}1 = 2$$

$$\text{df Within} = (\text{The number of subjects}) - (\text{number of groups})$$
$$= 15 - 3 = 12$$

$$\text{df Total} = (\text{Total number of subjects}) - 1 = 15\text{-}1 = 14$$

$$\text{MS (Between)} = (\text{SS Between})/\text{df Between} = 90/2 = 45$$

$$\text{MS (within)} = (\text{SS Within})/\text{df Within} = 54/12 = 4.5$$

$$F = (\text{MS Between})/\text{MS Within} = (45)/4.5 = 10$$

Look up the F with $df_1 = 2$ and $df_2 = 12$

Please see Appendix R for a brief discussion and an example of a correction for multiple comparisons.

APPENDIX G

COMPUTATION OF A 3 X 3 FACTORIAL ANALYSIS

AN EXAMPLE OF HOW TO COMPUTE A

3 x 3 FACTORIAL ANALYSIS OF VARIANCE

A (Methods

	Method X 1	Method X 2	Method X 3	
Low	9 12 12 X_1 13 14 — $X_1 = 60$	4 8 9 X_2 11 12 — $X_2 = 45$	9 4 5 X_3 9 8 — $X_3 = 30$	$X_{Row_1} = 13$
Med.	8 7 10 X_4 11 14 — $X_4 = 50$	12 12 13 X_5 13 15 — $X_5 = 65$	7 6 9 X_6 10 13 — $X_6 = 45$	$X_{Row_2} = 16$
Hi	5 5 6 X_7 10 9 — $X_7 = 35$	6 8 9 X_8 10 12 — $X_8 = 45$	9 11 11 X_9 12 12 — $X_9 = 55$	$X_{Row_3} = 13$

B (IQ)

$\Sigma X_{Col(1)} = 145$ $\Sigma X_{Col(2)} = 155$ $\Sigma X_{Col(3)} = 130$ $\Sigma X_{Tot} = 430$

N_{Tot} $= 45$

SS_{Total} $= \Sigma X^2 - \dfrac{(\Sigma X_{Tot})^2}{N_{Tot}}$

SS_A $= \Sigma \dfrac{(\text{ of all A's})^2}{n_i} - \dfrac{(\Sigma X_{Tot})^2}{N_{Tot}}$

SS_B $= \Sigma \dfrac{(\text{ of all B's})^2}{n_i} - \dfrac{(\Sigma X_{Tot})^2}{N_{Tot}}$

$SS_{Treatment}$ $= \left[\Sigma \dfrac{(\Sigma X)^2}{n_i}\right] - \dfrac{(\Sigma X_{Tot})^2}{N_{Tot}}$

$SS_{A \times B}$ $= SS\ Treatment - (SS_A + SS_B)$

SS_{Within} $= SS_{Tot} - SS_{Treatment}$ Between

$$SS_{total} = \sum X^2 - \frac{(\sum X_{Tot})^2}{N_{Tot}}$$

X_1	X_1^2	X_2	X_2^2	X_3	X_3^2	X_4	X_4^2	X_5	X_5^2	X_6	X_6^2	X_7	X_7^2	X_8	X_8^2	X_9	X_9^2
9	81	4	16	4	16	8	64	12	144	7	49	5	25	6	36	9	81
12	144	8	64	4	16	7	49	12	144	6	36	5	25	8	64	11	121
12	144	9	81	5	25	10	100	13	169	9	81	6	36	9	81	11	121
13	169	11	121	9	81	11	121	13	169	10	100	10	100	10	100	12	144
14	196	12	144	8	64	14	196	15	225	13	169	9	81	12	144	12	144
60	734	45	436	30	202	50	530	65	851	45	435	35	267	45	425	55	611
$\sum X_1$	$\sum X_1^2$	$\sum X_2$	$\sum X_2^2$	$\sum X_3$	$\sum X_3^2$	$\sum X_4$	$\sum X_4^2$	$\sum X_5$	$\sum X_5^2$	$\sum X_6$	$\sum X_6^2$	$\sum X_7$	$\sum X_7^2$	$\sum X_8$	$\sum X_8^2$	$\sum X_9$	$\sum X_9^2$

$\sum X_{Tot} = 60 + 45 + 30 + 50 + 65 + 45 + 35 + 45 + 55 = 430$

$\sum X_{Tot}^2 = 734 + 426 + 202 + 530 + 851 + 435 + 267 + 425 + 611 = 4481$

$SS_{Total} = 4481 - \frac{(430)^2}{45} = 4481 - \frac{184900}{45} = 4481 - 4109 = 372$

$SS_{Total} = 372$

$$SS_{Treatments} = \left[\sum \frac{(\Sigma X)^2}{n_i}\right] - \frac{(\Sigma X_{Tot})^2}{N_{Tot}}$$

(we'll have as many terms as # of groups--
in this Case 9)

$$= \left[\frac{(60)}{5} + \frac{(45)}{5} + \frac{(30)}{5} + \frac{(50)}{5} + \frac{(65)}{5} + \right.$$

$$\left. \frac{(45)}{5} + \frac{(35)}{5} + \frac{(45)}{5} + \frac{(55)}{5}\right] - \frac{(430)}{45}$$

$$= [720 + 405 + 180 + 500 + 845 + 405 + 245 +$$

$$405 + 605] - 4109$$

$$= 4310 - 4109 = 201$$

$$\boxed{SS_{Treatments} = 201}$$

SS_A (Col)
$$= \sum \frac{(\Sigma \text{ of all A's})^2}{n_i} - \frac{(\Sigma X_{Tot})^2}{N_{Tot}}$$

[you will have as many of these terms as
A-main effects--in this case 3)

SS_A (Col)
$$= \left[\frac{\Sigma(60 + 50 + 35)^2}{15} + \frac{(45 + 65 + 45)^2}{15} + \right.$$

$$= \left. \frac{(30 + 45 + 55)^2}{15}\right] - \frac{(430)^2}{15}$$

$$= \left[\frac{(145)^2}{15} + \frac{(155)^2}{15} + \frac{(130)^2}{15}\right] - 4109)$$

$$= [1402 + 1602 + 1127] - 4109$$

$$= 4131 - 4109 = 22$$

$$\boxed{SS_A = 22}$$

$$SS_B \text{ (Row)} = \Sigma \frac{(\Sigma \text{ of all B's})^2}{n_i} - \frac{(\Sigma X_{Tot})^2}{N_{Tot}}$$

[you will have as many of these terms as B-levels--in this case 3]

$$SS_B \text{ (Row)} = \Sigma \left[\frac{(60+45+30)^2}{15} + \frac{(50+65+45)^2}{15} + \frac{(35+45+55)^2}{15} \right] - \frac{(430)^2}{45}$$

$$= \left[\frac{(135)^2}{15} + \frac{(160)^2}{15} + \frac{(135)^2}{15} \right] - \frac{(430)^2}{45}$$

$$= [1215 + 1707 + 1215] - 4109$$

$$= 4137 - 4109 = 28$$

$$\boxed{SS_B = 28}$$

$$\boxed{SS_{AB} = SS_{Treatment} - (SS_A + SS_B)}$$

$$SS_{AB} = 201 - (22 + 28)$$

$$201 = 50 = 151$$

$$\boxed{SS_{AB} = 151}$$

$$\boxed{\begin{array}{c} SS_{Within} = SS_{Total} - SS_{Treatment} \\ = 372 = 201 = 171 \end{array}}$$

$$\boxed{SS_{Within} = 171}$$

Source	SS	df	mS	F	Sign.
A	22	$(a-1)=3-1$ $= 2$	$SS_A/df_a =$ $22/2 = 11$	$mS_A/mS_w =$ $11/4.75 = 2.32$	NS
B	28	$(b-1)=3-1$ $=2$	$SS_b/df_b =$ $28/2 = 14$	$mS_B/mS_w =$ $14/4.75 = 2.95$	NS
AB	151	$(a-1)(b-1)=$ $(3-1)(3-1)=4$	$SS_{Ab}/df_{ab} =$ $151/4 = 37.35$	$mS_{AB}/mS_w =$ $37.75/4.75 = 7.95$	S
Within	171	$N-K = 45-9$ $= 36$	$SS_w/df_w =$ $171/36 = 4.75$		
Total	372	$N-1 = 45-1$ $= 44$			

df_A $=$ a-1 = (levels of A main effect) - 1 = 3 - 1 = 2

df_B $=$ b-1 = (levels of B main effect) - 1 = 3 - 1 = 2

df_{AB} $=$ (a-1) (b-1) = (3-1) (3-1) = 4

df_W $=$ N-K = (number of subjects) - (number of groups)

$=$ 45 - 9 = 36

mS_A $=$ SS_A/df_A = 22/2 = 11

mS_B $=$ SS_B/df_B = 28/2 = 14

mS_{AB} $=$ SS_{AB}/df_{Ab} = 151/4 = 37.75

mS_W $=$ SS_W/df_W = 171/36 = 4.75

F for A main effect = mS_A/mS_W = 11/4.75 = 2.32

F for B main effect = mS_B/mS_W = 14/4.75 = 2.95

F for AB interaction = mS_{AB}/mS_W = 37.75/4.75 = 7.95

F for A effect is looked up with df_1 = 2 & df_2 = 36

F for B effect is looked up with df_1 = 2 & df_2 = 36

F for AB effect is looked up with df_1 = 4 & df_2 = 36

APPENDIX H

EXAMPLE OF AN SAS COMPUTER SETUP FOR

A CORRELATION PROBLEM

```
//JOBNAME JOB REQ#,'YOUR NAME',CLASS=H,MSGLEVEL=(2,0)
// EXEC SAS
DATA PROBI;
INPUT ID 1 SCOREX 3-4 SCOREY 6-7;
CARDS;
1  10   8
2   6   5
3   4   5
4   8   9
5   7  11
;
PROC PRINT;
PROC      CORR DATA=PROB1;
     VAR SCOREX SCOREY;
     TITLE 'PROB1 CORRELATION';
```

Welcome to Version 6.07 of the MVS SAS System.
To access the SAS Training tutorials, type: CRWT
at the CMS Ready; prompt during any VM/CMS session.

NOTE: The SASUSER library was not specified. SASUSER library will now be the same as the WORK library.
NOTE: All data sets and catalogs in the SASUSER library will be deleted at the end of the session. Use the
NOWORKTERM to prevent their deletion.

NOTE: SAS system options specified are:
SORT=5   DEVICE=CALCOMPV

NOTE: The initialization phase used 0.17 CPU seconds and 2523K.
1   DATA PROBI;
2   INPUT ID 1 SCOREX 3-4 SCOREY 6-7;
3   CARDS;

NOTE: The data set WORK.PROBI has 5 observations and 3 variables.
NOTE: The DATA statement used 0.05 CPU seconds and 3016K.

9   ;
10   PROC PRINT;

NOTE: The PROCEDURE PRINT printed page 1.
NOTE: The PROCEDURE PRINT used 0.02 CPU seconds and 3105K.

11   PROC CORR DATA=PROB1;
12   VAR SCOREX SCOREY;
13   TITLE 'PROB1 CORRELATION';

NOTE: The PROCEDURE CORR printed page 2.
NOTE: The PROCEDURE CORR used 0.02 CPU seconds and 3283K.

NOTE: The SAS session used 0.28 CPU seconds and 3283K.
NOTE: SAS Institute Inc., SAS Campus Drive, Cary, NC USA 27513-2414

OBS	ID	SCOREX	SCOREY
1	1	10	8
2	2	6	5
3	3	4	5
4	4	8	9
5	5	7	11

Correlation Analysis

2 'VAR' Variables: SCOREX SCOREY

Simple Statistics

Variable	N	Mean	Std Dev	Sum	Minimum	Maximum
SCOREX	5	7.000000	2.236068	35.000000	4.000000	10.000000
SCOREY	5	7.600000	2.607681	38.000000	5.000000	11.000000

Pearson Correlation Coefficients / Prob > |R| under Ho: Rho=0 / N = 5

	SCOREX	SCOREY
SCOREX	1.00000 0.0	0.55737 0.3290
SCOREY	0.55737 0.3290	1.00000 0.0

APPENDIX I

EXAMPLE OF AN SAS COMPUTER SETUP

FOR AN INDEPENDENT T-TEST

```
//JOBNAME JOB REQ#,'YOUR NAME',CLASS=H,MSGLEVEL=(2,0)
// EXEC SAS
DATA PROB3;
   INPUT SCORE 1-2 GROUP $4;
   CARDS;
05 C
07 C
09 C
09 C
01 C
00 E
02 E
03 E
04 E
06 E ;
PROC PRINT;
PROC TTEST DATA=PROB3;
       CLASS GROUP;
       VAR SCORE;
```

Welcome to Version 6.07 of the MVS SAS System.
To access the SAS Training tutorials, type: CRWTH
at the CMS Ready; prompt during any VM/CMS session.

NOTE: The SASUSER library was not specified. SASUSER library will now be the same as the WORK library.
NOTE: All data sets and catalogs in the SASUSER library will be deleted at the end of the session. Use the
NOWORKTERM opti prevent their deletion.

NOTE: SAS system options specified are:
SORT=5   DEVICE=CALCOMPV

NOTE: The initialization phase used 0.17 CPU seconds and 2523K.
1   DATA PROB3;
2   INPUT SCORE 1-2 GROUP $4;
3   CARDS;

NOTE: The data set WORK.PROB3 has 10 observations and 2 variables.
NOTE: The DATA statement used 0.04 CPU seconds and 3016K.

14 ;
15   PROC PRINT;

NOTE: The PROCEDURE PRINT printed page 1.
NOTE: The PROCEDURE PRINT used 0.02 CPU seconds and 3105K.

16   PROC TTEST DATA=PROB3;
17   CLASS GROUP;
18   VAR SCORE;

NOTE: The PROCEDURE TTEST printed page 2.
NOTE: The PROCEDURE TTEST used 0.02 CPU seconds and 3141K.

NOTE: The SAS session used 0.28 CPU seconds and 3141K.
NOTE: SAS Institute Inc., SAS Campus Drive, Cary, NC USA 27513-2414

The SAS System

OBS	SCORE	GROUP
1	5	C
2	7	C
3	9	C
4	9	C
5	10	C
6	0	E
7	2	E
8	3	E
9	4	E
10	6	E

The SAS System

TTEST PROCEDURE

Variable: SCORE

GROUP	N	Mean	Std Dev	Std Error	Minimum	Maximum	Variances	T	DF	P
C	5	8.00000000	2.00000000	0.89442719	5.00000E+00	10.00000000	Unequal	3.7268	7.9	0.0060
E	5	3.00000000	2.23606798	1.00000000	0.00000E+00	6.00000000	Equal	3.7268	8.0	0.0058

For H0: Variances are equal, F' = 1.25   DF = (4,4)   Prob>F' = 0.8340

APPENDIX J

EXAMPLE OF AN SAS COMPUTER SETUP

FOR AN ANOVA

```
//JOBNAME JOB REQ#,'YOUR NAME',CLASS=H,MSGLEVEL=(2,0)
// EXEC SAS
DATA PROB4;
INPUT GROUP 1-2 SCORE 4-5;
CARDS;
01  09
01  12
01  12
01  13
01  14
02  06
02  08
02  09
02  11
02  11
03  04
03  04
03  05
03  09
03  08
;;
```

```
PROC PRINT;
PROC ANOVA;
     TITLE 'ONE WAY ANOVA PROB4';
     CLASSES GROUP;
     MODEL SCORE=GROUP;
     MEANS GROUP;
```

Welcome to Version 6.07 of the MVS SAS System
To access the SAS Training tutorials, type: CRWTH
at the CMS Ready; prompt during any VM/CMS session.

NOTE: The SASUSER library was not specified. SASUSER library will
now be the same as the WORK library.

NOTE: All data sets and catalogs in the SASUSER library will be deleted
at the end of the session. Use the NOWORKTERM op prevent
their deletion.

NOTE: SAS system options specified are:
SORT=5 DEVICE=CALCOMPV

NOTE: The initialization phase used 0.17 CPU seconds and 2523K.
1   DATA PROB4;
2   INPUT GROUP 1-2 SCORE 4-5;
3   CARDS;

NOTE: The data set WORK.PROB4 has 15 observations and 2
variables.

NOTE: The DATA statement used 0.04 CPU seconds and 3016K.

19   ;
20   PROC PRINT;

NOTE: The PROCEDURE PRINT printed page 1.
NOTE: The PROCEDURE PRINT used 0.02 CPU seconds and 3105K.

```
21    PROC ANOVA;
22         TITLE 'ONE WAY ANOVA PROB4';
23         CLASSES GROUP;
24         MODEL SCORE=GROUP;
25         MEANS GROUP;
```

NOTE: Means from the MEANS statement are not adjusted for other terms in the model. Eor adjusted means, use the LSMEANS

NOTE: The PROCEDURE ANOVA printed pages 2-4.

NOTE: The PROCEDURE ANOVA used 0.05 CPU seconds and 3555K.

NOTE: The SAS session used 0.31 CPU seconds and 3555K.

NOTE: SAS Institute Inc., SAS Campus Drive, Cary, NC USA 27513-2414

The SAS System

OBS	GROUP	SCORE
1	1	9
2	1	12
3	1	12
4	1	13
5	1	14
6	2	6
7	2	8
8	2	9
9	2	11
10	2	11
11	3	4
12	3	4
13	3	5
14	3	9
15	3	8

ONE WAY ANOVA PROB4

Analysis of Variance Procedure
Class Level Information

Class	Levels	Values
GROUP	3	1 2 3

Number of observations in data set = 15

ONE WAY ANOVA PROB4

Analysis of Variance Procedure

Dependent Variable: SCORE

Source	DF	Sum of Squares	Mean Square	F Value	Pr > F
Model	2	90.00000000	45.00000000	10.00	0.0028
Error	12	54.00000000	4.50000000		
Corrected Total	14	144.00000000			

R-Square	C.V.	Root MSE			SCORE Mean
0.625000	23.57023	2.12132034			9.00000000

Source	DF	Anova SS	Mean Square	F Value	Pr > F
GROUP	2	90.00000000	45.00000000	10.00	0.0028

ONE WAY ANOVA PROB4

Analysis of Variance Procedure

| Level of GROUP | N | ------------------SCORE----------------- | |
		Mean	SD
1	5	12.0000000	1.87082869
2	5	9.0000000	2.12132034
3	5	6.0000000	2.34520788

APPENDIX K

EXAMPLE OF AN SAS COMPUTER SETUP

FOR A 3 X 3 FACTORIAL ANALYSIS

```
//JOBNAME JOB REQ#,'YOUR NAME',CLASS=H,MSGLEVEL=(2,0)
// EXEC SAS
DATA PROB5;
INPUT METHOD 1 IQ $3 SCORE 5-6;
CARDS;
1 L 09
1 L 12
1 L 12
1 L 13
1 L 14
2 L 04
2 L 08
2 L 09
2 L 11
2 L 12
3 L 04
3 L 04
3 L 05
3 L 09
3 L 08
1 M 08
1 M 07
1 M 10
1 M 11
1 M 14
2 M 12
2 M 12
2 M 13
2 M 13
```

```
2 M 15
3 M 07
3 M 06
3 M 09
3 M 10
3 M 13
1 H 05
1 H 05
1 H 06
1 H 10
1 H 09
2 H 06
2 H 08
2 H 09
2 H 10
2 H 12
3 H 09
3 H 11
3 H 11
3 H 12
3 H 12 ;

PROC PRINT; PROC ANOVA;
TITLE 'THREE-WAY ANOVA';
CLASSES METHOD IQ;
MODEL SCORE = METHODIIQ;
MEANS METHODIIQ;
```

```
51      PROC ANOVA;
52          TITLE 'THREE-WAY ANOVA';
53          CLASSES METHOD IQ;
54          MODEL SCORE=METHODIIQ;
55          MEANS METHODIIQ;
56

NOTE:   Means from the MEANS statement are not adjusted for other terms in the model. For adjusted means,
        use the LSMEANS statement.

NOTE:   The PROCEDURE ANOVA printed pages 2-4.
NOTE:   The PROCEDURE ANOVA used 0.06 CPU seconds and 3555K.

NOTE:   The SAS session used 0.34 CPU seconds and 3555K.
NOTE:   SAS Institute Inc., SAS Campus Drive, Cary, NC USA 27513-2414
```

The SAS System

OBS	METHOD	IQ	SCORE
1	1	L	9
2	1	L	12
3	1	L	12
4	1	L	13
5	1	L	14
6	2	L	4
7	2	L	8
8	2	L	9
9	2	L	11
10	2	L	12
11	3	L	4
12	3	L	4
13	3	L	5
14	3	L	9
15	3	L	8
16	1	M	8
17	1	M	7
18	1	M	10
19	1	M	11
20	1	M	14
21	2	M	12
22	2	M	12
23	2	M	13
24	2	M	13
25	2	M	15

26	3	M	7
27	3	M	6
28	3	M	9
29	3	M	10
30	3	M	13
31	1	H	5
32	1	H	5
33	1	H	6
34	1	H	10
35	1	H	9
36	2	H	6
37	2	H	8
38	2	H	9
39	2	H	10
etc.			

THREE-WAY ANOVA
Analysis of Variance Procedure
Class Level Information

Class	Levels	Values
METHOD	3	1 2 3
IQ	3	H L M

Number of observations in data set = 45

THREE-WAY ANOVA
Analysis of Variance Procedure

Dependent Variable: SCORE

Source	DF	Sum of Squares	Mean Square	F Value	Pr > F
Model	8	202.40000000	25.30000000	4.82	0.0004
Error	36	188.80000000	5.24444444		
Corrected Total	44	391.20000000			

R-Square	C.V.	Root MSE	SCORE Mean
0.517382	24.02177	2.29007520	9.53333333

Source	DF	Anova SS	Mean Square	F Value	Pr > F
METHOD	2	19.60000000	9.80000000	1.87	0.1690
IQ	2	28.93333333	14.46666667	2.76	0.0768
METHOD*IQ	4	153.86666667	38.46666667	7.33	0.0002

THREE-WAY ANOVA

Analysis of Variance Procedure

Level of METHOD	N	SCORE Mean	SD
1	15	9.6666667	3.03942350
2	15	10.2666667	2.93906367
3	15	8.6666667	2.94392029

Level of IQ	N	SCORE Mean	SD
H	15	9.0000000	2.50713268
L	15	8.9333333	3.43233920
M	15	10.6666667	2.79455252

Level of IQ	Level of METHOD	N	SCORE Mean	SD
H	1	5	7.0000000	2.34520788
L	1	5	12.0000000	1.87082869
M	1	5	10.0000000	2.73861279
H	2	5	9.0000000	2.23606798
L	2	5	8.8000000	3.11448230
M	2	5	13.0000000	1.22474487
H	3	5	11.0000000	1.22474487
L	3	5	6.0000000	2.34520788
M	3	5	9.0000000	2.73861279

APPENDIX L

EXAMPLE OF AN SAS COMPUTER SETUP

FOR A CHI SQUARE

```
//JOBNAME JOB REQ#,'YOUR NAME',CLASS=H,MSGLEVEL=(2,0)
// EXEC SAS
DATA PROB2;
INPUT SEX $1 CLASS 3;
CARDS;
M 1
M 1
M 1
M 1
M 1
M 1
M 1
M 1
M 1
M 1
M 1
M 1
M 1
M 1
M 2
M 2
M 2
M 2
M 2
F 1
F 1
F 1
F 1
F 1
F 1
F 1
F 2
F 2
F 2
F 2
F 2
F 2
F 2
F 2
F 2
F 2
F 2
F 2
F 2;
PROC PRINT;
PROC FREQ;
        TABLES SEX*CLASS / CHISQ;
```

Welcome to Version 6.07 of the MVS SAS System.
To access the SAS Training tutorials, type: CRWTH at the CMS Ready;
prompt during any VM/CMS session.

NOTE: The SASUSER library was not specified. SASUSER library will
now be the same as the WORK library. NOTE: All data sets and catalogs
in the SASUSER library will be deleted at the end of the session. Use the
NOWORKTERM to prevent their deletion.

NOTE: SAS system options specified are:
    SORT=5 DEVICE=CALCOMPV

NOTE: The initialization phase used 0.18 CPU seconds and 2523K.
```
1       DATA PROB2;
2       INPUT SEX $1 CLASS 3;
3       CARDS;
```

NOTE: The data set WORK.PROB2 has 39 observations and 2 variables.
NOTE: The DATA statement used 0.05 CPU seconds and 3016K.

```
43      ;
44      PROC PRINT;
```

NOTE: The PROCEDURE PRINT printed page 1.
NOTE: The PROCEDURE PRINT used 0.03 CPU seconds and 3105K.

```
45      PROC EREQ;
46        TABLES SEX*CLASS / CHISQ;
```

NOTE: The PROCEDURE FREQ printed page 2.
NOTE: The PROCEDURE EREQ used 0.04 CPU seconds and 3376K.

NOTE: The SAS session used 0.31 CPU seconds and 3376K.
NOTE: SAS Institute Inc., SAS Campus Drive, Cary, NC USA 27513-
2414

The SAS System

OBS	SEX	CLASS
1	M	1
2	M	1
3	M	1
4	M	1
5	M	1
6	M	1
7	M	1
8	M	1
9	M	1
10	M	1
11	M	1
12	M	1
13	M	1
14	M	1
15	M	2
16	M	2
17	M	2
18	M	2
19	M	2
20	F	1
21	F	1
22	F	1
23	F	1
24	F	1
25	F	1
26	F	1
27	F	2
28	F	2
29	F	2
30	F	2
31	F	2
32	F	2
33	F	2
34	F	2
35	F	2
36	F	2
37	F	2
38	F	2
39	F	2

The SAS System

TABLE OF SEX BY CLASS

SEX	CLASS		
Frequency Percent Row Pct Col Pct	1	2	Total
F	7 17.95 35.00 33.33	13 33.33 65.00 72.22	20 51.28
M	14 35.90 73.68 66.67	5 12.82 26.32 27.78	19 48.72
Total	21 53.85	18 46.15	39 100.00

STATISTICS FOR TABLE OF SEX BY CLASS

Statistic	DF	Value	Prob
Chi-Square	1	5.867	0.015
Likelihood Ratio Chi-Square	1	6.036	0.014
Continuity Adj. Chi-Square	1	4.414	0.036
Mantel-Haenszel Chi-Square	1	5.717	0.017
Fisher's Exact Test (Left)			0.017
(Right)			0.997
(2-Tail)			0.025
Phi Coefficient		-0.388	
Contingency Coefficient		0.362	
Cramer's V		-0.388	

Sample Size = 39

APPENDIX M

EXAMPLE OF AN SPSSX COMPUTER SETUP FOR

A DESCRIPTIVE PROGRAM ON FREQUENCIES

```
//JOBNAME JOB REQ#,'YOUR NAME',CLASS=H,MSGLEVEL=(2,0)
// EXEC SPSS
DATA LIST /1 VARA 1 VARB 3-4
FREQUENCIES VARIABLES=ALL / STATISTICS=ALL
BEGIN DATA
1  09
1  12
1  12
1  13
1  14
2  06
2  08
2  09
2  11
2  11
3  04
3  04
3  05
3  08
3  09
END DATA
FINISH
```

18-Mar-93 SPSS RELEASE 4.1 FOR IBM OS/MVS
Page
22:91:00 The University of Akron IBM 3090-200   OS/MVS

For OS/MVS The University of Akron   License Number 17
This software is functional through February 28, 1999.

Try the new SPSS Release 4 features:
* LOGISTIC REGRESSION procedure   * CATEGORIES Option:
* EXAMINE procedure to explore data   * conjoint analysis
* FLIP to transpose data files   * correspondence analysis
* MATRIX Transformations Language   * New LISREL and PRELIS Options
* GRAPH interface to SPSS Graphics   *
See the new SPSS documentation for more information on these new features.

    1 0   DATA LIST /1 VARA 1 VARB 3-4
This command will read 1 records from the command file
    Variable   Rec Start End   Format

    VARA   1   1   1   F1.0
    VARB   1   3   4   F2.0

    2 0   FREQUENCIES VARIABLES=ALL / STATISTICS=ALL
There are 955,872 bytes of memory available. The largest contiguous area has
949,768 bytes. Memory allows a total of 32,767 values accumulated across all
variables. There may be up to 8,192 value labels for each variable.

18-Mar-93 SPSS RELEASE 4.1 FOR IBM OS/MVS
Page 2
22:41:01   The University of Akron IBM 3090-200   OS/MVS

VARA

Value Label	Value	Frequency	Percent	Valid Percent	Cum Percent
	1	5	33.3	33.3	33.3
	2	5	33.3	33.3	66.7
	3	5	33.3	33.3	100.0
	Total	15	100.0	100.0	

Mean	2.000	Std err	.218	Median	2.000
Mode	1.000	Std dev	.845	Variance	.714
Kurtosis	-1.615	S E Kurt	1.121	Skewness	.000
S E Skew	.580	Range	2.000	Minimum	1.000
Maximum	3.000	Sum	30.000		

Valid cases   15   Missing cases   0

VARB

Value Label	Value	Frequency	Percent	Valid Percent	Cum Percent
	4	2	13.3	13.3	13.3
	5	1	6.7	6.7	20.0
	6	1	6.7	6.7	26.7
	8	2	13.3	13.3	40.0
	9	3	20.0	20.0	60.0
	11	2	13.3	13.3	73.3
	12	2	13.3	13.3	86.7
	13	1	6.7	6.7	93.3
	14	1	6 7	6 7	100.0
	Total	15	100.0	100.0	

Mean	9.000	Std err	.828	Median	9.000
Mode	9.000	Std dev	3.207	Variance	10.286
Kurtosis	-1.002	S E Kurt	1.121	Skewness	-.210
S E Skew	.580	Range	10.000	Minimum	4.000
Maximum	14.000	Sum	135.000		

Valid cases   15   Missing cases   0

APPENDIX N

EXAMPLE OF AN SPSSX COMPUTER SETUP

FOR A CORRELATIONAL PROBLEM

```
//JOBNAME JOB REQ#,'YOUR NAME',CLASS=H,MSGLEVEL=(2,0)
// EXEC SPSS
TITLE 'CORRELATION COEFFICIENT'
DATA LIST /1 X 1-2 Y 4-5
PEARSON CORR X WITH Y
STATISTICS 1,2
BEGIN DATA
10    8
6     5
4     5
8     9
7     11
END DATA
FINISH
```

18-Mar-93 SPSS RELEASE 4.1 FOR IBM OS/MVS
Page
22:40:50 The University of Akron IBM 3090-200   OS/MVS

For OS/MVS The University of Akron   License Number 17
This software is functional through February 28, 1999.

Try the new SPSS Release 4 features:
* LOGISTIC REGRESSION procedure   * CATEGORIES Option:
* EXAMINE procedure to explore data   * conjoint analysis
* FLIP to transpose data files   * corresondence analysis
* MATRIX Transformations Language   * New LISREL and PRELIS Options
* GRAPH interface to SPSS Graphics   *
See the new SPSS documentation for more information on these new features.

    1 0   TITLE 'CORRELATION COEFFICIENT'
    2 0   DATA LIST /1 X 1-2 Y 4-5
This command will read 1 records from the command file
Variable   Rec   Start   End   Format

X   1   1   2   F2.0
Y   1   4   5   F2.0

    3 0   PEARSON CORR X WITH Y
    4 0   STATISTICS 1,2
PEARSON CORR problem requires 80 bytes of workspace.

18-Mar-93 CORRELATION COEFFICIENT
Page 2
22:90:51   The University of Akron   IBM 3090-200   OS/MVS

Variable	Cases	Mean	Std Dev
X	5	7.0000	2.2361
Y	5	7.6000	2.6077

18-Mar-93 CORRELATION COEFFICIENT
Page 3
22:40:51 The University of Akron   IBM 3090-200   OS/MVS

Variables		Cases	Cross-Prod Dev	Variance-Covar	Variance-Covar
X	Y	5	13.0000	3.2500	

18-Mar-93 CORRELATION COEFFICIENT
Page 4
22:40:51   The University of Akron   IBM 3090-200   OS/MVS

- - Correlation Coefficients - -

                    Y

X   .5579
* - Signif. LE .05
** - Signif. LE .01   (2-tailed)
" . " printed if a coefficient cannot be

APPENDIX O

EXAMPLE OF AN SPSSX COMPUTER SETUP

FOR A CHI SQUARE

```
//JOBNAME JOB REQ#,'YOUR NAME',CLASS=H,MSGLEVEL=(2,0)
// EXEC SPSS
TITLE 'CHI SQUARE (CONTINGENCY TABLE)'
DATA LIST /1 GROUP 1 SEX 3
VALUE LABELS GROUP 1 'LOW' 2 'HIGH' /
              SEX 1 'MALE' 2 'FEMALE'
CROSSTABS TABLES=SEX BY GROUP
STATISTICS ALL
BEGIN DATA

1 1
1 1
1 1
1 1
1 1
1 1
1 1
1 1
1 1
1 1
1 1
1 1
1 2
1 2
1 2
1 2
1 2
2 1
2 1
2 1
2 1
2 1
2 1
2 1
2 2
2 2
2 2
2 2
2 2
```

```
2 2
2 2
2 2
2 2
2 2
2 2
2 2
2 2
END DATA
FINISH
```

18-Mar-93 SPSS RELEASE 4.1 FOR IBM OS/MVS
Page 1
22:40:51 The University of Akron IBM 3090-200 OS/MVS

For OS/MVS The University of Akron   License Number 17
This software is functional through February 28, 1999.

Try the new SPSS Release 4 features:
* LOGISTIC REGRESSION procedure   * CATEGORIES Option:
* EXAMINE procedure to explore data   * conjoint analysis
* FLIP to transpose data files   * correspondence analysis
* MATRIX Transformations Language   * New LISREL and PRELIS
Options
* GRAPH interface to SPSS Graphics   *
See the new SPSS documentation for more information on these new
features.

1 O TITLE 'CHI SQUARE (CONTINGENCY TABLE)' 2 0 DATA LIST /1
GROUP 1 SEX 3
This command will read 1 records from the command file
Variable Rec Start End   Format

GROUP   1   1   1   F1.0
SEX   1   3   3   F1.0

3   0   VALUE LABELS GROUP 1 'LOW' 2 'HIGH' /
4   0   SEX 1 'MALE' 2 'FEMALE'
5   0   CROSSTABS TABLES=SEX BY GROUP
6   0   STATISTICS ALL

There are 955,856 bytes of memory available.
The largest contiguous area has 999,752 bytes.
Memory allows for 31,658 cells with 2 dimensions for general
CROSSTABS.

18-Mar-93 CHI SQUARE (CONTINGENCY TABLE)
Page 2
22:90:52 The University of Akron IBM 3090-200 OS/MVS

SEX by GROUP

GROUP   Page 1 of 1

	Count	LOW 1	HIGH 2	Row Total
SEX MALE	1	14	7	21 53.8
FEMALE	2	5	13	18 46.2
Column Total		19 48.7	20 51.3	39 100.0

Chi-Square	Value	DF	Significance
Pearson	5.86710	1	.01543
Continuity Correction	4.41377	1	.03565
Likelihood Ratio	6.03590	1	.01402
Mantel-Haenszel	5.71667	1	.01680
Minimum Expected Frequency -	8.769		

18-Mar-93 CHI SQUARE (CONTINGENCY TABLE)
Page 3
22:40:52 The University of Akron   IBM 3090-200

Approximate Statistic	Value	ASEI	T-value	Significance
Phi	.38786			.01543 *1
Cramer's V	.38786			.01543 *1
Contingency Coefficient	.36162			.01543 *1
Lambda :				
symmetric	.35135	.17480	1.82634	
with SEX dependent	.33333	.20286	1.37372	
with GROUP dependent	.36842	.19168	1.57538	
Goodman & Kruskal Tau :				
with SEX dependent	.15044	.11404		.01680 *2
with GROUP dependent	.15044	.11399		.01680 *2
Uncertainty Coefficient :				
symmetric	.11191	.08728	1.28162	.01402 *3
with SEX dependent	.11212	.08744	1.28162	.01402 *3
with GROUP dependent	.11169	.08714	1.28162	.01402 *3
Kappa	.38583	.14682	2.42221	

Kendall's Tau-b		.38786	.14705	2.63270
Kendall's Tau-c		.38659	.14684	2.63270
Gamma		.67742	.18962	2.63270
Somers' D :				
symmetric		.38786	.14705	2.63270
with SEX	dependent	.38684	.14690	2.63270
with GROUP	dependent	.38889	.14740	2.63270

Pearson's R		.38786	.14705	2.55966	.01470
Spearman Correlation		.38786	.14705	2.55966	.01470
Eta :					
with SEX	dependent	.38786			
with GROUP	dependent	.38786			

*1 Pearson chi-square probability

*2 Based on chi-square approximation

*3 Likelihood ratio chi-square probability

Statistic	Value	95% Confidence Bounds	
Relative Risk Estimate (SEX 1 / SEX 2) :			
case control	5.20000	1.31652	20.53897
cohort (GROUP 1 Risk)	2.40000	1.07414	5.36245
cohort (GROUP 2 Risk)	.46154	.23634	.90131

APPENDIX P

EXAMPLE OF AN SPSSX COMPUTER SETUP

FOR A DEPENDENT T-TEST

```
//JOBNAME JOB REQ#,'YOUR NAME',CLASS=H,MSGLEVEL=(2,0)
// EXEC SPSS
TITLE 'T-TEST (DEPENDENT SAMPLES)'
DATA LIST /1 SCOREI 1-2 SCORE2 4-5
T-TEST PAIRS=SCOREI WITH SCORE2
BEGIN DATA
25  16
25  11
23  13
20  14
20   7
17  30
16   8
14  15
13   5
11   6
END DATA
FINISH
```

18-Mar-93 SPSS RELEASE 4.1 FOR IBM OS/MVS
Page
22:28:51 The University of Akron IBM 3090-200   OS/MVS

For OS/MVS The University of Akron   License Number 17
This software is functional through February 28, 1999.

Try the new SPSS Release 4 features:
* LOGISTIC REGRESSION procedure   * CATEGORIES Option:
* EXAMINE procedure to explore data   * conjoint analysis
* FLIP to transpose data files   * correspondence analysis
* MATRIX Transformations Language   * New LISREL and PRELIS Options
* GRAPH interface to SPSS Graphics   *
See the new SPSS documentation for more information on these new features.

1 0   TITLE 'T-TEST (DEPENDENT SAMPLES)'
2 0   DATA LIST /1 SCORE1 1-2 SCORE2 4-5
This command will read 1 records from the command file
Variable   Rec Start End   Format

SCORE1   1   1   2   F2.0
SCORE2   1   4   5   F2.0

3 0   T-TEST PAIRS=SCORE1 WITH SCORE2
There are 955,872 bytes of memory available.
The largest contiguous area has 818,000 bytes.
T-TEST requires 64 bytes of workspace for execution.

18-Mar-93 T-TEST (DEPENDENT SAMPLES)
22:28:52   The University of Akron   IBM 3090-200   OS/MVS

Variable	No. of Cases	Mean	Std. Dev.	Std. Error	Std. (Difference) Mean	Std. Dev.	Std. Error	Corr.	2-tail Prob.	t Value	2-tail df	Prob.
SCORE1		18.4000	4.993	1.579								
	10				5.900	7.866	2.488	.223	.536	2.37	9	.042
SCORE2		12.500	7.292	2.306								

APPENDIX Q

EXAMPLE OF AN SPSSX COMPUTER SETUP FOR

A TWO-WAY (3 X 3) ANALYSIS OF VARIANCE

//JOBNAME JOB REQ#, ' YOUR NAME ', CLASS=H, MSGLEVEL=   (2 ,

0) // EXEC SPSS

TITLE 'TWO-WAY ANOVA 3 X 3 FACTORIAL' DATA LIST /1 METHOD

1 IQ 3 SCORE 5-6

VALUE LABELS METHOD 1 'METHOD 1'

2 'METHOD 2 '

3 'METHOD 3' / IQ 1 'LOW'

2 'MED'

3 'HIGH'

ANOVA SCORE BY METHOD, IQ (1,3) STATISTICS 1

BEGIN DATA

1 1 09

1 1 12

1 1 12

1 1 13

1 1 14

2 1 04

2 1 08

2 1 09

2 1 11

2 1 12

3 1 04

3 1 04

3 1 05

3 1 09

3 1 08

1 2 08

1 2 07

1 2 10

1 2 11

1 2 14

2 2 12

2 2 12

2 2 13

2 2 13

2 2 15

3 2 07

3 2 06

3 2 09

3 2 10

3 2 13

1 3 05

1 3 05

1 3 06

1 3 10

1 3 09

2 3 06

2 3 08

2 3 09

2 3 10

2 3 12

3 3 09

3 3 11

3 3 11

3 3 12

3 3 12

END DATA

FINISH

18-Mar-93   SPSS RELEASE 4.1   FOR IBM OS/MVS
Page
22:38:53 The University of Akron IBM 3090-200 OS/MVS

For OS/MVS The University of Akron   License Number 17
This software is functional through February 28, 1999.

Try the new SPSS Release 4 features:
* LOGISTIC REGRESSION procedure   * CATEGORIES Option:
* EXAMINE procedure to explore data   * conjoint analysis
* FLIP to transpose data files   * correspondence analysis
* MATRIX Transformations Language   * New LISREL and PRELIS Options
* GRAPH interface to SPSS Graphics

See the new SPSS documentation for more information on these new features.

        1   0   TITLE 'TWO-WAY ANOVA 3 X 3 FACTORIAL'
        2   0   DATA LIST /1 METHOD 1 IQ 3 SCORE 5-6

This command will read 1 records from the command file

Variable   Rec Start End   Format

METHOD   1   1   1   F1.0
IQ   1   3   3   F1.0
SCORE   1   5   6   F2.0

        3 0   VALUE LABELS METHOD
        4 0   1 'METHOD 1'
        5 0   2 'METHOD 2'
        6 0   3 'METHOD 3'
        7 0   IQ
        8 0   1 'LOW'
        9 0   2 'MEDIUM'
       10 0   3 'HIGH'
       11 0   ANOVA SCORE BY METHOD, IQ (1,3)
       12 0   STATISTICS 1

18-Mar-93 TWO-WAY ANOVA 3 X 3 FACTORIAL
Page 2
22:38:54   The University of Akron   IBM 3090-200OS/MVS

*** A N A L Y S I S O F V A R I A N C E ***

SCORE
by METHOD
IQ

Source of Variation	Sum of Squares	DF	Mean Square	F	Sig of F
Main Effects	48.533	4	12.133	2.314	.076
METHOD	19.600	2	9.800	1.869	.169
IQ	28.933	2	14.467	2.758	.077
2-Way Interactions	153.867	4	38.467	7.335	.000
METHOD IQ	153.867	4	38.467	7.335	.000
Explained	202.400	8	25.300	4.824	.000
Residual	188.800	36	5.244		
Total	391.200	44	8.891		

45 cases were processed.
O cases (.0 pct) were missing.

18-Mar-93 TWO-WAY ANOVA 3 X 3 FACTORIAL
Page 3
22:38:54 The University of Akron   IBM 3090-200   OS/MVS

MULTIPLE CLASSIFICATION ANALYSIS

         SCORE
by   METHOD
         IQ

Grand Mean = 9.53

Variable + Category	N	Unadjusted Dev'n Eta	Adjusted for Independents Dev'n Beta
METHOD			
1 METHOD 1	15	.13	.13
2 METHOD 2	15	.73	.73
3 METHOD 3	15	-.87	-.87
		.22	.22
IQ			
1 LOW	15	-.60	-.60
2 MED	15	1.13	1.13
3 HIGH	15	-.53	-.53
		.27	.27
Multiple R Squared			.124
Multiple R			.352

APPENDIX R

EXAMPLE OF CORRECTION OF MULTIPLE
COMPARISONS

EXAMPLE OF CORRECTION OF MULTIPLE COMPARISONS

One should note that when an overall F is significant and there are more than two groups, the question of where the difference is always arises. To find out where the difference is, one generally runs multiple comparisons between the groups. That is, Group 1 is compared to Group 2, Group 1 is compared to Group 3, Group 2 is compared to Group 3, etc. As the number of comparisons (tests of significance) increases, the more likely one will find significance. This is referred to as Alpha error buildup. You are increasing the probability of making a Type I error that is greater than the alpha level originally set.

When making multiple comparisons, a variety of corrections may be used to control for alpha error buildup. Some of the most common tests are Dunnett's, Tukey's, Newman-Keul's, Duncan's, Dunn's, and Scheffe's. Definitions of each will be presented and a brief sample of the Scheffe will be given.

Dunnett's correction is generally used when one is interested in comparing a variety of experimental groups to a single control group.

Tukey's is a highly desirable correction when one is interested in all possible pair-wise comparisons, that is, comparing each group with every other group.

The Newman-Keul and Duncan tests are also used when one is interested in pair-wise comparisons. Duncan's test tends to be more powerful in that its corrections tend to be less severe. However, Tukey's test has a better reputation in the field.

Scheffe is probably the most widely used correction and it is the most conservative. That is, it is harder to get significance after using a Scheffe than it is using the other corrections.

The Scheffe allows you to make all possible pair-wise comparisons as well as comparisons between a group and the average of the other groups.

An Example of a Scheffe

Assuming we have three groups of ten people each (N = number of people = 30, K = number of groups - 3), some of the comparisons that could be made would be:

> Group 1 to Group 2
> Group 1 to Group 3
> Group 2 to Group 3
> Group 1 to the average of Groups 2 and 3

Etc. The F needed for the significance for any of these comparisons will have to be larger than the original F run on the original three groups. This F is referred to as F'. F' = F (K - 1).

For example, let's assume the F needed for significance in the overall F test was 2.96. This means that if a calculated F is larger than F = 2.96, the calculated F is significant. In order for any of the comparisons to be significant, the calculated F (or t^2) for that specific comparison must be larger than the F'. That is:

> F' = F (K-l)
> F' = 2.96 (3-1)
> F' = 5.92

Keep in mind that all of the comparisons can be made with t tests. One can square the t and that is equal to F ($t^2 \bullet$ F).

An example of $\alpha' = \dfrac{\alpha}{n-1}$ (Newman-Fry, 1972)

This is a correction used for only the number of comparisons the researcher is interested in making, not necessarily all possible comparisons. For example, if there are three groups, the total number of comparisons that could be made is six but the researcher may only be interested in three of the six. He would then only correct for three comparisons. For example, if he set the alpha level at $\alpha = .05$ and wanted to hold his Type 1 error constant at the 05 level for all comparisons, all he has to do is take the number of comparisons he is interested in making ($n_c - 1 = 3-1 = 2$) and then divide this (2) into alpha $\alpha/2$. This yields the new adjusted alpha $= \alpha'$.

To be significant originally p has to be equal to or less than alpha ($p \leq \alpha$). Now p has to be less than or equal to α' ($p \leq \alpha'$).

p is the probability associated with any of the tests of significance. The larger the obtained value of the tests of significance (the F, t, x2, etc.) the smaller the p (the less likely it will occur by chance alone)).

Newman, I., & Fry, John. "A Response to 'A Note on Multiple Comparisons' and Comment on Shrinkage." Multiple Linear Regression Viewpoints, 1972, Vol. 2, No. 1, pp. 36-39.

*This test has also been called a Bonferroni or Dunn's test.

GLOSSARY

active variable - an independent variable that is under the control of and can be manipulated by the experimenter.

age norm - represents the average score received in a given test by a specific age group; typically reported on a table which depicts the average score on a given test by various age groups.

assigned variable - sometimes referred to as an attribute, it is an independent variable not under the control of the experimenter. Generally, sex, race, and intelligence are assigned variables.

average - typically used to refer to a measure of central tendency of a group of scores; an arithmetic mean would represent an average score.

biased sampling - each person in the population did not have an equal chance of being selected for the sample.

canonical correlation - an extension of multiple regression analysis which predicts a set (2 or more) of dependent variables from a set (2 or more) of independent variables. This is a technique that estimates the relationship between two sets of continuous variables--a predictor set and a criterion set. One can think of these two sets as principal components. Each set of principal components is weighted to maximize the prediction of the other set.

cluster analysis - this is also a data reduction technique like principal components. The puropse of cluster analysis is to group persons or objects into a smaller number of groups. Based upon their similarities. (It is a classification procedure.) That is, objects or persons who are in a cluster are more similar to each other than persons or objects from different clusters.

common factor variance - variance (variability) shared by two or more variables. It is related to the concept of correlation and covariance (see r^2).

concept - an abstraction, it is a generalization of specific qualities; for example, weight, height age.

confounding - the mixing of the variance of one or more independent variables of interest with one or more extraneous variables.

construct - a concept with added meaning, such as I.Q. See intervening variable.

content validity - a test which displays this characteristic would be typified by questions which are drawn from subject matter which is of concern and interest and has data to support that the items are representative of the subject matter.

continuous variables - a variable with many different values; for example, I.Q. scores, anxiety scores, or motivation scores.

contrast (pair) comparisons - probability of making a Type I error for any specific comparison.

counterbalanced design - a design in which experimental precision is enhanced by having all treatments responded to by all subjects, but in a different order; for example, crossover design and Latin Square design.

covariance - the extent that two or more variables are correlated with each other and how much variability in the measurements can be attributed to the commonality between the variables.

covary - two or more variables are correlated and they vary systematically with other, either positively or negatively.

criterion - see dependent variable.

crosstabs - a procedure in which data can be tabulated, usually frequencies (nominal data) or percentages; it is used when analyzing the relationship between categorical or nominal data.

crossed-design - is a factorial design in which all levels of one factor can be found in all levels of the other factor or factors.

degrees of freedom - related to the total number of independent replications (n) which can be the subject, items, groups, etc.; the number of replications free to vary when holding the total constant.

dependent variable - is referred to as the criterion, the "then" part of the 'if-then' hypothesis statement; it's the inferred effect that is being measured due to the independent variable; it is what is always statistically analyzed.

dichotomous variable - a variable that has only two values assigned to it (see variable); examples of dichotomous variables are sex (male or female) or the sides of a coin (heads or tails).

discriminant analysis (DA) - purpose is to predict group membership based on some weighted linear set of predictor variables. (The dependent variables are the groups.) For example, one can use principal components to predict group membership.

disordinal interaction - interaction in which when the lines are plotted, they cross in the area of interest.

empirical - objective observation (or tests).

error of measurement - variance due to lack of reliability in the measurement instrument.

error variance - uncontrolled variance, considered to be a function of random variation in measures due to chance

eta - symbolized by η^2. Eta is only interpreted in terms of Eta^2. It is also called the correlation ratio. It ranges from a score of O (no relation) to a score of 1 (perfect relation). There are no negative signs. Eta measures the total degree of relationship both linear and non linear. That is, it measures straight line and curved line relationships.
$(\eta^2_{yx} = 1 - (SSwithin/SStotal))$

evaluation - this would represent the sum total of the measures of student achievement within a given class; also represents the total plan for treating all measures obtained by a teacher for a given student or class.

experimental operational definition - defines a variable or construct in terms of its procedures or operations; it details how the variable was manipulated.

experimental research - differs from ex post facto research in terms of control; there must be at least one active variable under the experimenter's control and to which he can randomly assign.

experimental variance (between group) - see systematic variance; variation in measures on the dependent variable attributed to systematic differences between our independent variables; for example, group, treatments, etc.

ex post facto research - the independent variable is not under the control of the researcher and/or has already occurred.

external validity - the extent that a study is generalizable to other people, groups, investigations, etc.

extraneous variables - variables that one does not want to include in the study, and one wants to control for their possible contamination of the study.

face validity - a measurement instrument characteristic which indicates that the questions being asked either do or do not appear to represent the content of the instruction: this represents a visual examination of the items and instrument.

factor analysis - a multivariate method which helps the researcher to determine and interpret how many dimensions (factors) exist for a particular set of measures; this is done through a mathematical procedure of analyzing sets of correlations. A factor is a hypothetical construct that underlies a set of variables (items). A factor is made up of items that load on the factor (correlated with the factor). An item is considered to load on a factor if it is highly or relatively highly correlated with that factor. If the item is only highly correlated with one factor, it is called factor pure. A factor is interpreted based on the item that loads on the factor.

factorial design - a design made up of at least two actors (main effects), the purpose of which is to control variance while testing the effects of the independent variables in terms of different dependent variable scores.

family-wise comparisons - the probability of making a Type I error in a set of contrasts (family).

fixed design - all levels of a factor in a factorial design are fixed. That is, one is not allowed to generalize to any level other than the one that has been tested.

heterogeneity - this term refers to the degree of difference or dissimilarity of students or items; a heterogeneous group of students would represent people with very little in common insofar as the examined characteristics are concerned.

heuristic - the research's potential value for further discovery or investigation; this aspect of science differentiates it from technology.

homogeneity - this term refers to the degree of similarity or commonality among students or items; a group of students or items which are similar in terms of the examined characteristics would be referred to as being highly homogeneous.

hypothesis - a statement of the relationship between two or more variables in an if-then form.

independent variable - there are two types - see active and assigned variable; the presumed cause of the dependent variable; the 'if' part of the 'if-then' hypothesis statement.

interaction - the differential effect across the area of interest (it is the simple effects that are plotted; the lines will be nonparallel).

internal validity - a study has internal validity to the extent that one can say the independent variable causes the effects of the dependent variable; in other words, a study has this to the extent it can assume causation.

interquartile range - is an estimate of how much the scores in the distribution deviate from the measure of central tendency as measured by the median. It is the 75% - 25%, sometimes also called quartile deviation.   2 interval - numbers which represent equal units of measurement; for example, distance between 2 and 4 is equal to the distance between 10 and 12; such scales can be added, subtracted, multiplied and divided; these scales do not have an absolute zero; for example, a thermometer.

intervening variable - sometimes called constructs, a term invented, that is assumed to account for unobservable internal psychological processes; it is generally inferred from behavior.

law of large numbers - as you increase the size of the sample, the more accurately your sample value is representative of the population value.

least square solution - is the general statistical computational procedure on which tests of significance are calculated. The least square solution is a procedure in which the sum of all the deviation scores squared are as small as possible.

main effects - the factors that make up a factorial design, they must have at least two levels.

maxicon principle - maximize experimental variance while minimizing error variance.

mean - this measure of central tendency is computed in the same manner as the arithmetic average; sum of all the scores divided by the number of scores.

measurement - this term refers to the assessment of student behavior in quantitative terms; an evaluation plan will normally encompass several measures of student behavior.

measured operational definition - defines a variable or construct in terms of how it is being measured.

median - this measure of central tendency indicates the middle score of a group of scores; it divides in half the number of higher scores with a like number of lower scores; it is a point in a distribution in which half of the scores fall below and the other half of the scores fall above that point.

metaphysical explanation - a relationship or proposition that cannot be empirically tested.

mixed design - a factorial analysis of variance design in which at least one factor is random and at least one factor is fixed (see random & fixed design).

mode - this measure of central tendency refers to the score which occurs most frequently; for example, in a group of scores in which no more than two people received the same mark, excepting one score which four people received, that score would represent the mode.

multiple regression - a method for predicting a dependent variable by two or more independent variables that may be continuous, dichotomous or both.

multivariable - when there is one dependent variable being predicted by two or more independent variables.

multivariate - when there are two or more dependent variables being predicted by two or more independent variables.

nested design - is when all levels of one factor are not found in all levels of another. The levels of one factor are confounded in levels of another factor. Sometimes called split-plot design.

nominal - a measurement scale made up of numbers used to designate a class or category; they cannot be added, subtracted, multiplied, or divided; for example, use numbers to classify people by sex, religion, race, etc.

nonparametric statistics - are statistics that don't make the same stringent assumptions as do parametric statistics. (See definition of parametric statistics). Nonparametric statistics are also called distribution free tests (i.e., they are free of the assumptions about the distribution of the population and sample [normal, skewed, etc.]). Nonparametrics also do not make the assumption that requires the measurements to be at least interval in nature and also do not require homogeneity of variance. However, nonparametric statistics tend to be less powerful than parametric statistics.

non-probability sampling - sampling that does not use random sampling procedures.

norm - this term is used to refer to typical scores obtained by relatively large groups of people with similar characteristics; a test may be "normed" by compiling typical scores for a certain grade level or age level or other common base.

normal distribution - this is a theoretical distribution of scores in which a plotted frequency distribution will result in a smooth bell-shaped curve. Such a distribution of scores will result in approximately 68% of the scores between $\pm$ one standard deviation; 95% of the scores between $\pm$ two standard deviations; and 99.7% of the scores between $\pm$ three standard deviations.

null hypothesis - states that there is no relationship between two or more variables.

objectivity - a method of measurement that is not affected by the researcher's biases.

operational definition - defines a variable or construct in terms of how it is being measured or its activities (procedures).

ordinal - scales that are rank ordered; numbers are assigned to represent rank ordered positions; they can not be added or subtracted, multiplied or divided; for example, size, places, I.Q.

ordinal interaction - interaction in which when the lines are plotted, they do not cross in the area of interest, but the lines are not parallel.

orthogonal - variables are at right angles to each other, zero correlated with each other and totally independent of each other.

orthogonal comparisons - a set of contrasts that are independent (nonredundant) for K number of groups. Only K-1 orthogonal contrasts can be moded.

parameter - the actual population value.

parametric statistics - are statistics that make certain assumptions about the population from which the sample comes. It assumes: normal distribution of the population and sample, homogeneity of variance, and equal intervals of its measures. (However, most of those assumptions can be violated with little effect on the accuracy of the statistic, i.e., most of the parametric tests are very robust.)

path analysis - method for studying the relationship between direct and indirect effects assumed (causes) of the dependent variables (endogenous). It is a procedure used to test the causal relationship formulated by a theoretical model. (Theory is needed before one can effectively use path analysis.) Path analysis generally uses path annalytic diagrams to display the pattern of the causal relationships among a set of predictor variable (exogenous) and dependent variable (endogenous). Path analysis is used to possibly better understand "causal relationships" when non-experimental conditions exist.

percentile rank - this is a method of expressing individual scores in terms of relative rank among the total group of scores; a particular numerical percentile rank indicates the percentage of scores which fall below the given rank.

power: the power of a test is the ability of a test to detect a difference when a difference exists. Mathematically, this can be stated:

power = 1 -   (the probability of
              making a Type II error)

(Type II errors are also called beta errors.)

practical significance - differs from statistical significance, deals with whether the difference is large enough to be useful, and sometimes is measured in terms of the proportion of variance accounted for (r^2).

principal components analysis (PC) - a special case of factor analysis. It is a data reduction procedure where variables (items, etc.) are transformed into a smaller set of linear combinations of these variables (items). These linear combinations are called principal components (factors) and these principal components are uncorrelated with one another. The first step in doing principal component analysis is to start with a correlation matrix. Conceptually, it creates PC by putting together the most highly correlated set of items, and each set of highly correlated items is calculated in such a way to create a zero correlation with every other set.

<u>probability</u> <u>sampling</u> - sampling that uses random sampling procedures.

<u>problem</u> - a question statement asking what relationship exists between two or more variables; many hypotheses can be derived from a problem statement.

<u>quasi-experimental research</u> - there is an active variable but the investigator does not have total control over scheduling or he can't randomly assign.

<u>qualitative measures</u> - assessments of this type are more subjective in that one is attempting to assess levels of quality instead of quantity rank; ordering free-responses on essay examinations, in terms of the reader's estimate of the best to the poorest, would be an example of a qualitative measure.

<u>quantitative measures</u> - measures of this type are more objective in nature in that weights or values are assigned for specific levels of a characteristic or performance; such weights or values are typically expressed in a numerical form; measurement is virtually impossible to perform without quantitative values identified for a given characteristic or performance.

<u>quota samples</u> - a form of non-probabilistic sampling in which quotas or proportions of particular objects or groups are used for representatives; it appears similar to the probabilistic technique of stratified random sampling but it is generally not as accurate.

r^2 - also referred to as the coefficient of determination; the proportion of variance that one variable can account for in another variable (common factor variance).

random assignment - a procedure in which subjects or objects are assigned to different groups using random procedures (see randomization).

randomization - assignment of subjects, objects, treatments, etc., in such a way that each of these has an equal chance of being assigned by using random procedure.

randomized design - the levels of a factor are randomly picked from a population for the purpose of generalizing from these levels to the "infinitely large" population from which they were picked.

random sample - method of drawing a sample so that every person in the population being sampled has an equal chance of being drawn.

range - this term reflects a measure of variability of a group of scores in that it expresses the difference between the highest and lowest scores on a given measure.

ratio - scale that has equal intervals and an absolute zero; one can add, subtract, multiply, and divide and one can say something is twice as much as something else, for example, a ruler.

regression effect - simply stated, this term describes the tendency of extreme scores to move toward the average on subsequent measures. Regression also means the same as correlation.

reliability - this is a value indicating the consistency of results of a given measure; a reliable instrument will yield a constant relative rank for people within a given group on each administration of the instrument.

robust - this is a term that has been used to indicate that the underlying assumption of a test of significance can be violated with having very little effect on the accuracy of the test.

sampling - taking of a portion of a population or a universe.
score - this is a quantitative expression of a student's performance on a given measure; a score in and of itself has little meaning until it is combined and compared with a total group of scores.

simple effects - the individual groups that make up a factorial design.

source of variation - first column of an analysis of variance table which is made up of the components of variability for that particular study, the main effects, interaction, and total.

split-plot designs - see nested design.

standard score - this type of score reflects a transformation of a relatively meaningless single score into a form which expresses the score in terms of the scores of the total group, thus providing a relative meaning to the single score.

standard deviation - this is a measure of variability of a group of scores; within a normal distribution, the standard deviations (S.D.) will be a value in which $\pm$ four S.D. will encompass approximately 100% of the scores, and $\pm$ one S.D. will include approximately 68% of the scores.

statistic - a measure calculated on a sample to infer certain characteristics of the parameters of the population.

statistical significance - the probability that something is likely to occur other than by chance.

systematic variance - variability in measurements due to some known or unknown causes that effect the dependent scores to lean in one direction more than another; there are two types, biased and experimental (between group) variance.

substantive hypothesis - (sometimes called a research hypothesis) states that a relationship between two or more variables exists.

theory - a set of constructs and definitions stating the relationship among certain events or variables for the purpose of predicting and explaining the relationships between the variables.

trend analysis - is a curve fitting technique in which one tries to fit either a straight or curved line that tend to best reflect the relationship over a number of repeated measures or observations.

unbiased sampling - a sample that uses randomization procedures.

univariate - when there is one variable being predicted (dependent variable) by another variable (independent variables).

validity - simply stated, this test characteristic refers to the quality of actually measuring the behaviors which the instrument is designed to measure.

variable - something that has measurements attached to it and is under investigation; for example, IQ is a variable and the numbers may range from 0-180, sex may be a variable with numbers ranging from 0-1 or 1-2, etc.

<u>variance</u> - any set of measurements that has attributed to it a total amount of variance; total variance can be broken into two major components: error variance and systematic variance (see error and systematic variance); the standard deviation squared is also called variance.

INDEX